BODY AND BIBLE

BODY AND BIBLE

Interpreting and Experiencing Biblical Narratives

Edited by

Björn Krondorfer

Trinity Press International   Philadelphia

First Edition 1992

Trinity Press International
3725 Chestnut Street
Philadelphia, PA   19104

Cover design by Jim Gerhard

Library of Congress Cataloging-in-Publication Data

Body and Bible : interpreting and experiencing biblical narratives /
edited by Björn Krondorfer.
       p.   cm.
    Includes bibliographical references and index.
    ISBN 1-56338-048-X (pbk.) :
    1. Theater—Religious aspects.   2. Religion and drama.   3. Bible
plays.   4. Narration in the Bible.   I. Krondorfer, Björn.
PN2049.B6   1992
792.1'6—dc20   92-33157
                                                               CIP

Printed in the United States of America

92   93   94   95   96   97   6   5   4   3   2   1

Contents

Preface

The sea looked and fled, Jordan turned back.
The mountains skipped like rams, the hills like lambs.
What ails you, O sea, that you flee?
O mountains, that you skip like rams?

                                                    Psalm 114

When I conceived of this book, I asked Katya Delakova, a teacher, dancer, and choreographer of modern dance, to write about her work with biblical narratives. Katya has taught both in the United States and in Germany, and she has inspired many people to listen to their bodies and become aware of their movements. She has influenced countless people during her long career. (Even in my family, two generations were exposed to her charisma and teachings: my mother in the mid-1970s in Frankfurt, Germany, and myself twenty years later in her studio in Trenton, New Jersey).

Before Katya could complete her manuscript for this book, she lost her courageous struggle against cancer in the spring of 1991. Her contribution would have provided the vision and wisdom of an accomplished artist. To show the breadth and depth of her work (as well as the vitality of her spirit), I want to quote from a letter she wrote a few months before her death:

Dear Björn,

Yes, I am interested to contribute to such a book as you plan to do. Right now, however, I am writing a scenario for Psalm 114, which we took as a theme for a group at the Summer institute of Havuroth in Philadelphia. We improvised with the parting of the Sea, with the Mountains that leap like goats, with the Rock that transforms into a Pool of Water . . .

vii

Did you know that Gerhard Marcel Martin . . . had a fellowship at the Union Theological Seminary in New York [and] worked with me in this year? We produced the Tower [of Babel], and as he returned to Germany he continued with the work and called it Bibliodrama. . . . My inspiration for "The Tower" came out of visits and discussions with Adin Steinsaltz in Jerusalem, one of the foremost thinkers of the Jewish people. Our question to Adin was: why [did God] confuse the languages? Adin brought us a Midrash, which said: And as their tower grew higher, also their arrogance grew, and it was so, that when a buildingstone dropped from the height, they lamented and tore their clothes because it took more than a year to bring the stone so high—but when a human being fell from the heights, no one even turned.

The plays of good and evil that were done in front of churches in medieval times were topics that stirred the soul—I saw Jedermann *with Moshe in front of the cathedral in Salzburg and will never forget it. Another of these unforgettable pieces was the play of Daniel done in the church by New York's "Pro Musica." But in both these cases it was not only what was done but how it was done. . . .*

We had in recent two weeks such moving experiences, one indoors, Schoenberg's opera "Moses and Aaron" at City opera, and one outdoors at an Indian Pow Wow: there was a flute player, a young Indian, who also did a "hoop-dance." He played with 36 hoops painted in the 4 colors of Indian directions: red, yellow, black and white. After he played and twirled and swung these hoops in the most surprising formations, they suddenly formed in his arms a huge sphere. Carefully, he took this Roundness and put it in front of himself on the ground. There it stood absolutely still and firm; then he said: Only when one culture will learn to support the other, can the World hold Balance.

This could be performed in front of any house of worship!

Take care! With warm greetings!

Katya

Katya's life bridged different cultures and religions (although she never left her European and Jewish roots); her work reconciled the body-mind split. Her remark that the *how* is as important as the *what* can serve as a general dictum for this book. Those of us who have met Katya know how much energy and rigor she dedicated to the "how": medium and message are interwoven.

I also want to thank other sources of inspiration and support. Katharina von Kellenbach and Samuel Laeuchli gave me encourgement and help from the beginning to the end of this project. My thanks also go to the members of the Jewish-German Dance Theater. In our four-year experimental work on Jewish and German history and reconciliation, I learned more about the power of performance than anywhere else. I am also indebted to Alan Paskow and Robin Bates, who read parts of the manuscript; to Gerhard Elston for his help in translating Tim Schramm's manuscript; and to Billi Yalowitz for his cooperation on my chapter of Jacob and Esau. Finally, special thanks go to Harold Rast, whose encouragement and assistance exceeded by far my expectations of a publisher's task.

BODY AND BIBLE

Introduction

Björn Krondorfer

"Play," Victor Turner observed, "can be everywhere and no-where, imitate anything, yet be identified with nothing" (1986:168). Given this description, play seems to provide an ideal model for postmodernity—the representation of culture as scattered and polymorphic, as *simulacra*, and as incomplete and creative. Indeed, we have lost a universe that has hitherto provided coherent meaning systems and given us a sense of being protected by a sacred canopy. This loss has not only unleashed great anxieties but also released powerful creative energies. For better or worse, the twentieth century has procured more playful modes of living. As individuals and communities, we have played with new forms of experiencing ourselves in relation to our traditions, cultures, and realities.

The rapid growth of therapeutic, theatrical, and religious networks is a case in point. Therapeutic services reach from Freud's psychoanalysis to Moreno's psychodrama, from Gestalt therapy to logotherapy, from Reich's or Lowen's body therapies to encounter groups and sensitivity training (cf. Corsini 1984). In theater, the avant-garde has embraced both therapy and religion, experimented with ritualistic theater and liturgical dance, and moved into the area of paratheatrical events. At the same time, drama and dance therapies have emerged. In religion, scholars and clergy have begun to play with therapeutic and dramatic elements, and have developed methods variously called bibliodrama, Bible-theater, or mimesis. In addition, a vast number of hybrid, often ephemeral workshops and seminars have emerged, dissolving boundaries between the academic, religious, medical, and theatrical institutions, and wedding spirituality, shamanism, witch-

1

craft, healing, and ritual. These "countercultural ritualizations" have focused on the recurring ideas of "self, experience, and creativity" (Grimes 1990:110).

Today we can choose from innumerable organizations, communities, and networks that promise self-exploration, release, healing, and salvation. We can playfully weave our way through vision quests and tele-evangelism, shamanistic centers and psychoanalysis, pararituals and sacramental rites, theater workshops, and covens. We are encouraged to create our own stories by putting together experiences gained in religious, theatrical, and therapeutic environments. We truly are, as twentieth-century literature has emphasized, *homo ludens*, the playing human; or, as others have said, a *bricoleur*, the postmodern human who playfully rearranges the world from fragments and debris of the past without claiming truth or origin.

As the twentieth century draws to an end, we experience life as *bricolage*. Coherent meaning systems are replaced by a coincidental accumulation of *objets trouvés*. The meaning created in all those spaces of self-exploration is often transient, temporary, playful, and fictional (though we still take them seriously). We have become self-reflexive beings, knowing that we create what we believe in. However, the dark side of self-reflexivity is our anxiety at getting lost in a meaningless universe; so we cling to our beliefs even more vigorously. The growing religious Fundamentalism is as much a response to this loss of meaning as are the crowded waiting rooms of psychotherapeutic and medical institutions, or the mushrooming of workshops on "parashamanism, paratheatre, or pararituals" (Grimes 1990:121). The flip side of *bricolage* is religious Fundamentalism and spiritual consumerism.

Considering this predicament, we ought to ask ourselves whether this book, which wholeheartedly endorses the notion of play, does more harm than good. Is it not actually play itself that contributes to our *bricolage* style of living and the loss of meaning? Is it, therefore, legitimate to combine the Bible—which is for many a sacred, authoritative voice—with the elusive, equivocal nature of play? Why would we turn to play to interpret biblical narratives? Is it not play that circumvents the seriousness and sacredness of life?

Play is neither nonserious nor antisacred. Play, as the contributions to this volume demonstrate, provides spaces in which the modern human is in search of meaning or, to adopt a Jungian phrase, "in search of a soul." Religion, theater, therapy, or other hybrid spaces are perhaps the few remaining forums within an increasingly technological and pragmatic society in which meaning can be created, reinvented, rearranged, probed, and played with. In playing, we become human.

The authors presented in this volume have all "played." They have used or invented creative methods to approach and interpret biblical narratives, and they have (re)discovered innovative ways of relying on and employing the body in the task of "meaning-making." Hence the title, *Body and Bible*. However, the authors are also respected and serious theologians, scholars of religion, therapists, and artists. Most work within academic institutions, but some do not. They live in the United States, Great Britain, or Germany; they are Christian, Jewish, or unaffiliated. What unites them in this volume is their willingness to share methods and reasons for *how* and *why* they conduct plays with biblical narratives.

The book opens with a chapter in which the editor traces the cultural forces and ideas that have shaped the current diversity of playful experimentations with biblical narratives. It is followed by Samuel Laeuchli's comprehensive introduction to the hermeneutic and existential dimensions of play. He shows how the Genesis account of the Expulsion of Adam and Eve contains experiences which, if reenacted, can confront us with our dark sides—an encounter Laeuchli calls "mythic shock." Tim Schramm's contribution moves into the world of the New Testament. Step by step, he takes us through a bibliodramatic workshop on a healing story (conducted near Hamburg) and shows how the participants were able to renew their understanding of themselves and the figure of Jesus. His detailed report serves as a good introduction to readers unfamiliar with actual play processes; other readers will be inspired by Schramm's ability to mediate between text and play.

Gerhard Marcel Martin also belongs to the German school of bibliodrama. He traces the origins of this movement and presents his own approach which always leads him back to the text itself. Playing, for him, is always a chance to learn something new about biblical narratives.

David Rhoads revitalizes oral traditions of the Gospels by combining storytelling and performance. Like Tim Schramm, he reflects on the story of the Syrophoenician woman, thus inviting us to compare two distinct approaches to the dramatic rendering of the same text.

The contributions of Walter Wink and Arthur Waskow show how play, body, and movement can be applied to working within religious and liturgical communities, both Christian and Jewish. They strive toward "human transformation," or *tikkun olam* (to heal the world), and thus introduce a political and liberating dimension.

In his article, Waskow also argues for renewing the traditional Jewish method of "midrash-making." Alix Pirani's reflection on Cain and Abel is the result of such a modern midrashic process. She approaches the Genesis story from a therapeutical perspective but transplants it into rural England. It is a playful and thoughtful fantasy about her (and other psychotherapists') attempts to heal the "first" family.

Tom Driver takes us back to the reality of a graduate seminar in New York and reflects on the power and hazard of playing biblical narratives. Exploring the depth of a story about a victimized woman (Judges 19), Driver reports that the "mythic shock," to use Samuel Laeuchli's phrase, was greater than some students could bear. The narrative, so to speak, overpowered play and players. Björn Krondorfer's subsequent chapter also addresses the power of play and shows how play retrieves the emotional and sensual quality of narrative structures. Working with two dancers on the story of Jacob and Esau, they confronted problems relating to male identity.

Women's lives are at the center of Evelyn Rothchild-Laeuchli's concluding chapter. In "Lot's Wife Looks Back," she explains how she integrates the playing of biblical stories in her therapeutical practice. We can also take her title as a fitting maxim for the ending of this book. When we play, we look back to the anguish, pain, and joy stored in our memories and culture, and as we play, we also move— we move on without being paralyzed by fear and shame, weaving our present into the past and future.

This book has a double purpose. On the one hand, it presents the current diversity of ideas, methods, styles, and applications in this new field of research. On the other, it hopes to convey the excitement that people experience when entering biblical narratives through play, reenactment, and embodiment. In this sense, the book reaches out to the educator and scholar, artist and therapist, theologian and layperson. If Turner is correct in assuming that "play is everywhere and nowhere," then play occurs in places where we least expect it: in the classroom, therapy session, church, family, and work—or when we make theology or art, or write a scholarly article or sermon. Whenever we construct our society and reality, there is a good deal of playing involved. This book makes us conscious of our playing so that we discover, once again, that playing is a passionate and creative way of relating to the world.

References

Corsini, Raymond J., ed. 1984. *Current Psychotherapies.* 3d ed. Itasca, Ill.: F. E. Peacock Publishers.

Grimes, Ronald L. 1990. *Ritual Criticism: Case Studies in Its Practice, Essays on Its Theory.* Columbia: University of South Carolina Press.

Turner, Victor. 1986. *The Anthropology of Performance.* New York: PAJ Publications.

The Whole Gamut of Experience: Historical and Theoretical Reflections on Play

Björn Krondorfer

From *Eutrapelia* to *Liminality:* What Is Play?

In the history of Western civilization, play has been variously idealized or degraded, praised or cursed, and turned into a scientific object or a means of self-forgetfulness. It has been described as an innocent and enjoyable activity of children or, depending on the value system, as a reproductive (or disruptive) and creative (or regressive) activity of adults. "Play," anthropologist Turner wrote, "is a transient and is recalcitrant to localization, to placement, to fixation."

> Play is [not] just "having fun;" it also has a good deal of ergotropic and agonistic aggressivity in its odd-jobbing *bricolage* style. . . . Play draws material from all aspects of experience, both from the interior milieu and the external environment. . . . Play deals with **the whole gamut of experience** both contemporary and stored in culture. . . . Play is perhaps [humans'] most appropriate mode of performance. (Turner 1986:168–70)

Play, Turner suggests, is categorically elusive and yet deals with the "whole gamut of experience both contemporary and stored in culture." How did Turner arrive at a definition that seems to juxtapose—or perhaps reconcile—such different qualities as transient and basic, and fleeting and foundational? What historical and theoretical assumptions have preceded a statement exhibiting so much confidence in the wide-ranging applications and implications of play? If we look at the changing historical attitudes towards play, we begin to understand the current diversity of perpectives on the nature and function of play; we will also understand why, in the twentieth century, various cultural phenomena, including religion, therapy, and theater, have been described as forms of play.

5

My major arguments in this chapter are the following: Prior to the nineteenth century, the agent of play was the adult civilized man who used play for his aesthetic sophistication. Play was accepted as the virtue of *eutrapelia* (literally, "happy turning" [Ardley 1967:228]). However, during the nineteenth century, a radical shift in the cultural and social perception of the value and agent of play occurred. A new paradigm, "evolutionism," (cf. Goudge 1973:178–81) developed, which began to replace the classical notion of play as the aesthetic sophistication of the adult with a definition of play as a biologically and culturally inferior activity of children and savages. Theories assuming the accuracy of this evolutionary model reached their peak in the 1890s. However, during the same decade, definitions emerged which started to question the validity and dominance of evolutionism. At the dawn of the twentieth century, the adult was rediscovered as the agent of play. Freud and Moreno prepared the ground for looking at patients as adult players in therapeutic environments; philosophers and social historians acknowledged the foundational value of *homo ludens*; anthropology and avant-garde theater saw adult players as being engaged in social, sacred, and experimental drama, calling the latter "liminal" events; historians of religion and theologians looked at *sacer ludus,* "sacred play," thus paving the way for experiential and playful appropriations of religion. It became legitimate to interpret therapy, ritual, theater, and religion as psychological, social, dramatic, and sacred forms of play.

I will now trace these historical and theoretical observations in more detail and, at the end, show how playful experimentations with biblical narratives emerged in the second half of the twentieth century.

From Aesthetic Sophistication to Cultural Inferiority: The Value and Agents of Play Prior to the Twentieth Century

The main ideological forces shaping the occidental idea of play were Greek antiquity and the church's rejection of play as vain activity. Plato's rather derogatory remarks against play both as imitation and a child's activity (*mimesis* and *paidia*), and Aristotle's affirmation of play as a necessary rest and virtue (*eutrapelia*) were introduced into Christian culture by Augustine and Aquinas. Play was tolerated as long as humans did not become protagonists in a universe confined to a transcendental reality or authority. Because both Platonic thought and Christian theology anchored human actions and knowledge with an absolute essence or God, they embedded the ludic apprehension of reality into a larger, transcendental reality. Humans, so to speak, were "the playthings of the gods" (Ardley 1967:235; Rahner 1972:11).

Within this scheme, play served the purpose of strengthening morality and enhancing spirituality; it was a device for the aesthetic refinement of one's personality. Aesthetic education was largely synonymous with the virtue of *eutrapelia*, the ability of a man to be both serious and nonserious, a man of inner serenity who "brings a lightness . . . to every situation" (Ardley 1967:229). The proponent of this virtue was the *eutrapelos*, the adult male, "the old man who plays just like a boy" (Hincmar of Reims, quoted in Rahner 1972:3). Children, supposedly, possessed the quality of being absorbed in free, nonserious, and innocent activity outside of the demands and the pursuits of gain in the material world. The glorification of these childlike qualities, however, was more of a sentiment on the part of adults than recognition of a child's real needs. The actual agent of this virtuous play behavior was the *eutrapelos*, the civilized, free, adult man.

Children themselves, however, especially throughout the medieval age, were treated as little adults. It was not until the sixteenth century that the concept of "the child" as someone who is in need of special attention emerged. Certainly Rousseau (1712–1778), who admired children for their alleged proximity to nature, and Pestalozzi (1746–1827), who praised the purity of children, modified the general consciousness (cf. Aries 1965; Boas 1966:29–38). Yet it was a long struggle until the public recognized play's significance for the physical and mental development of children. A school regulation of eighteenth-century Germany read as follows: "The children shall be instructed in this matter in such a way as to show them, through the presentation of religious principles, the wastefulness and folly of play." An American church discipline of 1792 echoed: "We prohibit play in the strongest terms. . . . The students shall be indulged with nothing which the world calls play" (Lehman and Witty 1927:1).

However, the voices that called for different attitudes toward children and that considered play important for their development could no longer be subdued. In 1787, the German anatomist Friedrich Tiedemann published his *Beobachtungen über die Entwicklung der Seelenfähigkeiten bei Kindern*, one of the first developmental studies on children, followed by three other significant German works in the 1850s.[1] However, it was not until the 1890s that the bulk of work on child education and child psychology appeared simultaneously in many European countries and in America. Educational reforms, which acknowledged children in their own right and promoted education on large demographic scales, were inventions of modernity.

Yet at the dawn of evolutionary theory and shortly before the child fully emerged as the new agent of play, the German humanist Friedrich Schiller launched an attempt to reverse a process that treated play increasingly in scientific and pragmatic terms. In 1795, Schiller wrote his famous letters *On the Aesthethic Education of Man* in which he

insisted that the adult man was the primary agent of play, the *eutrapelos*. In these letters, he envisioned an aesthetic education that
would transcend restrictions placed on humankind by both natural
and moral conditions. He regarded these restrictions as the result of
two conflicting drives governing human life: the "sense-drive" (*Stoff-
trieb* or *sinnliche Trieb*), which represented the human dependency on
nature and material, and the "form-drive" *(Formtrieb)*, which referred
to the dependency on reason and form. Both drives Schiller thought,
were inadequate means for achieving aesthetic education. Only a
third drive, the "play-drive" *(Spieltrieb)*, could account for the possibility of an aesthetic education. The play-drive would mediate between the physical laws of nature (sense-drive) and the moral laws of
reason (form-drive). Only in play, Schiller argued, where sense-drive
and form-drive are in harmony, do humans experience freedom from
physical and moral constraints. Only in play do humans become fully
human because the play-drive is neither determined by biological necessity nor moral reasoning: "For, to mince matters no longer, man
only plays when he is in the fullest sense of the word a human being,
and he is only fully a human being when he plays" (*Letter* 15:107).

Despite Schiller's advocacy for the aesthetic sophistication of
adults, his letters anticipated the transition from the classical humanistic ideal of play to its modern counterpart, the evolutionary ideology, which put play into the service of educating savages and
children. Schiller himself resisted the idea of using play for didactic
and moral purposes (cf. *Letter* 22:157), but his emphasis on the play-
drive as the basis for an aesthetic education unwittingly anticipated
educational reforms that turned children into the new agents of play.
Pedagogy became the test ground of aesthetic principles. Schiller's
letters thus represented a turning point between preevolutionary
thought, which had largely ignored play—except for the aesthetic refinement of man—and the new scientific mentality, which would
eventually sweep the nineteenth century and turn play into a cultural
deficiency and an object of scientific zest (Kowatzki 1973).

Schiller's ideas were taken up again in the twentieth century. Huizinga, Winnicott, and some "play theologians," for example, cor-
rectly noticed that Schiller's characterization of play as a foundational
and mediating drive constituted the first attempt to attribute anthropological and ontological significance to play. However, in the nineteenth century, Schiller's idealistic description of play was largely
ignored.

The transition from the (adult) virtue of *eutrapelia* to the education
of children, which took place in the nineteenth century, was a mixed
blessing. On the one hand, this period saw the democratization of
educational privileges which hitherto had only been available to the

aristocracy or bourgeoisie and recognized the different needs of children. The changes that occurred with the spreading of evolutionary theory were long overdue. No longer was the play of only the civilized, adult man (the *eutrapelos*) the object of reflection; the play of children became the topic of pedagogical and scientific concerns.

On the other hand, the newly emerging sciences, such as ethnography, anthropology, psychology, and pedagogy, were spellbound by evolutionism. As a result, they debased the concept of play and regarded it as a biologically and culturally inferior activity of children and "primitive" people. This debasement coincided with the need of redefining "man's" place within a seemingly ever-expanding universe, both in terms of hegemonic interests (such as colonialism) and the acquisition of scientific knowledge. To view play as an inferior activity that had to be controlled and disciplined was one of the responses of European androcentrism to the breakdown of a bygone monolithic universe.

The increasing interest in children and savages corresponded to the formation of other typologies such as "the imbecile," "the criminal," and "the woman." Those groups were on the same inferior level, all different from the virtuous European male. A new scientific discourse was established—perhaps best described as hegemonic evolutionism. The newly emerging scientist who reacted with "intolerance towards variety" and insisted "on uniformity" categorized and manipulated everyone who was other than himself (Aries 1965:415; Boas 1966; Drinka 1984; Manuel 1959).

With respect to play, the typologies of child and savage were of special significance. The (ontogenetic) development of children and the (phylogenetic) "undevelopment" of primitive cultures became models for understanding cultural and biological progress. Children were scrutinized in their European homes while savages were under investigation abroad. Both were interpreted as evolutionary links between animals and adults, and nature and culture. The infantile play of children and the ritual play of savages were considered to be of biological and cultural necessity, an activity of two agents who had not yet reached their full human potential.

Play was no longer a leisure activity of the privileged class (sport came to assume this function) but an unavoidable phase through which an organism passed. It was a transitory and inferior condition superseded by a higher and more serious activity. The latter, of course, corresponded to contemporary European civilization. The image of the wise man who aspired to an aesthetic sophistication had been successfully replaced by the model of a rational adult male striving for scientific knowledge. The *eutrapelos* had been replaced by the scientist who treated play as a relic from "man's" past. Play was relinquished to children and savages because of its assumed obsolete nature, and the scientist converted those newly defined agents of play into his objects of inquiry.

If play, at large, was seen as an immature form of adult behavior, it was only consequential to channelling this raw and uncultured energy by christianizing savages abroad and educating children at home. Already Schiller had stated that play, in its initial form, was raw and superfluous energy (cf. *Letter* 27:211). Educational theory combined Schiller's idealism with Darwin's system of selection and growth (his *Origin of Species* was published in 1859), and with Haeckel's biogenetic law ("phylogeny repeats itself in ontogeny"). Haeckel wrote in 1866 that "the development of the child is a brief recapitulation of the evolution of the race." Each child, according to Haeckel's logic, was a living testimony of the evolution of humanity. Only a few years later, in 1873, the British psychologist Herbert Spencer adopted and modified this idea: "Education must reproduce in miniature the history of civilisation" (all quotes from Claparede 1975:122,185). Every child, according to Spencer, had to learn each step of the human evolution. Children were filled with all the necessary genetic and biological information, but culturally, morally, and mentally they were empty and in need of being filled by education.

Play theories, which basically approved of evolutionary thought but shifted the emphasis to psychology and education, virtually mushroomed at the turn of the nineteenth century. There was Schaller's (1861) and Lazarus's (1883) recharge theory; Spencer's (1873) "surplus energy" theory inspired by Schiller; Stanley Hall's (1920) and Karl Groos's (1898;1901) theory of play as a time for practicing skills (they influenced Erikson's and Piaget's stage theories); or Ellen Key's plea for a "natural education" (1909) and Lilla Appleton's biological theory of education (1910). In 1893, *The National Association for the Study of Children* was set up by Stanley Hall in America, followed by *The British Child-Study Association* in 1894 (cf. Ellis 1973; Scheuerl 1975; Liebermann 1977).

Though all these theories differed in their assessment of what constitutes play, none was able to challenge the parameters set by hegemonic evolutionism. In 1911, Edouard Claparede, in his book *Experimental Pedagogy and the Psychology of the Child*, could still write that a scientific comparison of "man and the child, human beings and animals, the civilised man and the savage, the virtuous man and the criminal" would yield valuable information for psychology in general. Correspondingly, a comparison "between children and imbecile adults," "children and savages . . . and animals" would be valuable for child psychology (1975:82,85).

The value of play, according to nineteenth-century theory and pedagogy, was to lift the agents of play, namely, children and savages, to a more mature and civilized level. A real shift of this perception did not occur until Freud began his psychoanalytic work.

Play as Foundation of Culture: The Rediscovery of the Adult Player in Therapy and Philosophy

At the turn of the century, Freud continued to operate within the paradigms of his time, drawing on the phylogeny-ontogeny axis and the typologies of child and savage. Yet he also challenged and changed radically his intellectual environment: the infantile and savage features of adults were the objects of his inquiry. Like Schiller who had marked the shift from classical humanism (play as aesthetic sophistication of man) to evolutionism (play as cultural inferiority of the child), Freud was a seminal thinker who provided thought patterns leading to a reappraisal of both *homo ludens* and the *bricoleur*—the modern and postmodern version of the playing human.

Strictly speaking, Freud limited the term *play* to the realm of the child. He saw both the childhood of humankind (totemism) and the childhood of individuals (Oedipus complex) as of prime importance for the formation of civilization in general and one's personality in particular. Although his anthropological and psychoanalytic studies identified various kinships between child, savage, artist, and neurotic, he differed from hegemonic evolutionism insofar as he recognized the power of neurosis. His psychoanalytic journey into the interior space of the human psyche placed the child and the savage back into the personality of the European adult, thereby dismantling the illusion of civilization's grandeur. What had been projected onto the "other" returned as the repression of one's own aggressive and sexual impulses. Play, fantasy, and rituals could no longer be portrayed as the innocent virtue of *eutrapelia,* nor as infantile and archaic behavior of others; rather, they had to be viewed as a "civilized" person's obsession, substitution, regression, and delusion (cf. Freud 1908; Waelder 1932; Ricoeur 1970).

The tendency to refocus one's interest on the playing European adult grew even stronger with Moreno, a contemporary of Freud. Starting out as a religiously inspired poet, Moreno gathered his first impressions of the therapeutic power of play while telling stories to children in a public park in Vienna. In the 1920s, he shifted his focus to spontaneous role playing which he conducted with friends and actors. These experimentations, which he called *Stegreiftheater* (Theater of Spontaneity), aimed at creating a unity between audience and actors in which everyone became a participant engaged in acts of genuine creativity and conflict-resolving. Moreno's principles found their definite shape in his theory and method of psychodrama and sociodrama; they influenced other psychotherapies, especially the human potential movement, and they were often employed in theater, especially in experimental drama (Moreno 1973; Fanchette 1971; Mann 1979).

Winnicott, a child psychologist who blended psychoanalytic thought with Schiller's humanistic ideals, also claimed the adult as agent of play. "Cultural experience," he wrote, "begins with creative living first manifested in play." Playing equally applies to children and adults and is "a basic form of living" (1989:100,50). Playing is a form of therapy, and, in reverse, therapeutic processes are a form of playing.

> Psychotherapy takes place in the overlap of two areas of playing, that of the patient and that of the therapist. Psychotherapy has to do with two people playing together. . . . It is good to remember always that playing is itself a therapy. (Winnicott 1989:38,50)

Echoing Schiller's statement that "man is only fully a human being when he plays" (*Letter* 25:107), Winnicott argued that "it is in playing and only in playing that the individual child or adult is able to be creative and to use the whole personality, and it is only in being creative that the individual discovers the self" (1989:54). In play, humans become themselves.

Freud, Moreno, Winnicott, and the human potential movement recognized resemblances between play, therapeutic sessions, and dramatic reenactments. Therapy adopted dramatic play and turned the patient temporarily into an actor; theater, as we will see, adopted therapeutic play and turned the actor temporarily into a patient. The result of this kinship was the reacceptance of the adult as the agent of play.

The therapeutic embrace of the playing adult was paralleled by a renewed historical, theological, and philosophical interest in the phenomenon of play. When the historian Huizinga published his book *Homo Ludens* in 1938, he, like psychologist Winnicott, took up Schiller's notion of play as a basic human drive and emphasized the foundational function of play for culture. Culture, he wrote, "does not come *from* play like a babe detaching itself from the womb: it arises *in* and *as* play, and never leaves it" (1955:173). Similar to Geertz's suggestion of the interdependency of culture and humankind ("Without men, no culture, certainly; but equally, and more significantly, without culture, no men" [1973:491]), Huizinga viewed play as an essential appendage to human existence. Culture, he argued, cannot be conceived as an entity apart from play. The interplay of both is essential for the development of human civilization. We become human by playing.

Huizinga's serious scholarly interest in play was favorably received by theology and philosophy. Theology discovered play as a metaphor for doctrines of creation and redemption while philosophy vested play with essential hermeneutic functions. The theological and philosophical appropriation of play confirmed that theories of play had finally rid themselves of the nineteenth-century notion of play as an inferior activity of children and savages. Instead, soteriological and paradigmatic, and etiological and teleological qualities were now assigned to it.

Philosophy has regarded play as essential for apprehending reality; yet no consensus has been reached on the question of what constitutes this essence. Does play signify openness or constraint, freedom or stability, nontruth or truth? Philosophers inclined to modern worldviews responded in favor of play's structural constraints while those inclined to postmodern worldviews favored play's open-endedness—a discrepancy which deserves a brief investigation (Fink 1960; Derrida 1978; Gadamer 1979; Hans 1981).

Gadamer, a proponent of modernity, understood the relationship between play and reality as being based on objective structures and on truth. In his work *Truth and Method*, he argued that reality is something "untransformed," and, as such, inaccessible to humans. Only certain approaches to the world, such as art and religion, would be able to transform reality, "to raise it up to its truth" (1979:102), and thus make it accessible. However, transformed reality, as we encounter it in art and religion, remains meaningless unless humans appropriate them through play. Music needs to be performed, drama staged, and religious rites enacted to be understood. Without play, they have no meaning. It is in this sense that Gadamer, like Schiller and Huizinga, claims that "play is an elementary function of human life" and that "human culture is inconceivable without a play-element" (1977:29).

Gadamer, however, depreciates the individual contribution of human players, because, as he argues, only the truth or essence of what is being played out in art or religion has any relevance. When humans play, he wrote, they only play out the "superior truth" (1979:101).

> The players are not the subject of play; instead play merely reaches presentation through the players. . . . [Neither] the separate life . . . of the performer who acts a work, nor that of the spectator who is watching the play, has any separate legitimacy in the face of the being of the work of art. (1979:92,113)

This slighting of the human player recalls the Platonic and theological notion of humans as "plaything of the Gods," with the only difference being that Gadamer replaces God with what he calls truth, structure, and essence. Despite his affirmation of a "hermeneutic universe, in which we are not imprisoned . . . but to which we are opened" (1979:xiv), Gadamer, like other thinkers whose worldviews are bound to modernity, establishes the relationship between play and reality on the grounds of an intact sacred canopy: Humans confirm in and through their play the existence of objective truth and meaning.

Contemporary critical theory aims at breaking away from such universal claims and, instead, reflects upon the postmodern condition. Proponents of postmodernity use play as a metaphor for affirming a radical open-endedness of reality. Derrida's deconstructionist philosophy, for example, suggests a nonteleological and antitheological model of "freeplay" and proposes the model of the *bricoleur* who playfully (re)arranges the world from the debris of the past. The *bricoleur*, according to Derrida, affirms the noncenter and nontruth within what humans interpret as structure or essence, thus allowing heterogeneous content and multiple truths to emerge. The *bricoleur* is a "mythopoetic" being whose epistemological paradigm is not essence but play. Play is "the joyous affirmation of the play of the world and the innocence of becoming, the affirmation of a world of signs without fault, without truth, and without origins" (Derrida 1978:292).

With respect to assessing actual play processes (such as therapeutic sessions, religious rituals, or dramatic enactments), both Gadamer's objectivism and Derrida's deconstructionism are rather impractical. Gadamer's claim of objective truth behind all (subjective) interpretations cannot do justice to the psychological and cultural validity of multiple, heterogeneous, and innovative forms of human play; Derrida's concept of the "innocence of becoming" in freeplay empties actual play processes of their emotional, ethical, and political content and impact. However, as impractical as both philosophical conceptions may be, the discrepancy between Gadamer and Derrida is a good indicator for the current controversy on the significance of play: Is play at the basis of culture or is it *simulacrum*, a sign of the ultimate artificiality of all human activity? Is play grounded in a sacred canopy or a nonteleological universe? Are we, as *homo ludens* who generate culture and apprehend reality, still bound to some generic truth, or do we, as the self-reflexive *bricoleur*, always invent, reinvent, and examine our own productions? In one word, does play signify the *meaningfulness* or *meaninglessness* of human existence?

Play as Transgression of Culture:
The Adult Player in Theater and Ritual

Unlike historical, philosophical, or theological theories that assign foundational qualities to play, both theater and anthropology drew attention to the performative and transgressive qualities of play. During the late nineteenth century, the text-centeredness of Western philosophy and theology could no longer hold exclusive attraction for the arts and human sciences. Europeans became interested in the primitive, the exotic, and the tribal. While scientists labeled primitive cultures inferior, artists began to cherish them as relics of their own ceremonial and mythic past (cf. Boas 1973:593–98; Rubin 1985:1–79).

At the turn of the century, avant-garde theater started to experiment with archetypal, sacred, and ritual material. Informed by anthropological studies of so-called savage cultures and by psychoanalytic explorations of the savage dwelling within the European psyche, avant-garde theater searched for a certain metaphysical and ontological rawness of the human experience and for the expression of the irrational, the hidden, the unconscious, and the mythic. Avant-garde artists reacted against the naturalism of the turn-of-the-century theater which seemed to have lost all ritualistic aspects. For them, the emotional relevance of theater was at stake; rituals and myths would transgress and invert normative structures and thus revitalize the stage and society as a whole.

Christopher Innes, who has investigated the history of avant-garde theater, concluded that experimental drama borrowed both from therapy and ritual. It adopted therapeutic play and turned the actor temporarily into a patient; it adopted ritual and turned the actor into a priest, a holy actor, and an initiand.

> Beneath variations in style and theme there appears a dominant interest in the irrational and primitive, which has two basic and complementary facets: the exploration of dream states or the instinctive and subconscious levels of the psyche, and the quasi-religious focus on myth and magic, the experimentation with ritual and the ritualistic patterning of performance. (Innes 1981:3)

Historically, the reritualization of avant-garde theater began with the staging of Jarry's *Ubu Roi* in 1896. Jarry portrayed the fictitious European King Ubu as an infantile and savage creature. The play's inflated images of savagery and infantilism, the "scatological obscenity and gratuitous violence," appalled the aesthetic sensibility of the nineteenth-century audience (Innes:26; cf. Schumacher 1985; Driver 1970:140f). Jarry had dared to mirror the childish and brute nature of bourgeois society at a time when the normative scientific discourse had seized upon play and ritual, linking them to the typologies of child and savage. The irreverent and ritualistic play of *Ubu Roi* playfully mocked and inverted the nineteenth century's scientific devotion to play.

In the 1920s and 1930s, Antonin Artaud, who followed in Jarry's footsteps, became one of the most ardent supporters of a primal theater that aimed at synthesizing the religious, dramatic, and therapeutic horizons. Artaud intended to create a "Theater of Cruelty" which, like the plague, was to be "contagious" and "immediate and painful." Artaud despised "the modern humanistic and psychological meaning of the theater" and suggested a theater that "disturbs the senses' repose, frees the repressed unconscious, [and] incites a kind of virtual revolt." He did not object to psychoanalysis, however, because it would assist in creating a "religious and mystic" theater, bringing forth "the exteriorization of a depth of latent cruelty" (1958:28–47).

> I propose to bring back into the theatre this elementary magical idea, taken up by modern psychoanalysis, which consists in effecting a patient's cure by making him assume the apparent and exterior attitudes of the desired condition. (1958:80)

Artaud aimed at reritualizing theater by blending it with the discoveries of psychoanalysis. By and large, however, Artaud failed to realize his own dramatic ideas. This failure and his nine-year confinement to mental asylums resulted in his work, outside of France, falling into oblivion (Sellin 1968; Knapp 1969; Esslin 1976). However, in the 1960s, Artaud's vision of a Theater of Cruelty forcefully resurged in Europe and the United States, exerting great influence on experimental drama.

In New York, Julian Beck's and Judith Malina's "Living Theater" was the first to integrate aspects of a Theater of Cruelty (cf. Brown 1965:34); other innovative theater groups, like Schechner's "Performance Group" or Chaikin's "Open Theater," also turned to Artaud's writings for inspiration (cf. Blumenthal 1984). In Great Britain and France, director Peter Brook experimented with Artaud's scripts and searched for the basic elements of performances which he characterized as energy, danger, and simplicity (Brook 1968; Heilpern 1977). At the same time, Grotowski's theater experiments in Poland aimed at "creating a secular *sacrum* in the theatre" (Grotowski 1968:49). His demand that actors surrender to complete discipline and strenuous physical training came perhaps closest to a Theater of Cruelty. "Like the mythical prophet Isaiah," Grotowski praised Artaud, "he predicts for the theatre something definitive, a new meaning, a new possible incarnation" (1968:125; cf. Kumiega 1987:19).

Assessing the development of experimental drama, performance theorist Schechner concluded that "Western theatre has become increasingly ritualized during the last eighty years, moving into areas of human interaction once reserved for religion" (1977:160). Religion, of course, was not understood as pious, doctrinal, or institutional religiosity; rather, experimental drama explored the raw, dangerous, and ambiguous nature of the sacred which it discovered in both Western

and non-Western religious traditions. "The theater of cruelty ex-
pulses God from the stage," Derrida once remarked; yet, it is "sacred
theater" (1978:235,243).

Analogous to Freud's discovery of the savage inside the European
adult, experimental drama revealed the sexual and aggressive drives
behind religious symbols, rituals, and narratives. For example, almost all of Grotowski's early performances, such as *Faustus* (1963),
The Constant Prince (1968), and *Apocalypsis cum Figuris* (1968) reversed
Christian symbolism and portrayed its sexual, violent, and sadomas-
ochistic undersides; the Living Theater's spectacles, like *Frankenstein*
(1965) and *Paradise Now* (1968), mixed Jewish mysticism with Yoga
and Native American rituals; Schechner's *Dionysus in 69* (1968) combined Greek drama and a New Guinea rite of passage; Chaikin's
Open Theater produced *The Serpent: A Ceremony* (1968), which reinterpreted the biblical narrative of the Garden of Eden.

By reritualizing theater, the stage became a space for experimenting with social and individual transformation. Acting techniques as
well as performance scripts incorporated religious, ritualistic, and
therapeutic elements. It seemed that experimental drama, especially
during the so-called poor theater phase of the 1960s and 1970s, saw itself as a synthesis of religion and psychotherapy, aspiring to heal social evil and individual wounds by transgressing normative structures
that were experienced as repressive and oppressive. What therapy
would do for individuals, rituals would do for communities, and experimental drama would be located somewhere in between.[2]

A "transformation of ritual into theatre is occurring today,"
Schechner wrote as he observed theater projects of the early 1970s
(1977:79). The affinity of theater and ritual, he claimed, was nowhere
as transparent as in rehearsal processes of experimental drama.

> Both rehearsals and [ritual] preparation employ the same means: repeti-
> tion, simplification, exaggeration, rhythmic action, the transformation of
> "natural sequences" of behavior into "composed sequences." . . . Thus it
> is in rehearsals/preparations that I detect the fundamental ritual of theatre.
> (1977:132,136)

Rehearsal periods promise to bridge the gap between ritual, theater, and therapy. "Rehearsals are centers of psycho-physical, sociological and personal research," Schechner wrote. "Theatre has fed
from and been a feeder of therapy" (1977:160,166).

Victor Turner provided an excellent theoretical framework for ac-
counting for the efficacy of rehearsal periods of stage drama (as, like-
wise, of "social drama" in general). He coined the term *liminality* for
periods of transition in which a culture, group, or individuals are put
to the test. *Liminality* (derived from Latin, meaning *threshold*) is a be-

twixt and between in time and space in which cultural values and the normative perception of reality are probed, transgressed, condensed, and intensified. More than just playful mockery, liminality is a serious activity, essential for the revitalization of social structure.

Originally, Turner reserved the term *liminality* for agrarian societies, contrasting it with liminoid phenomena of industrialized societies. In this scheme, liminality stands for collective experiences and is a necessary sociocultural construct of preindustrial societies; liminoid phenomena represent the more individualized, marginal, and fragmentary experiences of (post)modern society. While liminality is an effective ritual action, liminoid phenomena are leisure and entertainment (Turner 1977; 1982:20–60).

However, Turner did not consistently apply this distinction. In the broadest sense, liminality occurs whenever ritual processes facilitate crisis situations of "social dramas"—and that could happen in modern, industrialized societies as well.

Liminality generates creativity and transformation. It occurs outside of ordinary life and provides new impulses for society. "Liminality, marginality, and structural inferiority are conditions in which are frequently generated myths, symbols, rituals, philosophical systems and works of art" (Turner 1969:128f).

For Turner, liminality is at work in a variety of performative genres of society, including theater. "The public liminality of great seasonal feasts exhibits its fantasies and 'transforms' . . . to the eyes of all— and so does postmodern theatre" (1982:81). Because of its marginal status and its ritualized, antistructural, and playful moods, experimental drama constitutes one of the few occasions in which modern society restores its loss of liminality. "In my nomenclature," Turner wrote when addressing the differences between experimental drama and entertainment theater, "these would represent a contrast between 'liminal' and 'liminoid' modes of performance" (1982:122).

Turner once said that "one *works* at the liminal, one *plays* with the liminoid" (1982:55), but he did not uphold this work and play, and liminal and liminoid distinction. In one of his later works, he wrote that play is "a liminal and liminoid mode, essentially interstitial, betwixt-and-between. . . . Play can be everywhere and nowhere, imitate anything, yet be identified with nothing." In the same writing, we find the already quoted, memorable phrase that "play deals with the whole gamut of experience both contemporary and stored in culture" (1986:168–70).

Turner's theory is significant because it helps to examine the social, performative, and experiential dimensions of ritual and religion, and theater and play. Because the concept of liminality encourages interdisciplinary thinking and dissolves some of the boundaries between ritual, play, theater, and therapy, the newly emerging field of ritual and performance studies has eagerly embraced it. Doty, for example, has suggested broadening Turner's concept to "ludic liminality," thus emphasizing the efficaciousness of "ritual as play" (1986:129). For Grimes, play and ritual are inseparably intertwined: "Play is at once a root of ritual and a fruit of the same" (1982:48). Perhaps the best description of liminality in relation to play, ritual, transgression, and self-reflexivity is found in Abrahams's anthropological study of a West Indian ritual. Play, Abrahams wrote, is "exempted from full judgment on moral grounds" and becomes "the embodiment of the dark side of a culture."

> If play involves committing such transgressions . . . it occurs to me that the study of the processes and the expressive repertoire of playing then provides a primary means of mapping transgressions permitted or even encouraged by a group. . . . The community agrees to the fiction that play is a liberating activity, but not because it represents a cultural retreat from being orderly or even moral. Rather, it is freeing because play establishes this zone of betweenness, one we could call a free-fire zone because of its enclosed dangers. (1986:30)

With Abrahams's description of play being foundational yet transgressive, fictional yet dangerous, and free yet enclosed, our reflections on play have come full circle. What Western culture had first tolerated as aesthetic sophistication of the adult man (*eutrapelia*), then dismissed as cultural inferiority of children and savages (hegemonic evolutionism), later reclaimed as foundational value (*homo ludens*) and praised for its self-reflexive and transgressive qualities (*bricoleur*), has, for the time being, reached its resolution in the theory of ludic liminality—"the human seriousness of play" (Turner 1982).

From *Sacer Ludus* to Bibliodrama: Religion, Play, and the Reenactment of Biblical Narratives

The religious community could not stay unaffected by the appreciation of play that occurred in secular society since the late eighteenth century. However, the religious and theological approval was impeded by the general suppression of playful impulses in the Christian Occident. Play had been considered to incite pleasures and passions of which neither Catholic ecclesiastical teachings nor a Protestant work ethic was too fond. We only have to think of Chrysostom's famous statement that "it is not God who gives us the chance to play, but the devil," to recall the church fathers' condemnation of play, dance, and theater which they identified with paganism, lust, and the devil (cf. Alt 1970). "Even now," Norbeck wrote, "these values are far from extinct in our nation, and the old admonition that play is the devil's handiwork continues to live in secular thought" (Turner 1982:39).

In the nineteenth century, historians of religion began to reexamine this strained relationship. In 1894, two years before Jarry had staged his scandalous *Ubu Roi*, Robertson-Smith gave his *Lectures on the Religions of the Semites* in which he favored ritual over myth, thus claiming priority of performative over narrative forms of religion. This indicated a significant shift in thinking about religion. No longer confined to texts, doctrines, and sacraments, it would now include religious experiences, mythologies, and rituals. Anthropological studies rivaled theological and exegetical methods, and put forth various theories on the origin and kinship of drama, ritual, and play. Jane Harrison, for example, studied the ritual origins of Greek drama; Gaster constructed an evolutionary model which progressed from ritual to drama to liturgy until it reached completion in literary composition; Burkert and Girard hypothesized that a primordial sacrificial ritual formed the center of religion and society; La Barre assumed that religion originated in shamanistic dances, and Van der Leeuw saw dance at the roots of *sacer ludus*, "sacred play" (cf. Doty 1986; Friedrich 1983).

The appreciation of the performative and experiential aspects of religion presupposed some intimation of the sacred, which was considered both an object and experience of something extraordinary and supernaturally powerful. The sacred, historians of religion claimed, manifests itself, for example, in religious ritual and sacred play. It generates an ambivalent feeling of fear and veneration that can be appeased and expressed through ritual embodiment and enactment. Religious experience was conceived of as a "numinous feeling" towards "the wholly other" (Otto [1923] 1980; cf. Van der Leeuw 1963 and 1986; Eliade 1970:1–37; for a critical assessment, see Ricoeur 1970 and 1974).

While Rudolf Otto's *mysterium tremendum* (the awe and dread felt towards the "wholly other") exerted great influence on the European conception of religious experience, William James's definition of religion as "feelings, acts, and experiences of individual men in their solitude . . . in relation to whatever they may consider the divine" ([1902] 1958:42) expressed the pious revivalism and individualism characteristic of the American continent. Religious experience was defined as either ontologically different from ordinary experience (Otto) or completely dependent on individual belief systems (James). In either case, it was beyond the grasp of more objective, social scientific criteria.

Despite these shortcomings, the way was paved for those in the religious community who were willing to reevaluate the strained relationship between text and experience, dogma and ritual, and theology and play. In the past decades, theologians, scholars, and educators began to develop play theories and to engage in the praxis of playful experimentations. This trend was supported by the growing acceptance of therapeutic models and social scientific theories of religion that no longer operated with either the sacred as "wholly other" or the radical individualism of William James. Geertz's *Interpretation of Cultures* is a case in point. He defines religion as a cultural and symbolic system that "establishes powerful, pervasive, and long-lasting moods and motivations in men" (1973:90), and thus contextualizes religious experience without reproaching it for its subjectivism. Religion, it was argued, is not a monolithic system representing one truth but is composed of multiple true experiences rooted in cultural systems. Like play, religion is fictive yet true (cf. Harrison 1977; Kliever 1981; Grimes 1990). It is, to borrow a concept from Foucault (1972), an *archive* of cultural experiences (cf. Krondorfer 1992).

Theology, too, has reconsidered its relationship to play. Beginning in the late 1940s, some liberal theologians from the Catholic and Protestant denominations affirmed the validity of play for contemporary theological discourse. These play theologians responded to the modern estrangement from doctrinal theology and began to incorporate psychological and playful elements to revitalize theology (Miller 1970 and 1971). More conservative play theologians, like German scholars Rahner (1972), Pieper (1952; 1973), and Moltmann (1972), who have been influenced by Schiller's idealism, proceeded largely within proper theological categories. There is, they claimed, a qualitative difference between *deus ludens* (the playing God) and *homo ludens* (the playing human). The more buoyant essays of American play theologians (Neale 1969; Cox 1969; Miller 1970; Keen 1970) focused on the playfulness of humans by adopting the positive outlook of popular psychology and the human potential movement.

Most play theologians, however, neither partook in actual play processes which rely on bodily participation, nor considered the hermeneutic assumptions of specific performances and dramatic reenactments; rather, they used play metaphorically to enhance theological thinking (Krondorfer 1990). Hence, play theology could offer encouragement but no practical assistance for those in the religious community who were interested in experimenting with play processes. The active fringes of religious institutions branched out into other areas, getting inspiration and stimulation from psychotherapies, dance, and experimental drama.

In Europe, especially in Germany, a movement developed over the past decade in which adults reenact Bible stories and embody biblical personae in order to learn about themselves and the text. This playful and dramatic approach to biblical narratives is called bibliodrama, a method that combines psychodramatic principles and exegetical interests, and sometimes relies on experimental drama techniques (Kiehn 1987; Martin 1976 and 1985). In the United States, similar experimentations take place. They are less of an organized movement and more a result of individual efforts employing a variety of styles and techniques (Wink 1973; Power 1979; Laeuchli 1987 and 1988). What these experimentations share is a playing with, embodying, enacting, or staging of sacred narratives, gestures, symbols, and rituals. *Homo religiosus* joined in the play and work of *homo ludens*. Many people engaged in the practical aspects of this work are not only involved in playful experimentations with biblical narratives but also committed to reflect on the methodological and hermeneutic implications and results of ludic liminality—in an attempt to further our comprehension of the human predicament.

Notes

1. The three German works are Löbisch's *Entwicklungsgeschichte der Seele des Kindes* (1851); Sigismund's *Kind und Welt* (1856); and Kussmaul's *Untersuchungen ueber das Seelenleben des neugeborenen Menschen* (1859). (See Claparede 1975; Millar 1968:13–38.)

2. Only recently have scholars begun to examine the complex relations between ritual, religion, performance, and experimental drama. The most comprehensive study is Innes's seminal work *Holy Theatre: Ritual and the Avant-Garde* (1981), which traces the historical development of the kinship of theater and ritual from Jarry's symbolism in the 1890s to postmodern productions of the late 1970s. Some scholars of religion have taken up similar research projects, such as Driver (1970) who focuses on the history of modern drama, and Grimes (1982; 1990) who looks at the expanded field of ritual studies, including experimental drama. Others have questioned the avant-garde's appropriation of ritual. Those critics regard ritual and performance as incompatible systems, or they accuse experimental drama groups of only pretending "to practice theatre as ritual" (Amankulor 1989:47) and of being overly ambitious by trying to revitalize both itself and ritual and religion. (See Kerr 1973; Graham-White 1976; Cohen 1980; Lee 1982.)

References

Abrahams, Roger D. 1986. "Play in the Face of Death: Transgression and Inversion in a West Indian Wake." In *The Many Faces of Play*. ed. Kendall Blanchard. Champaign, Ill.: Human Kinetics Publishers.
Alt, Heinrich. [1846]. 1970. *Theater und Kirche in ihrem gegenseitigem Verhältnis*. Reprint. Leipzig: Zentralantiquariat der DDR.

Amankulor, Ndukaku J. 1989. "The Condition of Ritual in Theatre: An Inter-cultural Perspective." *Performing Arts Journal* 33:45–58.

Appleton, Lilla Estella. 1910. *A Comparative Study of the Play Activities of Adult Savages and Civilized Children: An Investigation of the Scientific Basis of Educa-tion.* Chicago: University of Chicago Press.

Ardley, Gavin. 1967. "The Role of Play in the Philosophy of Plato." *Philosophy* 42 (July):226–44.

Aries, Philippe. 1965. *Centuries of Childhood: A Social History of Family Life.* Trans. Robert Baldick. New York: Vintage Books.

Artaud, Antonin. 1958. *The Theatre and its Double.* Trans. Mary Caroline Rich-ards. New York: Grove Press.

Blumenthal, Eileen. 1984. *Joseph Chaikin: Exploring at the Boundaries of Theater.* Cambridge: Cambridge University Press.

Boas, George. 1966. *The Cult of Childhood.* London: The Warburg Institute/University of London.

———. 1973. "Primitivism." In *Dictionary of the History of Ideas,* ed. Philip P. Wiener. 4 vols. New York: Charles Scribner's Sons.

Brook, Peter. 1968. *The Empty Space.* New York: Atheneum.

Brown, Kenneth H. 1965. *The Brig.* New York: Hill and Wang.

Claparede, Edouard. [1911]. 1975. *Experimental Pedagogy and The Psychology of the Child.* Reprint. New York; Arno Press.

Cohen, Hilary Ursula. 1980. "Ritual and Theatre: An Examination of Perfor-mance Forms in the Contemporary American Theatre." Ph.D. thesis, Uni-versity of Michigan.

Cox, Harvey. 1969. *The Feast of Fools: A Theological Essay on Festivity and Fan-tasy.* New York: Harper and Row.

Derrida, Jacques. 1978. *Writing and Difference.* Trans. Alan Bass. Chicago: Uni-versity of Chicago Press.

Doty, William. 1986. *Mythography: The Study of Myths and Rituals.* Tuscaloosa: University of Alabama Press.

Drinka, George Frederick. 1984. *The Birth of Neurosis: Myth, Malady and the Victorians.* New York: Simon and Schuster.

Driver, Tom F. 1970. *Romantic Quest and Modern Query: A History of the Modern Theatre.* New York: Delacorte Press.

Eliade, Mircea. 1970. *Patterns in Comparative Religion.* Trans. Rosemary Sheed. Reprint. Cleveland: Meridian Books.

Ellis, M. J. 1973. *Why People Play.* Englewood Cliffs, N.J.: Prentice-Hall.

Esslin, Martin. 1976. *Antonin Artaud.* New York: Pengiun Books.

Fanchette, Jean. 1971. *Psycho-drame et Theatre Moderne.* Paris: Editions Buchet/Chastel.

Fink, Eugen. 1960. *Spiel als Weltsymbol.* Stuttgart: Kohlhammer.

Foucault, Michel. 1972. *The Archaeology of Knowledge.* Trans. A. M. Sheridan Smith. New York: Pantheon Books.

Freud, Sigmund. 1908. "Creative Writers and Day-Dreaming." In *The Stan-dard Edition* 9, ed. James Strachey, 141–54. London: Hogarth Press.

Friedrich, Rainer. 1983. "Drama and Ritual." In *Drama and Religion,* ed. James Redmond, vol. 5. Cambridge: Cambridge University Press.

Gadamer, Hans-Georg. 1977. *Die Aktualität des Schönen: Kunst als Spiel, Symbol und Fest.* Stuttgart: Reclam.

_____. 1979. *Truth and Method*. London: Sheed and Ward.

Geertz, Clifford. 1973. *The Interpretation of Cultures*. New York: Basic Books.

Girard, Rene. 1977. *Violence and the Sacred*. Baltimore: John Hopkins University Press.

Goudge, Thomas A. 1973. "Evolutionism." In *Dictionary of the History of Ideas*, ed. Philip P. Wiener. 4 vols. New York: Charles Scribner's Sons.

Graham-White, Anthony. 1976. " 'Ritual' in Contemporary Theatre and Criticism." *Educational Theatre Journal* 28 (October):318–24.

Grimes, Ronald L. 1982. *Beginnings in Ritual Studies*. Lanham, Md.: University Press of America.

_____. 1990. *Ritual Criticism: Case Studies in Its Practice, Essays on Its Theory*. Columbia: University of South Carolina Press.

Groos, Karl. [1896.] 1898. *The Play of Animals*. New York: Appleton.

_____. [1899.] 1901. *Play of Man*. New York: Appleton.

Grotowski, Jerzy. 1968. *Towards a Poor Theatre*. New York: Simon and Schuster.

Hall, Stanley. 1920. *Youth*. New York: Appleton.

Hans, James S. 1981. *The Play of the World*. Amherst: University of Massachusetts Press.

Harrison, Paul M. 1977. "Toward a Dramaturgical Interpretation of Religion." *Sociological Analysis* 38, 4:389–96.

Heilpern, John. 1977. *Conference of the Birds*. London: Farber and Farber.

Huizinga, Johan. [1938.] 1955. *Homo Ludens: A Study of the Play-Element in Culture*. Trans. R. F. C. Hul. Boston: Beacon Press.

Innes, Christopher. 1981. *Holy Theatre: Ritual and the Avant-Garde*. Cambridge: Cambridge University Press.

James, William. [1902]. 1958. *Varieties of Religious Experience*. New York: Mentor Books.

Keen, Sam. 1970. *To a Dancing God*. New York: Harper and Row.

Kerr, Walter. 1973. *God on the Gymnasium Floor*. New York: Delta Books.

Key, Ellen. 1909. *The Century of the Child*. New York: G. P. Putnam's Sons.

Kiehn, Antje, et al., eds. 1987. *Bibliodrama*. Stuttgart: Kreuz Verlag.

Kliever, Lonnie D. 1981. "Fictive Religion: Rhetoric and Play." *Journal of the American Academy of Religion* 49 (December): 657–69.

Knapp, Bettina L. 1969. *Antonin Artaud: Man of Vision*. New York: Avon Books.

Kowatzki, Irmgard. 1973. *Der Begriff des Spiels als Ästhetisches Phänomen: Von Schiller bis Benn*. Bern/Frankfurt: Verlag H. Lang.

Krondorfer, Björn. 1990. "Play Theology as a Discourse of Disguise or Is the Crucifixion a Case of Child Abuse?" Paper presented at the American Academy of Religion, Mid-Atlantic, April.

_____. 1992. "Bodily Knowing, Ritual Embodiment and Experimental Drama: From Regression to Transgression." *Journal of Ritual Studies* 6 (Summer).

Kumiega, Jennifer. 1987. *The Theatre of Grotowski*. London/New York: Methuen.

La Barre, Weston. 1970. *The Ghost Dance: Origins of Religion*. Garden City, N.Y.: Doubleday and Company.

Laeuchli, Samuel. 1987. *Das Spiel vor dem dunklen Gott: Mimesis—ein Beitrag zur Entwicklung des Bibliodramas*. Neukirchen: Neukirchener Verlag.

_____. 1988. *Die Bühne des Unheils: Das Menschheitsdrama als mythisches Spiel.* Stuttgart: Kreuz Verlag.

Lazarus, M. 1883. *About the Attraction of Play.* Berlin: Dummler.

Lee, Ronald J. 1982. "Ritual and Theatre: An Overview." *Academy* 38:132–49.

Lehman, Harvey C., and Paul A. Witty. 1927. *The Psychology of Play Activities.* New York: A. S. Barnes and Company.

Liebermann, Nina. 1977. *Playfulness: Its Relationship to Imagination and Creativity.* New York: Academic Press.

Mann, John H. 1979. "Human Potential." In *Current Psychotherapies,* ed. Raymond J. Corsini. 2d ed. Itasca, Ill.: F. E. Peacock Publishers.

Manuel, Frank E. 1959. *The Eighteenth Century Confronts the Gods.* Cambridge: Harvard University Press.

Martin, Gerhard Marcel. 1976. *Fest: The Transformation of Everyday.* Trans. M. Douglas Meeks. Philadelphia: Fortress Press.

_____. 1985. "Das Bibliodrama und sein Text." *Evangelische Theologie* 45 (November):515–26.

Millar, Susanna. 1968. *The Psychology of Play.* Baltimore: Penguin Books.

Miller, David L. 1970. *Gods and Games: Toward a Theology of Play.* Cleveland: World Publishing Company.

_____. 1971. "Theology and Play Studies: An Overview." *Journal of the American Academy of Religion* 39 (September):349–54.

Moltmann, Jürgen. 1972. *Theology of Play.* Trans. Reinhard Ulrich. New York: Harper and Row.

Moreno, Jacob L. [1947.] 1973. *The Theatre of Spontaneity.* Ambler, Pa.: Beacon House.

Neale, Robert. 1969. *In Praise of Play: Toward a Psychology of Religion.* New York: Harper and Row.

Otto, Rudolf. [1923]. 1980. *The Idea of the Holy.* Trans. John W. Harvey. London: Oxford University Press.

Pieper, Josef. 1952. *Leisure: The Basis of Culture.* Trans. Alexander Dru. New York: Pantheon Books.

_____. 1973. *In Tune With the World: A Theory of Festivity.* Trans. Richard and Clara Winston. Chicago: Franciscan Herald Press.

Power, Joseph P. 1979. "Utilizing the Religious Experience for Personal Growth and Awareness Through the Psychodramatic Method." *The Journal of Pastoral Care* 33 (September): 197–204.

Rahner, Hugo. 1972. *Man at Play.* New York: Herder and Herder.

Ricoeur, Paul. 1970. *Freud and Philosophy: An Essay on Interpretation.* Trans. Denis Savage. New Haven, Conn.: Yale University Press.

_____. 1974. *The Conflict of Interpretations.* ed. Don Ihde. Evanston, Ill.: Northwestern University Press.

Rubin, William. 1985. "Modernist Primitivism." In *"Primitivism" in 20th Century Art: Affinity of the Tribal and the Modern,* ed. Rubin, vol. 1. New York: Museum of Modern Art.

Schaller, J. 1861. *Das Spiel und die Spiele.* Weimar: Bohlan.

Schechner, Richard. 1977. *Essays on Performance Theory, 1970–1976.* New York: Drama Book Publishers.

Scheuerl, Hans. 1975. "Alte und Neue Spieltheorien." *Der Evangelische Erzieher* 27:2–21.

Schiller, Friedrich. [1795.] 1967. *On the Aesthetic Education of Man in a Series of Letters.* Trans. E. M. Wilkinson and L. A. Willoughby. Oxford: Oxford University Press.

Schumacher, Claude. 1985. *Alfred Jarry and Guillaume Apollinaire.* New York: Grove Press.

Sellin, Eric. 1968. *The Dramatic Concepts of Antonin Artaud.* Chicago: University of Chicago Press.

Spencer, Herbert. 1873. *The Principles of Psychology.* 2 vols. New York: Appleton.

Turner, Victor. 1969. *The Ritual Process: Structure and Anti-Structure.* Chicago: Aldine.

———. 1977. "Frame, Flow, and Reflection: Ritual and Drama as Public Liminality." In *Performance in Postmodern Culture,* ed. Michel Benamou and Charles Caramello. Madison, Wis.: Coda Press.

———. 1982. *From Ritual to Theatre: The Human Seriousness of Play.* New York: PAJ Publications.

———. 1986. *The Anthropology of Performance.* New York: PAJ Publications.

Van der Leeuw, Gerardus. 1963. *Sacred and Profane Beauty: The Holy in Art.* Trans. David E. Green. New York: Holt, Rinehart and Winston.

———. 1986. *Religion in Essence and Manifestation.* Trans. J. E. Turner. Princeton: Princeton University Press.

Waelder, Robert. 1932. "Die Psychoanalytische Theorie des Spiels." *Zeitschrift für Psychoanalytische Pädagogik* 6:184–94.

Wiener, Philip P., ed. 1973. *Dictionary of the History of Ideas.* 4 vols. New York: Charles Scribner's Sons.

Wink, Walter. 1973. *The Bible in Human Transformation: Toward a New Paradigm for Biblical Studies.* Philadelphia: Fortress Press.

Winnicott, D. W. [1971]. 1989. *Playing and Reality.* Reprint. London/New York: Routledge, Chapman & Hall.

The Expulsion from the Garden and the Hermeneutics of Play*

Samuel Laeuchli

To play a text—the step from research to drama seems a wild tour de force in any academic forum. Understanding the Bible is a serious enterprise—the livelihood of professionals and the toil of graduate students and writers. Drama, a child's playful time, the creation of a piece of art—all this operates on such a different platform that the two worlds seem as far apart as one could imagine.

They are not. Dramatic reenactment is an authentic, integral process of our attempt to understand an ancient tale; it is at work even where there is no talk of play whatsoever. The connection between the two realms arises from the nature of myth and from the dynamic by which we try to understand it. The play element can make, if given clear parameters, an invaluable contribution to the dilemma of interpretation (Turner 1979; Laeuchli 1987). In order to present the case, I choose as paradigm Genesis 3, the Expulsion of Adam and Eve from the Garden of Eden—one of the famous tales in the history of myth and religion. I begin by recalling the exegetical dilemma.

How to "Think" About an Ancient Tale

We are confronted by the J-version (Yahwist) of creation. Yahweh created man out of clay, and with Yahweh's breath, he placed man in paradise and gave him a woman as companion. In the garden, God planted one tree, or two trees, depending on the reading of the sources, and told Adam and Eve not to eat from it. The serpent se-

---

*This chapter is a thoroughly revised version of an article published in *Religious Traditions* 14 (1991:1–57).

duced Eve into eating. She was promised to be like God. Eve gave Adam the fruit to eat, and they became conscious of their nudity; God found them hiding. He chided them, made them clothes, put a curse on them and on the snake as well, and banned the man and the woman from paradise. An angel with a flaming sword henceforth guards the garden.

Many scholars, rabbis, ministers, and priests have earned their credentials by struggling with this text. Who created that tale and who wrote it down? Where did it come from? Did it happen? Is it myth? What does it mean? What do we do with contradictions and riddles? How about parallel stories?

There seems nothing dramatic about such inquiries. We consider what the text says and examine images and sentences. We can question the story naïvely, accepting it literally, (Adam and Eve were historical individuals) or critically (Adam and Eve are symbols). As a result of such questioning, an extensive religious, scientific, and academic enterprise has evolved over the last 2,000 years. The roots of critique are the same for a teenager, who for the first time in life hears or reads the myth of Adam and Eve and wonders about it, or for an advanced scholar who has studied this tradition for thirty years. A process has begun its course.

Here is a tradition, originally transmitted orally, of the first man and woman's expulsion. One may call it text or Scripture, saga, myth, or literature. We hear it or read it, perhaps in the original language, perhaps in a translation. We hear words, sentences, idioms, or symbols. We question the tale: Were Adam and Eve historical people at all? The tale is heard symbolically even when we do not acknowledge a "field of symbolism": Few people assume that a god came walking through a garden physically, a figure looking behind the bushes to find naked culprits hiding.

An evaluating process is launched, guided by some kind of a method. The method may be highly naïve and simplistic in its submission ("the church says"; "the professor surely must know!") or sophisticated ("source criticism indicates"; "comparative studies show us"). With time, questions become more sterile or more daring: Is the story just a nomadic way to explain the world? Did God plan the rebellion, and did he know they would break the prohibition? The approaches vary, and schools and individuals contradict each other; however, we assume that the methods will open an access to the tale and that the text will become clearer.

The inquiry leads to a result. At the end, we have learned something we did not know before: that the Tree of Life is a widespread symbol in ancient mythology; that the second creation tale leads to the Expulsion, whereas the first one (Genesis 1) does not; that the tale is an ancient metaphor for the relationship between man and woman.

The results, like the methods, are often at odds with one another. From text to question to method to result—even if this is not the actual sequence by which we reach an insight, we tend to believe in it.

The evaluating process of response and appropriation does not differ radically between a critical philosopher and a devout investigator, and between an atheist and a believer although both camps dogmatically want us to think it does. We *believe* we enter—on both sides—a linear, cognitive endeavor that produces information, clarification, and explanation. Although to an adherent of a certain sect of science or religion the paths contradict one another, they have in common that they mean to access the tale by means of a diachronic, a seemingly rational transmittance. The story is "explained."

Such critical analysis, a crucial step in the human development of our faculty to think and disbelieve and to weigh and make judgments, has become immensely important to the study of the Bible. Text-critical investigations have identified different sources behind these tales; linguistic and historical analyses have shed a great deal of light on the partly nomadic, partly Mesopotamian origins and parallels of our tale. The following investigations would be unimaginable without such studies.

How to Understand . . .

Rational investigation promises results through a linear, cognitive process. Such a hermeneutic assumption (cf. Bleicher 1980) is highly misleading, and if its limitations are not understood, it will deceive us. The analytic explanation is part of a complicated hermeneutic enterprise (Palmer 1969:242). It was the failure of my own professional journey to have worked for a long time with a faulty model.

The linear cognitive process of investigation and research does not suffice—not simply because another access might also be possible or interesting. Even in direct confrontation with the text, a host of other factors is at work with very different laws of communication and reception, changing the character of transmittance profoundly. Entire spheres of activities, experience, and communication are left out. I mention three aspects of human inquiry that reveal the presence of highly differentiated processes.

A first alternative kind of transmittance takes place constantly through silence. We hear a story and for a moment we do not speak. Something is stirred up—a memory, a trauma, conflicts of value, or disturbing associations. We are thinking, but we also cannot clearly think as yet. We hesitate. We are stunned and pause; or we get up, walk around, and sit down again. Perhaps the words were too foolish, too powerful, or too enigmatic.

An important preinterpretative moment exists before the cognitive process takes over. It also can take place during or after the cognitive evaluation. Transmittance needs words, but it also goes on without words—not merely through what is said explicitly but through what is not said. We react through both language and silence. The scholar tends to ignore this pausing, perhaps even denies it in his own work. However, if we observe individuals reacting to texts, we recognize the importance of the nonspoken realm (Hall 1973).

In art, such silence is taken for granted. We listen to a Samuel Barber piece. It may not reach us at first. We pause, then we listen again. Then we try a third time. We look at a Paul Klee painting. We ask, what is it? We pause. We step back. We look again. We return to the museum another day. We may be given data about Barber and Klee, but information does not always help. Silence supports us as we attempt to hear or see.

Silence is not a momentary, disposable, even regrettable, absence of language, but an integral part of response and interaction. Silence is both passive and active. We may not answer a question at first. We may respond by staring into a wall, shaking our head, or touching someone's shoulder or face. We can be silent and thereby refuse to communicate; we can be silent and enter a powerful process of communicative contact. A sophisticated ritual takes place besides words, as Goffmann realized, in emotional contact and body language (Goffmann 1967).

The connection between language and silence is the daily bread of any human interaction, not merely of artistic, mystic, or ascetic creativity. In the social fabric, such transmittance plays a major role (Hall 1973:101). Someone tells us a story, and we hear a voice; or we do not want to hear that voice because it confuses us. Before we react or think, something is stirred in us. In that precognitive moment, language, thought, or explanation may *interfere* with our ability to hear or respond.

As in art or social interaction, the precognitive or postcognitive impact is at work as we deal with texts. We read Genesis and hear it against another individual in our past; or we read with the voices of teachers or preachers. We hear, and someone else is with us in the room. We find support; we may even need someone to help us tolerate the tale. We share or fence off uncomfortable memories. There are entire books, and not merely by graduate students, in which it is not the writer who writes but his teachers and foes.

The acknowledgment of silence is very old. The medieval monastic community experienced it as an integral aspect of its being and creativity, as do proponents of Yoga, the Quaker tradition, and transcendental meditation. In the theophany of Mt. Horeb, the major communication was the "voice of silence" (1 Kings 19:12). This voice has an autonomous role; it represents the counterpoint, as we try to comprehend a text. As in a baroque concerto, the tune sings with the force and rhythm of its counterpoint.

The linear interpretative model is unsatisfactory for a second reason. Beside words, there exists a powerful language of the body. As we read a tale, bodies tighten or loosen up. With taut lips or dark eyebrows, someone responds. While reading a page, people pause and lean back; they rise from their chair and walk around the room. When we talk or think about a text, whether we are conscious of it or not, we use our body. Hearing becomes physical. Individuals shake their head, or they move around the room. They crouch, turn around, laugh, or stretch. Transposition of meaning does not merely use thought or sentence; it includes physical clues (Benthall and Polhemus 1977).

Bertrand Russell walked for hours every day. I held my face in my hands for a long time when I read for the first time Paul Celan's powerful *Fugue of Death*. A graduate student told me the other day that she felt ill after she had to read, in her library carrel, a series of Holocaust documents describing atrocities done to the victims; she tried to control herself but suddenly ran to the bathroom and vomited. That woman's response was an authentic part of understanding and comprehending the document. If we ignore her response, we may barricade her and our own access to her text.

That we breathe, hearing or reading a tale, involves us already in bodily response. With our breath, we think, connect, or separate; we light up or withdraw. The *ruach*, the creative force of Genesis 1 and 2, has a spiritual and cognitive quality as well as a physical one. When we connect with a text positively, we breathe differently than when we are frightened by it. I have seen students in exams cramp their breath to near-asthmatic pains.

Communication is mental, and it is physical. Every actor and every director of a film or play knows of such "body language"—of jerking and hesitation and pause, the reluctance of a human shoulder, and the delicate or crass opening or closing of lips (Whorf 1956). What takes place on stage, takes place in the process of understanding. As we set out to comprehend, we turn to some kind of a gesture. Many a question in class is answered, not by the teacher's words but by his or her shrugging, by angry turning away, by the depressed or violent motion of a chin.

In a debate, a scholar challenged me cynically on this hermeneutic of body and play. He catechized us, saying that "understanding the truth" has nothing to do with art, Reichian psychology, or a theater department. Least of all, he said contemptuously, with the Shakers. It was to be only by reason. With frozen shoulders, he yelled into the room and made a fist. His lips were like ice, and his cheeks were the color of an enraged mask—so much for his rational hermeneutic (cf. Erickson and Rossi 1989:1).

The linear rational model is limited for a third reason. The process of transmittance takes along an entire underworld below the surface of things. We speak about God creating a paradise and about man losing that paradise, and our own loss of or hope for a paradise is lugged along. We read or think about Adam chiding Eve for having given him the fruit, and our own relationship to man and woman, our sexual conflicts, and our partnership or lack of partnership interferes, frequently unacknowledged.

Every poem contains a cosmos in itself—meaning and unspoken meaning, alliteration, sound, code, allusions, unconscious or half-conscious, at times quite hidden, the esoteric levels of Yeats or the enigma in the Sonnets of Shakespeare. Such levels, inevitably part of everyday life, are not merely present in the realms of myth, art, and symbol; they are operative in the act of exegesis itself.

An entire submeaning of the tale leads to a submeaning on the part of the interpreter. As we respond to a metaphor, we speak in metaphors (Siegelmann 1990). The explanation is itself a code, veiled and symbolic. The transmittance of the Genesis myth, as of every other body of literature, goes through a *Zwischenwelt*, an entire nebula or web of significance, poetic and coded. There are many concepts with which to name the coding: "depth meaning" assumes a certain stratification, "archetypal" seems too vague, to call it "unconscious" may coerce psychological categories on it, "esoteric" obscures the process, "code" may be too elusive, and "deconstructive" weakens the authentic power it possesses. I appreciate and work with all six concepts, and I recognize their limitations. Whatever we call that realm, we cannot escape what George Bachelard called the "rivalry between conceptual and imaginative activity" (1969:52).

The assumption that the hermeneutic process is a linear, conceptual event is limited by all three: silence, the body, and the unconscious. A descriptive process does not suffice (Achterberg 1985:51). "Reason is the logic even of the fool and of the madman," wrote Miguel de Unamuno (1977:331). This sentence holds true no less in the task of translation. For every linear and rational explanation, there are two others that defy it. The conceptual explanation buries an entire whirlpool of elusive, conflicting, competing forces. "Understanding" is in part a cognitive process, in part it is not; it does not suffice to "think" about a myth if we wish to understand it, and it does not even help to argue for or against rationality. The path from the myth to the interpreter leads back to the enigma or the substrata of communication; such is the drama through and beyond language.

The path from the text to the audience goes through a labyrinth of roads, across sound and rhythm, and through unexplained meta-phors, with the noise of unspoken and unfinished voices. The result does not lie in one specific "explanation"—we may not be given a fi-nal satisfactory explanation—but in the hermeneutic event itself.

I was invited to introduce a mimetic play in a Sunday academy of an alert church, and I chose the Expulsion of Genesis 3. A group of in-dividuals sat in a circle and listened to my introduction. One of the ministers in the church read the text. Then he closed the Bible. There was a moment of quiet.

Before we could begin with the work, one of the people arose nois-ily, walked over to the coffee urn and poured himself a cup of coffee. Nobody spoke. The man returned to the circle, sat down, and began to drink from the cup. He did not look up once. The entire group watched him in silence; it was like a pantomime by Marcel Marceau. For the unaware participant, there was nothing special to that little interlude. One man had a cup of coffee.

In fact, a powerful dramatic reaction to the text was taking place. How do I know? The man himself let me in on it. As we discussed the Expulsion tale privately after the play, he first objected violently to this "kids' stuff," which he said was irrelevant. Then he suddenly added, very darkly, that he was living in an all-out war with the woman he was married to: "I thought we had a paradise, and what we came out with was a suburban villa coated with poison." He looked at me in great anger and said, "So much for your garden!" When that man walked over to the urn and so ostentatiously poured himself a cup of coffee, he had really heard the tale and connected to its code. He acted out a painful, honest, and precise mimetic re-sponse.

When we posit the drama as a tool of investigation, we acknowl-edge what is happening anyhow. The drama exists and is played out, whether we want it or not. The step into research is a dramatic choice; intuitively, we enter a dramatic path. As we attempt to encounter and comprehend the mythic expulsion of the first humans, a rich, multi-leveled process takes place in which many aspects of our being are in-volved: speech, intuition, emotions, defense, the clothed body, the nude body, unconscious desires, social interactions, and political cli-ches. I need to look at this drama and at the exegetical event wrought by turmoil, society, and need before I can turn to the conscious play.

The Drama of Interpretation

Despite all theories, designs, and safeguards, the huge exegetical enterprise of the past centuries has not brought clarity, let alone con-sensus. The creation myths lead not only to serious conflicts of interpretations but also, as America demonstrates time and again, to spite, hate, and fanaticism. They tend to create wars of interpretation with many fronts and diverse weapons. In the most felicitous scenario, the debate on myth is fought with skill and humor and in good spirits; (Edmunds 1989) in numerous cases it turns bitter if not outright venomous. Were Adam and Eve historical individuals? Evangelists scream "yes" into microphones. Others have lost their livelihood for teaching the "wrong" answer to that question.

Any method, theory, or design contains the seeds of conflict because it is divisive; it breaks the text, coerces it, and makes demands on it. If we were to invite, in order to discuss our tale, a Freudian, a structuralist, and a Marxist representative of scientific investigation, confront them with a traditional historian, a Catholic or Anglican theologian, and a feminist critic of the text's patriarchal tendencies, we would be likely to watch the outbreak of a high drama among the six—a Scopes trial, perhaps, with renewed zeal and sharpened methodological weapons.

Books on Genesis at first do not look like declarations of war. They present critical analysis, documented textual research, and anthropological or theological theories, such as von Rad's, Drewermann's, Leach's. Interpretations sound logical to those who propose and accept them. On comparison from a distance, they contradict one another. The conflict is implicit; it goes on below the surface of things. It simmers in department and church meetings, and in book reviews and footnotes, and finally it affects decisions on tenure and pulpit.

The drama is there all along, but dishonestly. We give our pretense the coat of truth. The dissertations, liberal or conservative, quote those they need to quote. Students obey the teachers who have trained them (or they go against them and are stuck in the same mold); writers are subservient to the church, the publisher, the doctoral committee . . . to receive a job, professional acceptance, or grants. What guides "research into the expulsion" is a church, a tradition of scholarship, an emotional need, a political commitment, fear, anger, or hope. We might be expelled ourselves. The war of the priests has become the war of the scholars, in Feyerabend's brilliant formulation *extra scientiam nulla salus* (1978:306). Right now, in Germany, there has been launched what amounts to a crusade against Drewermann's psychoanalytic work on Adam and Eve (Drewermann 1977).

The conflicts, fears, and illusions—the liability of scholarship as of religion—lie in the tale itself, in its chaos and its mythic ambiguity. And this not only because, with Goethe, the so-called worldview of the past is the worldview of the scholar (*"Was Ihr den Geist der Zeiten heisst, ist doch meist nur der Herren eigner Geist."* Goethe, *Faust* I:577–

78). The hermeneutic wars are the war of the text itself. They begin with our very first step into the realm of research. A conclusive process of translation or interpretation of this story does not exist and cannot exist, because the myth that is multidetermined, ambivalent, and protean does not work on such an assumption. It contains an entire spectrum of issues.

The Genesis tale confronts us with a serious cognitive, social, and physical dilemma: Why would a god—cosmos, society, life—put Adam and Eve in the garden and then throw them out? It posits a sexual dilemma: When the god sees them naked and punishes them, is it really true that we pay a price sexually for growing up? The tale confronts me with my loss of innocence: Did God want me to eat from the apple, make my own choice, and grow up? If he did not want me to do it, why did he not prevent it? The tale confronts us with problems of origin, the meaning of evil, the possibility that a deity is limited, and the meaning of mythic or symbolic language. It raises serious questions: Is there a god behind the human predicament? Is there meaning, order, and purpose at the roots of our journey? Nietzsche, Kafka, and Gottfried Benn are all speaking in that tale.

Coming to terms with that story is by no means a sign of foolishness; it is, to the contrary, a sigh of honest response. Such response is an act, an event, and a deed. It includes our body, our emotions, our society, anger, social confrontations, urban and rural passions, and the fear and glory of social critique; and it takes place as encounter, with real and imaginary foes. The hermeneutic task consists, as Dilthey and his followers perceptively assumed, of a "transposition of inner experiences" (Palmer 1969:104). Such transposition consists of and is communicated by ideas; it touches on our emotions, and it leads to physical action—to symbol as well as concept and deed. Adam and Eve were thrown out. People have ostracized others because they disagreed with "correct" answers to the tale. In the tragedy of the tale, they saw their own predicament and despair.

If we assign the purely cognitive transposition a determining role, we cause great damage, not merely to the text but to us the hearers and to the society that must live with the questions. For if we miss the complementary emotional and somatic particles, we miss the whole. The conviction that conflicts of interpretation are solved by rational debate is wishful thinking to a terrifying degree, and with disastrous results.

In an academy in Hamburg, we played the tale of Genesis 3 just as the "Desert Storm" of the American army broke out. It destroyed the country which in antiquity contained the mythic paradise. Once again, there was talk of evil, of the devil, and of saving humankind. In the contemporary analogy, it became clear how much the war, fought with half a million troops, computers, bombs, and airplanes, was also fought with irrationally ambiguous imagery—crusade, evil, and defense of human rights. The war had little to do with any of them. We were faced with the same discrepancy of words and deeds as in the hermeneutic enterprise.

What makes such drama both intense and dangerous to the participants is the element of chaos. In Genesis, the two tales of creation are the response to the mythic chaos of water (Genesis 1) and desert (Genesis 2). The tale of the Expulsion returns us to the threat of chaos: Man and woman are chased from the garden again. As we work with this outcome, chaos does not remain a historic image; it becomes an undercurrent in the very process of interpreting these tales. Just as the mythic model was an attempt to master the fear and proximity of chaos, so the interpretative event is a response to that same fear and proximity. The scholars and preachers are as afraid of chaos as the mythmakers. They may fear the chaos of explanations but, even more so, they fear that very chaos of life which the Genesis text has addressed.

I present two recollections from my teaching experience in order to show the degree of fear about this chaos, how the drama breaks out, and how the dynamic of chaos and fear can be examined at raw and unguarded moments.

A group of scholars and students was debating problems of biblical creation, sources, "gods," and the roles of man and woman. One scholar felt visibly uncomfortable; he especially disliked the use of the word *myth*, and he was annoyed about such phrases as "God walking down Central Park in the dusk." He finally exploded and chided the audience for speaking about "two gods." It takes a pitiful ignoramus to speak that way about Genesis, he pontificated.

A student asked him politely if it was a matter of being "ignorant" when actually two distinct names for God did exist, one of them in the plural and the other clearly mythic and tribal. The names surely reflect two sources, she pointed out, and both of the gods were male. The West Semitic texts talk of *EL* and *YA*.

The professor looked at her, his eyes ready for the kill. At first, he rambled and mentioned the Mishnah. Then he turned to the woman and asked, "Is Hebrew your mother tongue?" The student turned bright red. She was a capable Jewish-American student, and her Hebrew was probably limited. "No," she replied. Then he said, "Why don't you go home and learn Hebrew first, before you pontificate on the Creation stories of Genesis?"

His attack was extremely vile, but it was on target. The man had to get away from the clear perception and questions of this student. A modern Eve, she challenged God's knowledge with her own. For whatever reasons, he was terrified and enraged by what was so obvious to many of us, and he stopped the discussion cold by an outright attack and by abusing a vulnerable student.

At that very moment, we watched scholarship turn into war. The drama of the tale turned into the drama of interpreters. Some observer might object, claiming that the professor's viciousness, defense, fear, and obvious terror about this woman's position had nothing to do with scholarship. I would suggest it has a great deal to do with scholarship.

He probably would not attack her like that in an article on Genesis. Instead, he would use sophisticated arguments—rabbinical and historical, linguistic, and textual—from archaeology, philosophy, or Torah. In the published manuscript, the war will have been swept under the table of rational discourse (otherwise the article might not be published). However, if we catch the man at unguarded moments, in times of vulnerability and fear, as at this panel, we are observing what was really taking place. We watched a spontaneous, sadistic, quite uncomfortable interaction of panic—the scholar against the woman. (As we parted, she had tears in her eyes.)

The second example dates back to one of my first years of teaching at Temple University. The study of religion was just beginning to enter state universities. A student from upstate had taken her first religion course with a not-very-radical colleague of mine. She went home for Christmas and took a vacation job as a waitress in a coffee shop.

One day a journalist from the town newspaper was her customer. He asked her jovially where she came from and what she was doing with her life, and she told him of her first semester at Temple University. He inquired about what she had liked best, and she mentioned a great course on the Bible.

Did she learn anything, the journalist wanted to know. Indeed, she had, she replied. He began raising his eyebrows. What did she learn down there about God that people up here could not have told her just as well? There were sources in Genesis, she exclaimed, and nobody had told her about them! He looked at her, speechless. Then he exclaimed, "and that is all they teach you down there!" He paid without leaving her a tip.

The journalist went home and wrote a venomous column against our department, about contaminating the poor kids of his solid town and perpetrating lies about God, revelation, Bible, and truth (and for that kind of garbage the folks of Pennsylvania pay taxes!). He sounded like Amos chiding the priests—or he was one of the priests running from Amos (Amos 7:10ff).

The young woman brought the clipping to a class the following semester, as we discussed the death of Socrates. He too had been accused, then killed with hemlock, for seducing the youth of the town. For many weeks, the tirade against seducing the young people from upstate hung in the office of our department.

A host of cultural, personal, economic, and political issues lies behind these incidents. They reveal the extent of unacknowledged emotions and the preponderance of fear and chaos in the conflicts of interpretation. The question is not whether to accept such fear and drama—they exist whether we like it or not—but whether we allow ourselves to see them and in one form or another incorporate them into the investigating process. We deal with the dilemma by entering it. I incorporate drama and chaos as fully present, consciously experienced elements in the study of the text. They are not simply refined, immaculate, or cleaned-up arguments—crucial in many sectors of research—but the raw reactions. If we want to examine the depth level of the tale, its basis to scholarship, and the discord of perception, we must enter the spontaneous moments, or the unguarded times. They contain the clue to the interpretative processes we examine in this chapter.

Instead of merely thinking about this conflict of interpretation, which would continue the discord unaware for another hundred years, I *enter* it. I accept the "hermeneutic war" as an authentic component of research. We do not agree about why we are expelled; perhaps we are angry about it, or afraid, distant, or even totally confused. We might not even agree *that* we are expelled. Instead of pretending to write a secure interpretation of this tale, we abandon this pretense. We do not know why we are expelled; we do not know if God wanted it or not; we do not know who to blame; we do not know if this tale is true and under what conditions it is true. The chaos and drama of this myth is our chaos and our tale.

How can this take place? We *play* the myth. In the play, whether concrete or merely in imagination, ambivalence is allowed and portrayed. We enter the elements of this tale; its symbols, its models, and its contradictions. We experience its force, its Kafkaesque gestalt, and its enigma. We may have to experience opposite camps of interpretation—recognize them and even allow them to induce into us their dynamic, their fear, and their hopes (Drewermann 1990). The drama exists whether we like it or not; we bring it to the surface by a replay.

If I wish to deal creatively with the drama of interpretation, I must become part of it, willingly and openly (Derrida 1978). I am participating in it anyhow; the task is to acknowledge this participation, and to reenact and share it. I do not deal with the text as if, for the time of my exegetical work, the conflict does not exist: I begin with the conflict, and with the chaos and drama itself. I dare to be part of the drama in a process of textual confrontation.

The dramatic hermeneutic is a difficult process: to watch the actualization of mythic imagination. We no longer merely read the books, but we observe events in which the books are transposed, exhibited, and acted out. The drama that goes on in history and society, in classrooms and pews, and among friends or family, is placed in our midst. We play, and from the experienced plays, we find patterns for our own replay.

The Play of The Expulsion

Finally I turn to the concrete play. It is the forum, the path and the event in which the conflict and impasse of interpretation can take place safely—in protected sequences—and can be turned into a potentially healthy and constructive activity.

Play creates and contains its own access, and its limits and code. It is not an easy path, and its results are often more disturbing than those of many a cognitive journey, because it leads us faster and more deeply into contradiction, pain, and conflict. The play arises from and reflects the trauma of life itself; in turn, the drama shows that myth is, in fact, but a metaphor for that very trauma (Winnicott 1989:100).

The person who investigates is *homo ludens,* or man at play and the child at play (Piaget 1962), humanity at its best (Schiller). It is connected to ritual, art, liturgy, and ancient and modern forms of imagination, including Greek tragedy and Renaissance drama. The process is spontaneous but it thrives on an order of its own; only in a protected space can a creative play evolve (Leutz 1974).

When I speak about play, I do not mean the play construct that has been posited by Gadamer and his school. It would be hubris to write a theology, philosophy, or psychology of the kind of play I present, for such would simply be another Docetic exercise, one more pretense or escape. The only way to play is to watch and experience play, and that is a concrete, ritualistic, and dramatic endeavor—an event or a deed. Only then can I speak about mimetic play. Otherwise, it remains a "concept" of play, an idea or theory. When Gadamer said in his *Wahrheit und Methode* that of course he does not play, he pulled the rug out from under the entire access (Gadamer 1975). It would be like a person writing on love and then declaring that he has never practiced love, nor does he ever intend to do so.

To enter play is not an Aristotelian accident, afterthought, afterdeed, or illustration. There is no concept of play that can substitute for the play itself and thereby lead us to "understand" the play; "play is a thing by itself" (Huizinga 1950:45). Such play is not the original text but juxtaposition, analogy, and metamorphosis; it is a new event—Dilthey's transmittance and the tale experienced. It lives from its ancient model, transforming it and incarnating it. The text is somatized or resomatized. We make observations afterwards; we share, reveal, hide, and realize the degree to which the play creates consciousness, growth, and community. If I could give a definition of playing, I would not need to play; I could simply write this chapter.

The parameters of this article do not allow me to present any kind of continuous and detailed presentation. I will mention a few examples of such play, and then I will make some observations on the process (cf. Moreno 1959).

At first, some kind of a scenario is designed—scenes, encounters, translations, and analogies—with which to enter the story of the Expulsion. The design can follow the text quite literally. In Germany, in a widespread movement called bibliodrama, the entry into the text is often on such literal terms (Kiehn 1987). The tale is played out as closely as possible to the original text.

The design can be less literal, include analogical scenes from other tales, treat the text in terms of comparative models and metaphors, and allow historical transmutations and modern analogies. We can play with just one paradigm, such as tree, snake, or garden; or we can stage the loss of innocence and the expulsion from childhood in a New York City neighborhood. A wide range of designs is open, from a very literal to a very broad replay of the text.

In either case, I must create a focus; I order the image world. The Creation of the cosmos in Genesis 1 was an act of focusing: bipolarities, six days, rhythm, and rest. Just as we order the universe in the scientific endeavor, we structure the text in the design of play. What is the center and what is periphery? We establish connections and analogies, and we see polarities, encounters, and parallels. What scholars, preachers, or hearers often do unconsciously, we do knowingly. We design an order of play. As the director of a theater production "blocks" his scenes, our text receives a visual order.

One initial way to order the myth and its replay is to follow and underline its numeric structure (Young 1976). Our tale can be seen through a quaternity of four figures: God, Adam, Eve, and Snake; or we shape the scenario in a pentagonal structure, with the Tree of Life in the center and the four figures around that tree.

We can also begin with the triangulation of power that is classic in relationship as well as in history and culture: God with Adam and Eve. As the snake is included, the triangle of the paradise turns again into a fourfold structure. The step from the triangle to the quaternion is an important symbolic evolution in the history of religion, thought, and symbolism.

However we proceed, we construct the play within a mythic, symbolic geometry. Such geometric structure is not merely "our" addition; it arises from the tradition. It is not an exercise in magic numerology; the ancient Christian church was violently torn apart because of a numerological symbolic impasse about the concept or image of the Trinity and the struggle between a unified and a triadic order. Whether the deity was one or three, and what one and three meant, was a matter of life and death for many of the ancient Christians.

Within such an order, we now turn to block some scenes; we create encounters or design a sequence. The group often throws the order out—and quite soon—because the participants will use their own imagination and analogies. In a few minutes, the play will have its own order, and the role players and observers will create their own code. We merely design a sequence from which to begin.

Imagine four chairs in the center of the room for the four roles—a scene from a recent course.

GOD

ADAM   EVE

SNAKE

Someone volunteers to play God. He rises from his chair, picks up an imaginary plant near the window, and places it in the middle of the scene. A man sits down inquisitively on the chair of Adam, and a vibrant young woman chooses to play Eve. Behind the mask of the snake hides a witty mind. There are numerous ways for such a play to evolve. The people who are about to play the myth of Genesis 3 bring along many different social and psychological variables, including their biographies and cultural traditions. Whatever they represent and however they choose to direct the scenes, a drama is about to be unleashed.

The person portraying God tells them not to touch the plant. Often the man does not challenge the prohibition; often the woman wants to know why she should not be allowed to eat from that tree. In fact, she demands to know. *How* she expresses her demand depends on her personality and mood; she may be timid, fearful, inquisitive, angry, or rebellious. Whatever she feels, the conflict is inevitable: God prohibits man and woman from eating from that tree, and he turns them against himself.

The person who is God has many options. He may point out that this is his garden (he can do in his park how he pleases). He may skirt the questions, or he may attack the woman. However he is portrayed, the confrontation has begun, and the variables determine the flow of events. Something happens in a few minutes. The people who play identify with the roles in the story. They become Eve, Adam, and God, often without realizing the quick transfer of the personae. They feel like Eve and Adam, and they speak as Eve, Adam, or God.

In one example from a recent university class, Eve turns to Adam and asks what he makes of that tree over there. Adam admits sheepishly that they are not allowed to eat from it. Eve becomes aggressive and asks, "How come you are such a wimp?" She turns to God and says, "You *did* plant the tree, after all!" She takes him to task for imprisoning them in this "sandpile of innocence." She does not want to stay in there for the rest of her life.

Almost inevitably, such opening exchanges stir up tensions between the man and woman. Something is askew, no matter how they play their scenario. They talk about sex, power, and obedience. They ask why God would plant such a tree, and whether or not they are happy in this zoo of Samoa. In one pointed exchange, Eve asked her man, "Are you happy, Adam? Are you *really* happy?" And the man came up with a rather unexpected response: "There is something in me, Eve, that does not like your asking that question of me." Freud knew what he meant when he talked about defense.

We observe at times a tense hesitancy on the part of the man and an intuitive streak of rebellion in the inquisitive sentences of the woman. Yet the roles can be reversed, with fear and submission being on the side of the woman. Whatever the distribution of power between them, the two know what is going to happen. In scene after scene, they have a premonition. They talk as if the rebellion has already taken place, as if there were no way they could escape playing the next scene. Adam and Eve, as much as God, are participants in the tragedy of the Fall before the Fall takes place (Schmiedt 1987).

This mutual sharing of the mythic depth experience goes on as we continue the tale, as God restates his power: This is *his* universe. The rules of that garden are his. He does not have many options. He must repeat the command: *You shall not eat from it!* If you do, you shall die. It is that simple. Does God know what is going to happen? If he tells them he does *not* know what is coming, what God is this? If he says he *knows* what is coming, what God is this? As one snake player put it to him: "In either case, you are in deep trouble!"

It is a spectacular moment to introduce the snake. It can be enacted in many roles—as an outright rebel, sneaky consciousness, sexual temptation, or shadow of the deity. The playfulness and the innate wisdom of the snake's role is a miracle in mythic imagination when played out in a group. Quite frequently, and exactly as in Faust, the counter-god makes the brightest remarks and has the most pointed insights.

I recall a black woman from North Philadelphia who was in my class. She came from a rather Fundamentalist background. She wanted to play the snake, and she played it quite piously and submissively. God was very nasty to her. Then suddenly she woke up and took God on. She talked back wittily, her body language changed, and she laughed and stood her ground: "You know, baby, if it hadn't been for me, you wouldn't have a world! How about that, baby!" She was Mephistopheles redivivus pure and simple, and she loved every sentence of hers.

All interactions between humankind and God lead to an impasse. However the God is actualized, he cannot answer the attacks without contradictions. That is why the arrival of the snake is such a phenomenal mythic intervention. God cannot really speak, act, or participate in this scenario without the snake. To have created this counterfigure to Yahweh is one of the most illuminating contributions in the history of religious symbolism, exactly as it has been in the case of Job and Faust. The snake comes off as an organic evolution in mythic logic (Jung 1956).

Finally Eve takes her bite from the apple. The man joins her in eating from it. They immediately realize that they did something irrevocable. As one Eve pointed: "Adam, we cannot go back, ever. At no time in our future. My future. Your future. It's in here. In my body." At times, it is Adam who wonders first if what they did was right; at times, Eve knows better than Adam that the choice is irrevocable.

In one angry exchange, Adam attacked Eve in retrospect for being what she was. Eve picked up the point and wondered, "Why then did God create me as I am? Did he want *me* to do *his* work without taking credit for it?" Is it, as some psychologists phrased it, the classic "double bind" so he could push her, then chide and punish her, to do what he wanted to do himself?

In another encounter, Adam wondered what the next day would feel like. Return to the grove, he mused, where they held each other. "I felt your body. We walked into the twilight. Now hiding. I wonder what I'll feel tomorrow morning when the sun rises. My flesh reflects its glow, and my mind is terrified about my courage." "*My* courage," responded Eve.

From the first sentence on, the biblical models and the contemporary concerns are intertwined. If we listen to their exchange, we hear them speak on two levels, as role figures in the myth and as contemporary individuals—a modern authority figure and a modern woman and man. Such intermingling of levels, a mixing of past and present comes about spontaneously and often after but a few seconds of play. A host of harsh conflicts has come to the surface surreptitiously: issues of power and parents, a father's attraction to his daughter, weakness and fear inherent in patriarchal society, a woman's insecurity, and her challenge to the man. An entire scenario of family and sexuality, and of submission, control, and loss has been brought up.

The scenes join the past with the present. The crossing of time and space and the exchange of antique and modern consciousness cannot be stopped. Individuals, observers as well players, constantly switch from one to the other, from tale to the present, and from the events there to the events now. The ancient mythic models easily invite and allow transfer, identifications, and projections. We speak through them, we put them on—clothes, masks, and ritual tools. No wonder the ancient Christians would use the Greek term for *mask* (persona) to designate the three faces of the Trinity. Play, mask, personality, and God are metaphors of consciousness.

As we start such a play, we discover how images become alive and relevant, and, at the same time, precarious or even dangerous. In the course of hours or mere minutes, a group entering that myth through play finds out, with surprise, what an explosive tool it has on its hands. The entire parameter of the mimetic entry arises in a few minutes—identifications, conflicts, projections, and spontaneity—and continues to work for days or years.

The responses by the participating group members are many. People disagree, break in, contradict, and ask questions. They have been mercilessly drawn into the tale. Many a tense exchange has broken out between some of the players and some of the observers. It is not this or that insight that matters, or this or that solution—be it theological, psychological, or historical—but the very presence of an enigmatic cosmic order, the extent of social cruelty and contradictions, and an entire imagistic spectrum. The tale, in all its riddles, is of one cast.

A Process of Play

The sketched process has been honed in an intense development over twelve years, in an institute named after the antique "mimesis," in cooperation with my wife, the clinical psychologist Evelyn Rothchild-Laeuchli. I conclude the presentation with a few theoretical remarks that are also related to the work in this institute (Laeuchli 1988:131–202).

When a group of people from various backgrounds replays an ancient tale, a hermeneutic drama is unleashed. With all the cultural patterns, metaphysics, or faith they bring to the tale, it captures their imagination—not everybody's and not under any circumstances; the play is no *opus operatum* of alternative access. Yet often something is working splendidly; the play with myth frees unexpected vitality.

I have watched many a class, as such a dramatic play was introduced, turn vivacious and controversial, and teem with passion and wit. A workshop vibrates with conflict and arguments. Individuals are stunned and participants disagree; they fight with one another and take sides. People stand up, move around, laugh, argue, or become upset or quiet. The class or workshop turns explosive and uncomfortable at times. The change is visible in those who act and in those who observe. As a tale comes to life, a group becomes engaged and concerned. Individuals ponder the play for days.

We discover through the enactment how the mythic model has a power of its own. It has the wisdom to draw us in and absorb us in its riddle, depth, sickness, brilliance, or whatever we see in it. Mircea Eliade was right when he said that myth is a cosmos—a cosmos of its own. The step from ritual to mimetic drama (Turner 1979) opens up this cosmos, which turns out to be the dark side of our life.

As we enter the cosmos of myth mimetically, we are struck by the constant confluence of languages. In his study on the literary transformation of myth, Erich Auerbach quotes a twelfth-century manuscript in which Adam and Eve speak vividly as a man and as a woman. However, they do not speak Hebrew (who would know Hebrew in early medieval Christian France?); they speak medieval French, and they speak in the vernacular (Auerbach 1959:148).

In that rare text, one of the first of its kind in Western literature, a process of far-reaching importance is sketched. The mythic tale is retold and thereby comprehended in the vernacular of the age. The text by Auerbach marks the crucial moment of transition from myth not merely into literature, drama, and poetry but toward spontaneous speech, and to "Commedia del'Arte" and experimental theater.

The modern workshop teaches us dramatically that this dual experience—between "then" and "now," between a given text and the reframing, newly spoken word—is no exception or mistake. Transformation into the vernacular is the daily experience of anyone reading that tale. When we think about it, of course, we use our own idioms. We receive and reconstruct it with our symbols, thoughts, and metaphors. Our sentences are poetic, academic, or the colloquial jargon of a group, depending on the way individuals process thought and express themselves. Auerbach's manuscript is repeated anytime a priest, scholar, poet, or layperson hears and appropriates a story.

Modern players use imagery, models, and metaphors from the tale: tree, snake, fruit, and angel. They accuse one another: God and Adam, Adam and Eve, Eve and the snake. As they evolve their play, modern "translators" also use their own language, weaving the mythic symbols into their own experiences, and into idioms, concepts, and social metaphors of the present, both personal and cultural. The tale is Hebraic, and it is experienced in New York, Newfoundland, and Niedersachsen; it is both an antique and a contemporary metaphor, and the two modes of meaning and experience intersect constantly.

Such juxtaposition of languages is in fact antique. The tragedy of Sophocles used two dialects, Doric and Attic. The confluence of diverse cultural speech patterns was present in the very Genesis cycle under discussion! The Creation tales contain two traditions that were centuries apart, two names for God, and two tales of the Creation (one nomadic and one Babylonian). The process of multilayered cultural transmittance and reformulation was at work in the ancient shaping of these tales. We cannot return to an "original" Creation tale because it never existed; we return to collected texts that are already part of the process we are examining here.

The process of textual juxtaposition and simultaneity is not limited to play; such intersecting happens in every single academic or nonacademic response to the story. The play makes it visible. Because of its spontaneous and dramatic quality, it has participants vacillate more obviously and more easily in the multiple spheres of speech and imagery, and experience and thought.

We not only encounter multiple "language levels" but also a confluence of language and body. When we enter the tale through the medium of spontaneous play, we enter it physically. There comes about a somatization of the text (Hanna 1970:213). We allow the body to participate (Delakova 1984; Yasuo 1988). We do not merely think; we experience and express. We feel. We respond with the shoulders, the lips, and the knees. We look at one another. We lean forward or backward; we crouch, laugh, or stare. Our hearts pound, and our faces flush. The stomach churns. We have difficulties breathing deeply (Fast 1970).

Somatization is to incarnate the text—to bring it down, home, or up—into our breath with which we pronounce it and into our bodies to which we connect it through analogy and metaphor (Birdswhistell 1970). We contain the tale. We dare to become its roles: Adam, Eve, the angel at the door, the snake and, yes, God. It is not merely the tale as a text, as "told" tale, but as experienced tale retold. Someone makes a fist; he responds to the tale. The man refuses to speak; he is afraid of what is happening. The woman flirts or turns away. She too connects to what is going on. The interpretative act or the cognitive event is joined to the physical reality—to flesh and breath and bones.

We do consciously what the ritual has always done. In the Seder, a community recited, questioned, and feasted. The Christian Eucharist ("This is my body") was not merely a formula, a statement of theology, or a text. It was an event. People assembled and sang; they ate and drank. In the spontaneous play, we act out consciously, or at least semiconsciously, what in the ritual goes on intuitively. To reframe a famous sentence by Socrates: *Unexamined ritual is not worth celebrating*. Replay leads to consciousness so that we know what we are playing (Turner 1982). In such replay we begin to comprehend—in part still intuitively and in part cognitively—what the tale may have conveyed and is able to convey.

The Genesis metaphor connects us with the dilemma of sexuality. Just as some churches have told their adherents that according to this tale their bodies are evil, so individuals who play the Expulsion tale at times feel "expelled." It is as if each individual's body is reliving the curse against the body (Lowen 1967). The translation of this myth into the framework of an individual can bring up physical issues, such as menstruation, childhood memories of being physically punished, sexual abuse of a girl, or ridicule of a man because of his body.

In a workshop, a woman played the role of Eve. God made her a dress and punished her for her nudity. She remembered in that very scene, with excruciating clarity, being called ugly by her first lover after having made love to him. She received an access through the metaphor of the tale, and she felt the hurt of Eve as well as her own. Such is an authentic translation in a moment of recognition.

The tale comes to us in layer after layer of culture and meaning. In Genesis, the strata have been identified by sources (Elohist, Jahwist, Priestly) and cultural origins (the nomadic and the Babylonian components of the tale). Such levels continue to intermingle in the interpretative event: first, those of the text itself, with its own strata of tradition, (the cosmological patterns in the two tales, and so on); second, the given traditional models and frameworks by which such texts have been passed on and are inherited (the scriptural models of Christians and Jews, and the cosmological frameworks of the Middle Ages, the Renaissance, and the modern world); and third, we come to it with our own contemporary framework of response (as American, Anglican, liberal, orthodox, critical, devout, secular, feminist, and so on).

Many interpretations can be given and have been given due to these levels. The play affirms the confluence of various frameworks of interpretation. Individuals have a right to deal in that story with justice, unfairness, good and evil, and sexuality. They may see the loss of innocence, the need and pain of growing up, the relation between man and woman, the emergence of adolescence, and the break with the parent. Problem after problem surfaces, of history, culture, patriarchal control, and sexual guilt.

The play cannot solve the dilemma of pluralism caused by these competing explanations; however, it demonstrates the transformation at work in the transmittance of tradition. I give an example, returning to geometric patterns. Historically, the tale presents Adam and Eve as being "thrown out" of the garden. An angel guards the entry. This is a horizontal event; it is an expulsion. In Christianity,

Christ became the "second Adam," descending even into hell. That symbol presupposed a vertical event. Christian imagery turned the Expulsion into a fall. It replaced the horizontal drama with a vertical one. In this view, Adam and Eve were not *driven out*, they *fell*.

When we watch the spontaneous play, we often observe how individuals use metaphors that are neither horizontal nor vertical. To be thrown out of the paradise means to lose childhood, home, country, innocence, or purity. The modern term of *loss* is not historical (it did not happen in some period of past human history) or cosmic (a supernatural event or fall between God and the world), but recurring, often personal—either as individual evolution or as social disintegration—and often connected to adulthood, revolt, maturity, and individuation.

We watch the move from horizontal to vertical to nonspatial metaphor. In one class, a student emotionally and dogmatically defended the tale of Adam and Eve as a "fall," as she had learned in church; she suddenly mentioned losing her parents. Someone else added that she too felt "lost in the world." The two began to talk about guilt (Reik 1975). We watched in front of our eyes the changing of metaphors. Expulsion became fall, and fall became loss. The metaphors changed in the moment of response, and the replay allowed the individuals to connect with one another.

The process of play is a laboratory for observation. It allows us to watch the process of spontaneous creation. Participants are not asked to submit a research paper ahead of time or a prepared statement on the Expulsion from paradise. They enter the paradigm without anyone telling them what to do or what to say. They are not asked for an "explanation." They spontaneously relate to the tale. Their language is often unexpected, poetic, coarse, sarcastic, and nonreligious. It tends to break acceptable patterns. Players curse, sneer, and flirt; they break consistency just as they follow their intuition (Moreno 1983).

Spontaneity allows us to be in touch with our physical and emotional experience. Perception changes. "The sacred world is that which exists spontaneously, naturally in the phenomenal world," wrote Trungpa (1988:126). The players act and communicate with their bodies. People rise, move their chair, shake hands, and wave their arms. They become witty or sad; they seek and think and prod. Bodies confront bodies. This act of spontaneity seems especially forbidden by the academic consensus. Spontaneity brings up streams of fear, conflicts of power, and political uncertainty. Yet there are traces of such spontaneity in the Platonic symposium, in religious debates of the Reformation, and in many a contemporary research seminar.

If we let individuals play spontaneously, without coercing them into believing and thinking and saying certain things, they discover an unexpected relevance in the cosmos of myth. It ceases to be an ancient illusion and becomes a fascinating paradigm dealing with urgent conflicts of justice, cruelty, poverty, and health. However, spontaneity evolves only on one condition: that the leaders do not manipulate the players into saying what they want them to say, but allow them to express what may not be acceptable to us, to the group, and even to themselves.

For instance, whenever this Genesis play gets going, there is bound to be a serious questioning of the god. She often speaks with an honesty we do not expect from such a role, expressing rage, fear, sadness, or hope. Some attack her for such honesty. Other participants are enraged and offended. To them such language is blasphemy. Others are delighted. If we punish or chide either the god or the attackers, we have lost our chance to enable a spontaneous play. The god is allowed to be sweet or nasty, and a tyrant, a philosopher, or a poet.

Spontaneity stands and falls with the safety of the process. The research group has to feel secure. To achieve this is no easy task. We must allow defense and walk the thin line between objective knowing and subjective experiencing. The process works only under such conditions. Under parental control—be it by a professor, priest, or group leader—spontaneity cannot flourish.

Often unacknowledged, a great deal of projection and analogy are at work in our encounters with history or text. The play intensifies the process and clarifies its rules. How naturally we translate the antique tale into the vernacular of our time, into our social framework, and into the realm of our body and emotions. By "acting out" the myth and entering it through our own tongue, we gain a considerably more immediate access to it than if we read or hear it as "text." We feel a sense of immediacy and physical identification; we are given a chance to participate. We are Adam; we are Eve; we meet Adam; we talk to God. The myth has become our world; our world has become mythic again (Rebilliot 1989). The tales allow us to be someone else and that "someone else" is so often in us.

The roles have many variables. Mythic metaphors, as all code, symbol, and paradigm, are multidetermined. God represents authority, but he also identifies with the son and expresses anger against the daughter. He is also a male parent without a partner. Adam is man and Eve is woman, but they are also children, teenagers, and parents. They all express male–female conflict and the dynamic of a dysfunctional family. The snake is not only the metaphor for evil but also the metaphor of sexuality, fertility, seduction, and freedom. None of these codes is univocal.

Projections are subtle. One individual identifies with God; another projects into the snake. Someone is Adam and accuses Eve—it has happened time and time again—for messing up his life. The player has not only identified with Adam but also incorporated the antique interaction between Adam and Eve. Adam lets Eve talk him into eating the fruit and then blames her for what she did. Someone plays Eve and seduces Adam in sensuous playfulness. She has introjected the mythic recognition that the woman can talk Adam into rebellion and sexuality. It was Eve, after all, who was the driving force in Adam's separating from the male parent.

The players and observers identify with the mythic roles. Such projections and identifications are not premeditated; they happen intuitively. The role players do not sit and decide: "Now I am going to identify with Adam, Eve, or God!" They are often amazed, discussing scenes in retrospect, at how easily they became Adam, Eve, or God without being aware of how it happened. Often the role players have little idea of what they are playing out. The spontaneity of the interactions allows them intuitive participation.

Players identify with more than one role. They change loyalties; first, they identify with God, then suddenly they attack him. Often they experience a strong ambivalence. Observers in the group side with one or the other, change their minds, side with two, like none of them, and finally throw up their hands in disgust since none of the players act to their satisfaction.

When we play the tale of the Expulsion, the most serious effect does not lie in any of the many possible psychological or cultural observations but in a basic, partly emotional, partly intellectual turnaround. This story is not what it seems at first sight. The play questions the traditional reading of the tale. It does not communicate what most people think it does. It provokes a reversal of meaning: When God planted the tree, he was not innocent.

As we act out the sequence, we connect to the darkness of the text. We come to realize that the god—he may be masculine or she may be a goddess—may or may not know what he is—or she is—doing. We also realize that the sexual conflict between man and woman is unbearable; and the paradigm of the Expulsion—be it loss of innocence, individuation, sexual awakening, or adulthood—is a far more precarious task than most people in religion dream of. The biblical story has a very dark side.

The result is often what I like to call a "mythic shock," because the tale is really quite horrendous. We watch the play of myth, and we turn away. We rage at the world, at the lack of justice, and at society. Perhaps we rage at nature itself. We are shocked. The god is setting the two young people up; he claims the world is good and then he throws his "image" out of the garden. I am often tempted to rephrase Dylan Thomas: "Do not go gently into that good garden!" The cosmos of myth is cruel, violent, and unfair.

What philosophers have debated for a long time, the play makes graphically lucid: Between the goodness of the god and the existence of evil, between his omniscience that knows the future and his failure to change the course of events, there is no rational solution. To tie goodness to the cruelty of the world remains—Voltaire felt it long ago—a farce.

The mythic shock is the crucial by-product in the depth experience of mimetic play. We are reminded not merely of depth psychology or psychoanalytic theories but of powerful poetic visions, Kafka, Jeremiah, and Dante. We come to experience a coincidence of opposites, or the ambivalence of the gods, which turns the seemingly naïve tale into a harrowing paradigm of sickness and perversion—God and Mephistopheles. This god is not imaginable without the serpent; if we allow honesty, the play connects the two and shows their interdependence. Not everyone tolerates their mutuality, and many observers seek to return—and quickly—to the surface tale that leaves them antagonists. In New Testament texts, we confront by the same process the precarious connections between Jesus and Judas, or the Savior and the tempter (Laeuchli 1992). Spontaneous play, if done in safety, does not lead to a sweet New Age; it leads to an ominous New Age.

I finally touch on two aspects that are especially important to me in this enterprise. The first realm is educational-hermeneutic (Courtney 1987). The process posits, under certain conditions, an alternative to traditional education. If we enter the dilemma of the Expulsion from the garden through play, we learn a great deal about Genesis and mythic tradition elsewhere. We get an inkling of its dynamics. Joseph Campbell wrote about myth in terms of "power" (1988). Enacting the story of the Expulsion has an innate force and is capable of addressing people outside any religious or academic setting. In the act of play, myth works on its own—an imagistic, artistic, dedifferentiated dynamic, as code or metaphor that does not need the prerequisite of historical or conceptual preparation.

Myth does not need advanced knowledge to work. I have played this myth in many classes which combined graduate students with college freshmen. Exceedingly few courses in a university can be designed to encompass both levels of students; yet, in dealing with myth in such a process, the degree of intellectual mastery of the material was not a crucial dividing point. It takes different emotional, artistic, and cultural stamina to experience and weigh the myth through the medium of play (Courtney 1968).

Among the scores of groups with which we have played were impoverished inner-city teenagers in a center for dysfunctional children. The young people, many of them hardly capable of attending school, entered these tales with vigor. They participated and were able to experience, interact, and even to discuss afterwards, unimaginable in a regular classroom setting. They talked about death and loss and the police (the gods) chasing them from the Pizza Hut (paradise). They entered the tales, at times brilliantly, on the intuitive levels for which the myths were originally designed. The play connected them to their daily life in the wasteland of poverty, racism, and abuse, which was their home after their expulsion (material also in Franzke 1977).

Interpreting the mythic play in retrospect and considering historical and conceptual information as well as psychological and therapeutic insights often enhances and contributes to the mastery of the process. I am doing it right now. Cognitive discussion after the play is not in vain. Social and political implications, cultural reverberations, the historical context, and all the connecting anthropological theories can throw light on many aspects of the interaction.

Play needs repetition. Adam and Eve have been repainted ad nauseam. Art historians tend to see repetition of subjects as a matter of "schools"—themes are in demand. That may be so, but there is a more primal dimension to repetition. The mythic imagery has extraordinary power the more familiar we become with it. Children love to have a fairy tale retold; they work through their predicament every time they hear it (Franzke 1989). Replay connects us with what we (almost) know and (almost) have forgotten. One can play the Expulsion time and time again.

Play also has ecumenical relevance. When different Christians, or Christians and Jews—rabbis, ministers, priests, or learned professors from many camps—debate that tale, communication let alone resolution is excruciatingly difficult. Ideologies create gigantic barriers. As we replay the myths mimetically, a mutual access can be opened which cuts across preconceived religious, confessional, and academic schemes.

The mimetic confrontation is not merely educational. There is a chance, tenuous and unpredictable, that we get touched by a tale, because it addresses, like the fairy tales, our deepest fears (Bettelheim 1976). As we enter the play of the Expulsion, we do not merely experience the "power of the expulsion," a paradigm of the loss of innocence or childhood; we also connect with our own expulsion. There exists a connection between hermeneutic and healing (Laeuchli 1987b). In the course of the play, the attempt to understand the lost paradise fuses with the attempt to do something about that loss.

When we think about the myth of the paradise, we may not care if anyone is thrown out of a paradise; we do not care what the rage of God implies, if anything at all. However, as we play the tale, we cannot help feeling its impact, because expulsion "implies" something lost, dark, and uncomfortable. Although the tale appears at first even more precarious and dangerous, the connection between the gestalt of the tale and some kind of a drive, meaning, or insight allows change, however tenuous, to become possible.

"The fear of God is the beginning of wisdom" is a sentence that connects understanding to experience and knowledge to catharsis. Where there is a consciousness of fear, there is a sign of hope. In the "drama of replay," the dividing lines between subjective experience and objective observation become fluid. They do not cease to exist; we are never totally the roles of the tale, and we always return to think and observe. However, the activities of playing out the tale and thinking about it merge.

When Aeschylus put the myth of Agamemnon on the stage of Athens (Grossman 1970), he performed one of the most far-reaching interventions in the history of Western literature. He gave myth a dark life of its own, no longer in a purely ritualistic framework, but as a new medium. It became mimesis (Koller 1953), reflection, mirror, and statement—a statement in its own right. Consciousness was connected with dramatic transformation (Melchinger 1990). Myth turned into tragedy.

In the modern replay, this process is carried one step further. Players and participants experience not merely dramatic transformation—the heritage of classical Athens—but a growing awareness about the extent of such tragedy. We no longer have an audience watching players and players playing for an audience; they are audience and players at the same time. This is why the Commedia del'Arte, psychodrama, and avant-garde theater are such important steps in this evolution. We are the play, and we are the mind that watches it; the dividing lines are in us. We have become the theater of Epidaurus.

As the liminal lines between subject and tale, and between experience and explanation are weakened, a therapeutic potential opens up (Axline 1969). That was the discovery not merely of the Greek dramatists, but of Aristotle watching their tragedies. We learn from the play that the problem of understanding myth is intertwined with some kind of a catharsis (see Aristotle's *Poetics* 6:1449, b27f). As we watch the Expulsion, we experience our loss. The combination of the two, the original mythic drama and the replay in our midst, gives us possibilities of personal and social change. As we play the loss, we connect with it. Such connecting is the beginning of growth (Laeuchli 1988). When I connect with what I lost, I do not need to fear it or deny it.

The drama frees me to reconnect with Adam, with Eve, with the god, and with the snake. Consciousness is then no longer a detached formula; it is an intellectual and personal bodily force (Gendlin 1962). It combines the cognitive-hermeneutic with the existential sphere of "healing." As I play my expulsion, I play my hope.

The mythic play, a tool of hermeneutic and a tool of catharsis, does not work all the time. For people who live on purely intellectual levels of creativity and response, the dramatic replay may be inaccessible. They may not be able to enter, and they should not be made to enter. Recognizing the pluralism of methods, I must not cram this process down an individual's throat. If someone wants to work in the library to find out about Genesis, I do not want to force a workshop on her. The presence and quality of mimetic change cannot be preached, much less coerced. Individuals have a right to defend against this approach, and their priorities should not be violated (Laeuchli 1987:171ff).

The mimetic play is no simple task. It takes strength, safeguards, preparation, and skill, and it would be destructive to try it out unprepared. The play unleashes enormous energies; precarious personal interactions surface quickly, and dark corners of the individual and society are opened. Elements of group work, therapeutic safeguards, and the wisdom of gentle prodding are basic for any successful process (Laeuchli and Rothchild-Laeuchli 1989:53ff). To lead this play is not an easy pastime.

At times, the replay seeks, even if unconventional understanding: *ludus quaerens intellectum*. And at times, it leads to change.

References

Abraham, Ralph. 1988. "Mathematical Hermeneutics." *ReVision* 10:3.

Achterberg, Jeanne. 1985. *Imagery in Healing; Shamanism and Modern Medicine.* Boston/London: Shambhala Publications.

Auerbach, Erich. 1959. *Mimesis: Dargestellte Wirklichkeit in der abendländischen Literatur.* Bern: Francke.

Axline, Virginia M. 1969. *Play Therapy.* New York: Ballantine Books.

Bachelard, Gaston. 1969. *The Poetics of Reverie; Childhood Language and the Cosmos.* Boston: Beacon Press.

Benthall, J. and T. Polhemus. 1977. *The Body as a Medium of Expression.* London: Allen's Lane.

Bettelheim, Bruno. 1976. *The Uses of Enchantment: the Meaning and Importance of Fairy Tales.* New York: Alfred A. Knopf.

Birdswhistell, R. L. 1970. *Kinesics and Context.* Philadelphia: University of Pennsylvania Press.

Bleicher, Josef. 1980. *Contemporary Hermeneutics.* New York: Methuen.

Brown, Peter. 1988. *The Body and Society.* New York: Columbia University Press.

Campbell, Joseph. 1988. *The Power of Myth.* New York: Doubleday and Company.

Courtney, Richard. 1968. *Play, Drama and Thought: The Intellectual-Background to Drama in Education.* New York: Drama Book Publishers.

——. 1987. *Dictionary of Developmental Drama: the Use of Terminology in Educational Drama, Theatre Education, Creative Dramatics, Children's Theatre, Drama Therapy and Related Areas.* Springfield, Ill.: Charles C. Thomas.

Delakova, Katya. 1984. *Beweglichkeit: Wie wir durch die Arbeit mit Körper und Stimme zu kreativer Gestaltung finden.* München: Kösel.

Derrida, Jacques. 1978. "Structure, Sign, and Play in the Discourse of the Human Sciences." In *Writing and Difference,* trans. Alan Bass. Chicago: University of Chicago Press.

Dilthey, Wilhelm. 1976. *Selected Writings.* New York: Cambridge University Press.

Drewermann, Eugen. 1977. *Strukturen des Bösen.* 3 vols. Paderborn.

——. 1990. *Tiefenpsychologie und Exegese.* Olten.

Edmunds, Lowell. 1989. *Approaches to Greek Myth.* Baltimore: John Hopkins University Press.

Erickson, Milton H., and Ernest Lawrence Rossi. 1989. *The February Man: Evolving Consciousness and Identity in Hypnotherapy.* New York: Brunner/Mazel.

Fast, J. 1970. *Body Language.* New York: Evans.

Feyerabend, Paul. 1978. *Against Method.* London: Verso.

Franzke, Erich. 1977. *Der Mensch und sein Gestaltungserleben.* Bern.

——. 1989. *Fairy Tales in Psychotherapy: The Creative Use of Old and New Tales.* Toronto: Hogrefe and Huber.

Gadamer, Hans-Georg. 1975. *Wahrheit und Methode: Grundzüge einer philosophischen Hermeneutik.* 4th ed. Tübingen.

Gendlin, Eugune T. 1962. *Experiencing and the Creation of Meaning.* New York: Free Press.

Goffman, Erving. 1967. *Interaction Ritual.* Garden City N.Y.: Doubleday.

Grossman, Gustav. 1970. *Promethie und Orestie.* Heidelberg.

Hall, Edward T. 1973. *The Silent Language.* New York: Anchor Books.

Hanna, Thomas. 1970. *Bodies in Revolt.* New York: Delta Books.

Huizinga, Johan. 1950. *Homo Ludens.* Boston: Beacon Press.

Jung, Carl Gustav. 1956. *Answer to Job.* New York: Pastoral Psychology.

Kiehn, Antje, et al., eds. 1987. *Bibliodrama.* Stuttgart: Kreuz Verlag.

Koller, H. 1953. *Die Mimesis in der Antike.* München.

Laeuchli, Samuel. 1987. *Das Spiel vor dem dunklen Gott: die mimetische Erfahrung als Forschung und Gestaltung.* Neukirchen.

——. 1987b. "Orpheus and Eurydice: the Healing Component of Myth." *Listening* 22/2:127–38.

——. 1988. *Die Bühne des Unheils: Das Menschheitsdrama als mythisches Spiel.* Stuttgart: Kreuz Verlag.

——. 1989. "Der Verlorene Groschen: hermeneutische Beobachtungen aus dem mythischen Spiel." *Der Evangelische Erzieher: Zeitschrift für Pädagogik und Theologie* 41:68ff.

———. 1992. *Jesus und der Teufel—BEGEGNUNG IN DER WÜSTE: Imagination, Spiel und Therapie in der Versuchungsgeschichte.* Mit klinischen Beiträgen von Evelyn Rothchild-Laeuchli. Neukirchen.

Laeuchli, Samuel and Evelyn Rothchild-Laeuchli. 1989. "The Mimesis of Myth." *Quadrant* XXII/2:53ff.

Lawson, J. 1957. *Mime: The Theory and Practice of Expressive Gesture.* London.

Leutz, G. A. 1974. *Das klassische Psychodrama nach J. L. Moreno.* Berlin: Springer.

Lowen, Alexander. 1967. *The Betrayal of the Body.* New York: Collier Books.

Melchinger, Siegfried. 1990. *Das Theater der Tragödie.* München D. T.

Moreno, J. L. 1959. *Gruppenpsychotherapie und Psychodrama.* Stuttgart: Thieme.

———. 1983. *Theater of Spontaneity.* Ambler, Pa.: Beacon House.

Palmer, Richard E. 1969. *Hermeneutics: Interpretation Theory in Schleiermacher, Dilthey, Heidegger and Gadamer.* Evanston, Ill.: Northwestern University Press.

Piaget, Jean. 1962. *Play, Dreams and Imitation in Childhood.* New York: W. W. Norton.

Rebilliot, Paul. 1989. "The Hero's Journey: Ritualizing the Mystery." In *Spiritual Emergency,* Stanislav Grof and Christina Grof. Los Angeles: Jeremy P. Tarcher.

Reik, Theodore. 1975. *Myth and Guilt.* New York: Universal.

Rossi, E. L. 1986. *The Psychobiology of Mind-Body Healing: New Concepts of Therapeutic Hypnosis.* New York: W. W. Norton.

Schmiedt, Helmut. 1987. *Regression als Utopie: psychoanalytische Untersuchungen zur Form des Dramas.* Würzburg: Königshausen & Neumann.

Siegelmann, Ellen Y. 1990. *Metaphor and Meaning in Psychotherapy.* New York/London: Guilford Publications.

Trungpa, Chögyam. 1988. *Shambala: The Sacred Path of the Warrior.* Boston/London: Shambhala Publications.

Turner, Victor. 1979. "Dramatic Ritual/Ritual Drama: Performative and Reflexive Anthropology." *The Kenyon Review New Series* I/1:80–93.

———. 1982. *From Ritual to Theatre: The Human Seriousness of Play.* New York: PAJ Publications.

Unamuno, Miguel de. 1977. *The Tragic Sense of Life in Men and Nations.* Princeton, N. J.: Bollingen.

Whorf, Benjamin Lee. 1956. *Language, Thought and Reality.* New York: Technology Press.

Winnicott, D. W. [1971.] 1989. *Playing and Reality.* Reprint. London/New York: Routledge, Chapman & Hall.

Yasuo, Yuasa. 1988. *The Body: Toward an Eastern Mind-Body Theory.* Trans. N. Shigenori and T. P. Kasulis. Albany, N.Y.: State University of New York.

Young, Arthur. 1976. *The Geometry of Meaning.* San Francisco: Delacorte Press.

THREE

Bibliodrama in Action: Reenacting a New Testament Healing Story*

Tim F. Schramm

A beautiful new flower has grown in the field of Bible study and practical work with biblical texts. It is called bibliodrama. Appealing to Christians and non-Christians alike, bibliodrama is a broad and inclusive label for a variety of methods and approaches to biblical (and sometimes nonbiblical) texts. "Theme-Centered Interaction," Bible theatre, biblical role play, and psychodrama can be mentioned as some of the elements that contributed to bibliodrama. Theology, pedagogy, Gestalt psychology, and play therapy are also predecessors of bibliodrama, not to mention meditation, dance, and body movement. The confluence of these has generated a new practical hermeneutics that can initiate holistic and existential encounters with the biblical tradition. Bibliodrama provides an opportunity to test, probe, and experience the possible meaning of what the Bible says with regard to our personal and professional existence. In brief, bibliodrama intends to understand the Bible with body and soul, and with heart and mind. It invites people who have more questions than answers, yet seek orientation and meaning in their lives (cf. Kiehn 1987).

In this article, I want to describe *my* bibliodrama and provide a firsthand account of how this new approach works. I divided my article into three parts. I will first talk about my own development and explain three key words (*amplification*, *play*, and *body*). Second, there will be a detailed report on a three-day bibliodrama workshop based on Mark 7:24–30, the story of the Syrophoenician woman. Third, I will conclude with some final hermeneutic reflections.

*Translated by Gerhard Elston and Björn Krondorfer.

I

The goal of our devotion to the Scriptures, the aim of all human endeavors at interpreting biblical texts, should be—as Martin Luther once said—to bring the Bible into our daily lives *("die Bibel in das Leben ziehen")* and to transform written words into living words *("Leseworte zu Lebensworten machen")*. However, for people who are trained in theology and philology at German universities, Luther's words are not easy to realize. Those people read the Bible as a historical source that speaks about ancient times and about issues remote from our contemporary experience. After finishing my doctoral thesis in the field of source criticism of the gospels, I too began teaching biblical exegesis and favored the historical-critical method. Undoubtedly, that was and still is an important task, but Luther's insight of "bringing the Bible into life—here and now!" fell more and more out of sight.

It was a happy coincidence, therefore, that I met Ruth Cohn, Norman Liberman, and John Brinley who came to Germany in the late 1960s to teach humanistic psychology, above all "Theme-Centered Interaction" (TCI) and "Gestalt-therapy" (Cohn 1983; Gordon and Liberman 1972; Perls 1974; Stevens 1975). I participated in several of their workshops, became acquainted with their alternative style of teaching and learning, and tried to translate it into my own field of study, that is, biblical exegesis. As a result, my bibliodrama has been greatly influenced by TCI.

TCI achieves a specific group culture characterized by nonjudgmental attitudes, mutual respect, and growing openness. A set of guidelines, not laws, provides groups with a sense of security. For example, the admonition to be responsible and in charge of your own behavior encourages self-esteem and autonomy; or to let people know why you are asking a particular question avoids artificial debates and reveals the background of the questioner.

TCI intends to create a dynamic balance of theme and interaction. Compared to more academic modes of teaching, TCI groups insist on interaction. Participants, teachers, and themes are all equally important. Participants get to know one another, and share their feelings, thoughts, knowledge, and ignorance. In other words, they interact freely as human beings. Interaction thus opens the door to genuine participation and involvement. Bibliodrama also values and appreciates every individual contribution, be it a word or a gesture (Schramm and Barth 1983:11–24). Friedrich Schleiermacher, a famous nineteenth-century theologian, was perfectly right in asserting that "all humans are artists."

Another aspect that is highly relevant for my bibliodrama is the TCI technique of amplification, meaning that all parts of a fully balanced interaction triangle (the individual, the group, and the theme) become enriched with personal and biographical data. All pieces belong to the patchwork of our life experiences; to share those experiences and their cognitive and emotional layers benefits the process of learning. It anchors the theme in the here and now and in us. I would describe amplification as a weaving of myself into a theme, or a grounding of the theme in myself, in you, and in all of us.

Amplification

Here is an example of how amplification works in New Testament stories. In a class, we read the parable of the fig tree in which Jesus encourages a vinedresser to wait for another year before cutting down a barren fig tree (Luke 13:6–9). Though it is important to recognize Jesus as the storyteller and to place this text in its particular historical setting, we do not fully understand the message unless we amplify the story with our own experiences. How do we do that? For example, we can meditate on trees in order to grasp the parable's central image (cf. Stevens 1975). A guided fantasy can help participants to remember trees in their lives:

> Remember places you lived before, the house in which you grew up, the surroundings, your neighborhood—and the trees which were there. Find the trees of your childhood, renew your acquaintance with them. (Pause). Now, move on and recall trees from your teenage years. Where did you live? Which trees come to mind? Look at them carefully. (Pause). Do you notice trees today? Think of your vacation. Did you perceive and encounter any trees? Is there a tree to which you feel a special bond, *your* tree? (Pause).

After returning to the here and now, many stories come to the surface. The class splits into small groups and further explores tree memories, enacts these images, and eventually plays the Jesus parable itself. As participants identify with the characters of the story, even with the fruitless tree, they become fully aware of how effective the parable is in light of their own experiences with trees. The owner of the vineyard might confront them with the demanding and harsh part within themselves; the gardener with their capacity to be patient and helpful; the tree with shadows we all have to confront. What happened when the owner returned a year later to look at the tree? As Jesus, how would we solve the problem? What about the owner, the gardener, and the tree? Did the tree recover? Is it still barren? Does it need yet another year? Through the method of amplification, participants connect the story with their lives, combine self-awareness with an understanding of the biblical text, and grow spiritually (Schramm and Barth 1983:147–53).

Play

There is a story in Buber's collection of Hasidic tales that demonstrates the difference between books and plays, and between reading and becoming entangled in an enactment.

> The Program and the Play: In the days when Rabbi Bunam still traded in lumber, a number of merchants in Danzig asked him why he who was so well versed in the sacred writings went to visit zaddikim; what could they tell him that he could not learn from his books just as well? He answered them, but they did not understand him. In the evening they invited him to go to the play with them, but he refused. When they returned from the theater they told him they had seen many wonderful things. "I know all about those wonderful things," he said, "I have read the program." "But from that," they said, "you cannot possibly know what we have seen with our own eyes." "That's just how it is," he said, "with the books and the zaddikim." (Buber 1970:241)

The point of Buber's story was brought home when I attended two different classes about the Jewish wedding tradition of "breaking glass." Years ago, when I took a course on Western religions, the instructor mentioned the breaking of the glass—a custom of which I had never heard before. He quoted a Talmudic story of Isaac Klein's famous *Guide to Jewish Religious Practice* in which a sage breaks a costly goblet at a wedding to remind everyone of the destruction of Jerusalem and of other calamities; folklorists added the explanation that the noise of breaking glass was believed to scare away the demons.

This was solid information but—as happens so often in the classroom—this information was more like feeding a computer, or storing up "cognitive data." Of course, it is important to know facts, but merely knowing them is not enough. Understanding, as Rabbi Bunam well knew, is more than and different from cognition.

I did not fully understand the Jewish custom of breaking glass until I attended a class titled "Ritual and Drama," taught by Samuel Laeuchli at Temple University in Philadelphia. He gave a brief introduction but no lengthy explanations. Instead, he invited us to reenact and play the ritual. One of us "became" a rabbi; others became the bride and bridegroom. Within seconds, a fascinating dramatic triangle was created, while the rest of the group sat in a circle and consciously or unconsciously identified with one of the three players. The glass was wrapped in a towel and put on the floor. On one side of it, the bridegroom and bride kept their distance and looked a little strained. On the other side, the rabbi stood and talked briefly about the meaning of getting married and the mutual responsibilities of husband and wife. There was a moment of silence and tension. Then the bridegroom took a step forward and crushed the glass with his foot. Again, there was silence, puzzlement, and consternation. The play came to a close.

After we wrote down our feelings and associations, we began to talk. Everyone was touched and personally moved. The glass, like all symbols, proved to be polyvalent and multidetermined. To some of us, the glass symbolized virginity, and the play was perceived as ritually working through the loss of childhood. Others saw the bridegroom "smashing" his mother's womb—as a son must break away from his mother to be ready for a mature marriage. Some women objected to the all-too-passive role of the female part—to them the story was about male domination and violence. A German student was reminded of what the Nazis had done to the Jews in 1938; the glass represented the shattered glass and destroyed lives of the so-called *Kristallnacht* (Night of Broken Glass). This spontaneous play of less than two minutes had unleashed delight and sadness, hope and fear, and memories and thoughts; and it had provoked active participation. I witnessed again that in playing we cannot but get involved, like in a Greek drama where chorus and audience are as much a part of the plot as the protagonists.

Body

As mentioned above, bibliodrama relies on a fascinating variety of approaches and techniques when working with texts. I have done this kind of work since the early 1970s, directing groups with students, teachers, ministers, and laypeople in church-related adult education programs. I started out by integrating my TCI experience with biblical issues. However, compared to what we do in bibliodrama today, my early work with groups, by and large, did not go beyond what might be called a lively "narration and discussion" circle, even though we used silence, guided fantasy, painting, role playing, and other creative methods. Verbal communication was still the main tool of both interaction and interpretation. Our bodies were present, and we adhered to the rule, "Pay attention to what your body says"; but we did not fully grasp the wisdom of this rule. Bodily postures, facial expressions, turning pale, blushing, throbbing of the heart, stiff necks, or pressure in the stomach were all signals we knew, but we were unable to overcome the culturally imposed overintellectualization in which we were imprisoned.

A breakthrough did not occur until movement exercises, which connected body and text, became an integral part of our endeavors of understanding biblical and nonbiblical texts. This happened in 1985 and 1986 when I began to study movement with teachers trained in Yoga, T'ai Chi, mime, Feldenkreis, dance, and theater (among others, Ellen Kubitza, a former student of Katya Delakova and Moshe

Budmore).[1] After my apprenticeship, I began to integrate the body into the hermeneutic process of understanding texts, coteaching with experts from these different fields. It was then that we really began to do bibliodrama. We started translating biblical stories into body language and searching for bodily equivalents to texts. The body began to play a central role in my definition and practice of bibliodrama. At the risk of oversimplifying a complex matter, I would say that bibliodrama is, first and foremost, a transformation of single words, sentences, and whole texts into the language of the body. Since the body is the most original, primary, and continuous source of awareness and learning, it should be no surprise that understanding is a bodily process. Hebrew thought and language knew about this connection for "knowing" was identified with "(making) love."

II

No conditions or prerequisites are attached to participating in bibliodramatic workshops. Participants do not have to be actors, mimes, or dancers, or theologians, writers, or scribes. Whoever is willing to be involved is invited to join. TCI-inspired bibliodrama groups create a realm of freedom in which participants decide for themselves whether to talk, play, and share, or to abstain from being involved (if that is what they feel they must do). There are many roles in a bibliodrama. Think again of Greek theater with the actors disguised and safely behind masks, the members of the chorus, and the audience itself. I usually tell a group that they should not do what they do not want to do. Though I might encourage them to speak and play, they should always follow their own voice and instinct. I also emphasize that there is no right or wrong, except that physical violence is not permitted.

The ideal size for a bibliodrama group is between eight and sixteen participants. It should never exceed twenty people because each individual needs time and space. We also have to respect the limits of our capacity to listen, perceive, and interact within a given time frame.

I will now describe in some detail a bibliodrama workshop with a group of middle school and high school teachers which met for three days in a parish hall of a rural congregation. The place was well suited for our purpose: A large hall under a thatched roof with a raised stage at one end. The floor was covered with a firm, warm carpet; there was plenty of room for gymnastic exercises. In short, the space was ideal for bibliodrama. I mention this because the space where we meet is part of the *globe* (a term used by TCI). It speaks to us without us being aware of it, and it can further or hinder our play and work.

In my description of this long and complex workshop, I will focus on four people whom I call Hannah, Dora, Carl, and Steve.

Arriving in the Group

The group gathers for its first session. We sit in a circle so that we can all see one another. The circle also provides a structure which, like a mandala, symbolizes and conveys wholeness and security. The first theme suggests itself: "We arrive—in this space, with these people, with our topic, with our text." Many groups, especially in academic settings, will ignore this initial phase, but those who jump too quickly into the subject matter are not likely to reach it. Our "prolonged way" is a more human and life-affirming alternative to the frequently dreary, everyday pedagogical approach. As the instructor, I usually look for exercises that allow me to say something about my background, to inject my voice and my body into this group, and to listen to the participants. In this particular group, we take the following steps.

After an initial greeting, I ask the participants to choose an "element" of their lives (a person, animal, plant, or object) and let this element introduce them. This exercise aims at sharing characteristics about ourselves without spelling them out directly. It is a first attempt at identification, role playing, and change of perspective, all of which are relevant to bibliodrama.

Hannah chooses her bike as her element. The bicycle reports:

> I'm an excellent, expensive bike with gear shift and an especially strong frame. I am beautiful. Hannah saw me three years ago in a bike shop and purchased me on impulse. She took me home right away, and I was surprised that she didn't ride me. She pushed me home and placed me in a dark shed. I stayed there sadly and unattended for several days. Then Hannah came and took me outside the village. I was astonished to find that Hannah couldn't bicycle: She learned painfully and slowly. She was 48 years old. During that time she came daily; it was a good time for both of us. But after a few weeks Hannah stopped coming. Two whole years I stood in the shed as if forgotten. Only during the past few months I have been used again. Hannah bicycles again, but somehow she is different. I don't know everything that happened in these two years, and I don't have to know. I just hope that I'll be needed now, so that I can go out and get some exercise. And I hope that Hannah will soon be again the way she was when she learned to bicycle.

Dora picks a special stone that lies on her night table. It is hollow inside and makes a peculiar sound when you shake it. The stone recalls:

> Dora likes sea-side vacations. While hiking at the North Sea shore, she found me and took me along. Since then I have held a place of honor: She often picks me up and sometimes she holds me up to her ear. I fascinate her, I can sense it. She ponders my age. She says I reach far back into the past. She would like to know my secret which is hidden inside me. But that's impossible because she would have to destroy me. She loves the

blend of "mysterious, yet touchable, audible, visible." Sometimes I think that Dora is a bit like myself—that's why she found me, and that's why she knows how to deal with me.

Steve is a farmer's son. His father owns a farm directly on the Baltic coast. He selects a bluff on the shore near his parent's home. The bluff recounts:

> I have known Steve a long time, almost all the 42 years of his life. Even when he was a baby his parents came to me for strolls with him. Later, he and his playmates often climbed all over me, much to the dismay of his parents and teachers who wanted to protect me. But I liked the playing children. Today, he owns the farm but leases it out. When children come to visit me, he gladly permits it. He says he loves me in my brokenness. He also says that one severe storm will damage me more than a hundred years of children's games, and he is right.

Carl is the father of two children. His 14-year-old boy is handicapped. Carl chooses his children to introduce himself, but he does not really manage to place himself in their shoes. He talks about his children, especially the ailing child. I do not correct him—that is a rule of the game. He and his wife must have endured a great deal. It is not easy to love this child, Carl says.

Physical Exercise

These brief introductions are followed by a physical exercise. First, we walk around the room, look at everything that catches our attention, touch the floor, the walls, and the stage, open and close the doors, stop in front of the windows, and take in the view. We take our time arriving in this space. We return to our protective circle but remain standing. We begin a second round of introductions, this time only with gestures. "Develop a gesture or a series of movements and show them to us; we will then respond by imitating them."

Each participant takes a step into the circle, pauses for a moment, and then performs a gesture or movement sequence. From the tiniest, barely perceptible movement of eyelids to wide-swinging arms, from an uneasy playing with a hand (palms, fingers, or fist) to kneeling or lying down—everyone finds a gesture and seduces us to imitation. As we repeat these gestures, we come to know one another a little more. We become aware of spatial dimensions: The above, the middle, and the below become visible and tangible. We have our first glimpse of playful spaces *(Spielräume)*, the playing that happens within and around us. Our space is multidimensional and so are we and the biblical text.

This brief exercise makes us aware of nonverbal communication, invites us to move, results in stimulation and creativity, and calls on our capacity to perceive. We see and feel what is being communicated. We know that our perception skills, like our ability to listen, are always selective, but we become more attentive to our diverse responses to nonverbal presentations, and we learn to critically review our own perceptions.

Names

Working with our names is another step of our task to "arrive." We take time to remember our names (cf. Schramm and Barth 1983:25ff), just as we will later take time for the text. I suggest that we add an imaginary name to our first names. We introduce ourselves as Dora Music, Hannah Courageous, Steve Clock, or Carl Engine Driver. We silently review these imaginary names, give a few thoughts to what they might convey, and then explain them. Dora talks about her love of music; Hannah says it is the first time that she has attended such a group and that she came with great trepidation but now feels her anxiety gradually subsiding; Steve mentions his problems with punctuality; and Carl thinks of a famous children's book that he is currently reading with his children.

Two or more hours have passed now. Depending on time and place, we can pose a serious question not attached to any game: What makes it easy or difficult to be here? What makes me want to leave and what allows me to arrive? In this workshop, however, we simply take a long break before entering the second unit.

Arriving at the Text

We listen to Mark's account of the Syrophoenician woman. The ear is a comprehensive organ that absorbs and receives; the eye, on the other hand, tends to analyze and deconstruct. The invention of writing certainly represented a cultural leap, but also limited the breadth of perception, as mythology so vividly describes (cf. Plato, 1933: 560ff). I read aloud the selected text. Then I ask one of the women to read the text. We listen to masculine and feminine intonations. Others will read the text again later, while we sit, listen, and hear more with each new reading. We refrain from any comments. The text is welcomed as a stranger in our midst, ever again a new guest. After those readings, all participants receive a copy of the text, and we take turns reading the text again, verse by verse and sometimes word by word. Sometimes we stand up and read while walking in a circle. We are beginning to play. Since biblical texts have a long history—ancient and venerable, yet contemporary and fresh—we read different translations, possibly in Greek, Latin, German, English, or French. The different translations show us some of the text's historic depth and present scope.

After listening we talk. We assume that comprehension is a complex process that needs to be slowed down. We also assume that we do not immediately understand a text or its linguistic components but that, instead, there will be a mixture of understanding and misunderstanding. Successful communication is a gift and anything but self-evident.

We start out with simple observations. We collect and repeat what we have heard. We reassemble the text. We restate as literally as possible and still without comment what the text told us. As a second step, we discuss our emotional reactions to the text. Since our understanding is influenced by our feelings, it is helpful to take them into account and explore them for a while. We will also discover how others are affected by the story that, in turn, helps us to understand one another.

We then proceed to brainstorming—a spontaneous collection of memories, images, thoughts, stories, other texts, songs, films, or whatever comes to mind—while listening to the text. Our musing knows no restrictions. All thoughts are genuine results of the participants' encounter with the text. Not until we acknowledge our insights and fantasies can we critically discern and name the unique characteristics of a story or those junctures where stories overlap.

The final step is a closure. Only after we have passed through the three steps of observation, feeling, and brainstorming do we try to come to a provisional conclusion (cf. Schramm and Barth 1983:67–76). This is the moment when I introduce the "exegetical journal." I ask the participants to write down their comments and reactions to the text. In the course of this workshop, there will be numerous opportunities to continue this journal. The journals document our journey with the text, and we will use them for our final discussion.

Our text is Mark's version of Jesus' encounter with the Syrophoenician woman:

> And from there he arose and went away to the region of Tyre and Sidon. And he entered a house, and would not have any one know it; yet he could not be hid. But immediately a woman, whose little daughter was possessed by an unclean spirit, heard of him, and came and fell down at his feet. Now the woman was a Greek, a Syrophoenician by birth. And she begged him to cast the demon out of her daughter. And he said to her, "Let the children first be fed, for it is not right to take the children's bread and throw it to the dogs." But she answered him, "Yes, Lord; yet even the dogs under the table eat the children's crumbs." And he said to her, "For this saying you may go your way; the demon has left your daughter." And she went home, and found the child lying in bed, and the demon gone. (Mark 7:24–30)

In this group, the emotional reactions are particularly interesting.

The group focuses on the narrator of the story ("Why are you telling us this?"), on the story itself ("I like you, you strange text"; or, "I do not like you; I find your depiction of Jesus unpleasant and unbelievable"), or on the characters in the story (sympathy for the woman; compassion for the sick child; astonishment and indignation regarding Jesus; criticism of the woman's importunity and of Jesus' arrogance).

One "exegetical journal" has the following entry:

> You are a tricky story! I understand you and I don't understand you: Do you want to tell me that I am not supposed to idealize "my" Jesus? He was human—is that what you are trying to say? A person with prejudices? I barely dare think that. In any case, it seems to me that you are a Brechtian wench among the stories of the New Testament, irreverent, street-wise, and impudent. You dance on the edge; you are a story at the margins, a story about a human encounter, a story with barbs.

Movement and Mobility

Before we can actually start playing, I need to introduce physical exercises to familiarize the group with body language.

In one relaxation exercise, for instance, we lie on blankets and entrust our weight to the floor. We no longer need to carry our own weight; the floor supports us. Since pelvic and neck regions are especially tense, we try to relax them with the aim of having our spine touch the floor. In a succeeding series of sitting exercises, we continue to work on the elasticity of the spine. We sit on our heals and put our head on the floor in front of our knees; more precisely, we let our head become heavy and fall forward so that it slowly pulls the upper body down until our head reaches the floor and rests there. Our breath pumps us back into a vertical sitting position. The goal is elasticity, permeability, and mobility; and we are always careful and kind to our body. Then we stand up and enjoy our upright position and mobility. We are trees swaying in the wind, moving forward and backward, and right and left, measuring the space we have at our disposal. We also stand on one leg with our eyes open and closed, and we gradually find our balance. Slower than normal, we begin to walk, a meditative walk through space, noticing every step and moving forward and backward with our "seeing feet."

Theme-Centered Interaction

We continue our journey toward the text. We now introduce the TCI technique of amplification. One of the central themes in the story of the Syrophoenician woman is, "Asking for help and accepting help," and we need to locate it in our own lives. We break into small groups, and each person silently reviews various stations in his life. We jot down a few notes about our memories and thoughts, and then we share our recollections about "asking for and accepting help."

It is a difficult subject. Some of us prefer to relate how we helped others. We are clearly reluctant to admit helplessness. Indeed, our own experiences emerge only gradually and painfully. Carl relates how much he admires the woman in our story. She appears to ask for help very matter-of-factly, something Carl finds incredibly difficult to do. He had waited a long time before forcing himself to see a doctor, whom he had to ask for help for his son and family. Dora says she cannot ask for help though, in the past, it would have saved her much misery. She says nothing else. Hannah talks about a problematic relationship. She says that she tried to avoid her problems by distracting herself and immersing herself in work. Then she began to have continuous nightmares, in which, each time, she managed to escape from danger, though she would always wake up in great agitation. She ignored these dreams until she finally got into a serious car accident on an open road without traffic. She says now that she made this accident happen. While still in the hospital, she found the courage to speak of her problem to a physician and ask for help. She says that she had to be pushed into accepting help.

I wrote the following lines in my exegetical journal:

> To become like children—they know how to ask for help. I can manage to ask peers for help. I think I could ask a good friend. Why do I not want to admit my need for help? When I finally went to the doctor, he was of great help and just a few words lifted my anxiety. What a woman in this story, asking for help against brusque rejection, not taking "no" for an answer.

This exercise on help fosters intimacy and trust among the participants. We allow some of our scars to be exposed, something that happens in intimate conversation and prayer, as the Hasidim say.

Translation into Body Language

We form new small groups. Each group's task is to express the theme of "asking for help" in body language, or to translate some of what we have said or heard into physical expressions. After a brief period of preparation, we meet again as a whole group and witness fascinating, disquieting, and powerful bodily performances. Some of the gestures with which we introduced ourselves in the first unit— the open hand, for instance—reappear, together with new and different ones. It is ever fascinating to discover how our body, that all-but-forgotten instrument, gradually awakens and comes to life. The courage to tolerate our own gestures and to slow down our movements grows, and the body's vocabulary increases. We respond to the performances by telling what we noticed, felt, and imagined. When Steve, for example, stands for a long time in the circle in a stiff and cramped posture, and when his knees finally give way and he allows himself to fall—not onto his knees but sideways, the face bitterly turned toward the floor—we physically experience how difficult it is for him to ask for help. We are relieved when, after a seemingly endless period of immobility, his left hand appears from under his prone body and forms an open bowl.

Narratio

After a long day with plenty of time to "arrive" in the group and at the text, we use the evening for an exercise that I call *narratio*. Generally, a text that explains everything and leaves no room for a reader's creative participation is boring. A text with gaps, on the other hand, stimulates our imagination. The power and efficacy of many biblical texts derive from their numerous gaps and openness to multiple interpretation (cf. Iser 1985:136ff, 1972; Sternberg 1985:186ff). The Markan story of the Syrophoenician woman is a good example, because it offers many openings for our imagination and invites diverse interpretations. This becomes evident, for instance, when we interview the characters of the story. Our questions compel them to provide additional information. We may ask the woman, "Has your husband played a role in this matter? Do you live alone with your daughter?" We ask Jesus, "Why did you want to hide?" We ask the child, "Please describe what is wrong with you." We can fill the gaps by identifying with one of the characters and retelling the story from his or her perspective. As we retell the story, we develop an intimate bond with the character we represent. The story plays us, and we play the story. We can hide behind the text and yet the text allows us to reveal ourselves.

In this group, we identify with the ailing daughter. Since she does not appear as a protagonist in Mark's account, exegetes and commentators have often entirely overlooked her. Our task is to retell the story from the daughter's perspective. We give ourselves thirty minutes to discover a story and write it down. Then we listen and marvel at the diversity of the stories.

I call Steve's version "The Anxious Mother." Steve imagines the daughter to be sick because the mother is overprotective. She observes each of her daughter's steps, suspects all kinds of dangers to body and soul, and finally destroys her spontaneity and freedom. The child is left in autistic isolation.

Hannah's story knows no miraculous healing. The daughter she envisions suffers from depression. Hannah senses that the daughter will have to live with it and that this is perhaps the other side of her sensitivity and creativity. By identifying with the daughter, Hannah experiences healing as a process, breaking through a vale of darkness, albeit knowing that there will be other dark valleys.

In Carl's version, the daughter suffers from epilepsy. She is miraculously healed and becomes a disciple of Jesus. Healing and discipleship appear as two sides of the same coin. As I listen to his story, it seems to me that Carl is protesting against Hannah's and Steve's psychologizing interpretations (Christology versus a Jesus-centered approach?).

I am particularly impressed by Dora's narratio:

The other day, when we were sitting together in the cafe, you asked me whether I have ever actually been sick. You said I always look so healthy. What shall I tell you? Yes, I have not been ill for a long time. I am really well, thank God. You are probably never ill, you said. Oh yes, yes—once, a long time ago, I was seriously ill, I was sick unto death. I must have been about 12 years old; I only remember dimly. For a long time I didn't want to know anything about it. It began with anxiety attacks before sleep. Yes, it sounds crazy, but that's what it was: I was afraid of falling asleep because . . . because once asleep I had terrible dreams or, rather, always the same terrible dream. In this dream I fall—I fall and fall into a bottomless abyss, and then I suddenly see rocks below me as I fall, and I know that I am plunging towards them. . . . This dream was so ghastly, so dreadful, that I did not want to fall asleep anymore; the dream reoccurred time and again. I tried to keep myself awake; I slept less and less, even jolting out of sleep. I grew gaunt, nervous, listless. Soon I was unable to listen to anyone. My girlfriends couldn't handle the situation and even my father talked to me less and less. I lost contact in school and within the family. I was much alone. I believe I would have been lost if my mother had not supported me. She was always looking after me, even when I stopped speaking entirely. She never gave up on me; she dragged me from doctor to doctor. None could help me, none did. One day, my mother had left and I sat alone in my room. Suddenly a great fatigue overtook me. I could not resist . . . then the dream . . . I'm falling, I'm plunging, there are the rocks, I'm dropping like a stone, down, down. All at once, I don't know from where and why, I am transformed. . . . Now I am no longer a stone but a bird . . . I can fly. I am no longer scared of the abyss, for I have wings . . . I must have slept deeply and for a long time after that. Toward evening my mother came into the room and saw me lying on the bed, relaxed. She must have known that I was healed. She looked at me kindly and caressed me. Then she said: "It is good, and dogs, dogs we are not; that much he understood." I didn't know what she was talking about, but I knew: It is good.

In the morning of the second day, we begin with extensive body work. We repeat yesterday's exercises (repetition and gradual intensification are fundamental to bibliodrama which, like meditation or

Yoga, requires continuous practice). Once again we are lying, sitting, standing, and walking—now with more awareness. New exercises are added but the goal remains the same: slowing down and discovering new spaces for play, awareness, and permeability. Breathing exercises allow us to experience our inner spaces while even the tiniest movement can teach us about external space. A wonderful phrase of Paul provides the spiritual background: "Do you not know that your body is a temple of the Holy Spirit within you, which you have from God?" (1 Corinthians 6:19)

Today I also suggest exercises that are specifically related to the story of the Syrophoenician woman, although I do not directly refer to the text as of yet. For instance, we spend time with the theme of "arising" (getting up like a cat, a child, or someone of old age); or with themes such as "hiding," "approaching," or "lying down." Sometimes these physical exercises, which were inspired by a textual reference, turn out to be the text itself: The text becomes incarnated.

Choosing a Word

After listening to the story of the Syrophoenician woman several times, I ask the participants to find their own word in this text—a single word to which they feel particularly attached. They write it down or paint it on large sheets of paper. After some time, I reread the text and ask the participants to place their words on the floor as they hear them. A new text emerges before our eyes. The story, now cut up into segments, is displayed on the floor (see Figure 3.1).

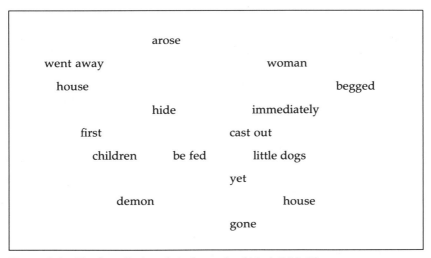

Figure 3.1   *The floor display of single words of Mark 7:24–30*

We look at the picture, or the single words and the total arrangement of this new "text." Did we miss certain words? Why were they not chosen? We split into groups of three and talk about what we see. Here again, the technique of amplification comes into play and is now applied to single words. Focusing on those words and phrases, we realize their power, multiple meanings, and openness. In this manner, words are resymbolized and remythologized, a phenomenon that is even more evident when we play. Hence, our next step is to play with these words.

Wordplay

We sit in a semicircle, and the open space in front of us is transformed into a stage. We take turns performing our word, translating it into body language. We can use props and accompany our playing with words or sounds. After the performance, we respond, like a chorus in Greek theater, to what we have seen and felt. The players also have the opportunity to comment on their play and on the group's reaction.

Steve has picked the word *arise*. He gets up, takes a step in the direction of our stage, and waits. When he steps onto the stage, he seems transformed. His body radiates tension and concentration. He walks in slow motion and stops decisively at center stage. It seems as if he is rooted there. Suddenly he flinches, and his face is tensing. He would like to move but cannot. He tries to lift the right foot from the floor, but his foot appears to be glued to the floor. He bends down, grasps his calf with both hands, and tries to uproot his foot. Again he fails. Steve is nervous and bewildered. He tries to raise the other foot, but to no avail. He begins to sway back and forth; perhaps the full weight of his body will loosen his feet. They still remain glued to the ground. Suddenly, as if a magnetic field had been switched off, Steve walks, runs, hops, and whistles happily.

The group responds to Steve's performance: "You had a firm position, too firm. Your arising was a liberation from the prison of immobility; the contrast between your struggle and the ensuing dance to music impressed me; I struggled and suffered along with you—the first step across a boundary is very difficult; when I saw how difficult it was for you to get started, I was reminded of the Exodus story." Steve says little after his play. He is exhausted. He has performed what he has experienced, leaving the century-old rural tradition to go to his own world. He had to struggle to give up agriculture and become a teacher, but he does not regret his decision.

Dora has chosen the word *begged*, but inspired by Steve's presentation, she wants to show how she envisions the *arising*. Calm and relaxed, she walks into the center, sits down, and rolls herself up into an embryo position. We see her breathing. Then she begins to move, like a chick in an eggshell or a flower bulb in the ground. The movements become fiercer; one arm stretches out straight into the air. Dora is now hunched on her knees, resembling a flower swaying in the wind which grew too fast.

The two performances stimulate our thoughts. Did we see a masculine and feminine variation on the theme? We certainly saw two different choreographies: Steve's upright posture and Dora's protective gesture. Steve's imagery showed determination, (rational) effort, and force, whereas Dora's presentation alluded to the world of the organic. Was rising an organic process or the result of willpower?

Like Dora, Hannah and Carl also chose the word *begged*. Hannah sits with both arms stretched forward, her eyes coyly turned to the ground, and her hands shaping a bowl. The image recalls Barlach's sculpture, *The Beggar Woman*. Carl tells a story in three acts. He furiously stamps his foot and curses, "Damn!" The next moment, he anxiously looks around and says, "Please, somebody help me!" Finally he folds his hands; we recognize a prayer in its distinct liturgical style: "God, please hurry to help me!" Both stories leave open whether their requests are answered.

Another participant performs the word *fed* ("Let the children first be fed") and shows us how eating can turn into gluttony and greed. He mimes grabbing food and stuffing it in his mouth until he can barely breathe. He suddenly stops and collapses. After a pause, he begins to shout: "Full, full, full—but never enough!" The group members react to what they felt—disgust, revulsion, and fear. The word *fed* seemed to be such a harmless word in the story; now it has attained a scary ambivalence. Just when are the children fed? Who decides? Are there any criteria?

A performance about the word *demon* concludes these wordplays. The performer is large and vigorous; he stops at the edge of the stage, leans against one of the beams, and slides down into a squatting position. He pulls his black leather jacket over his face. The leather, this animal skin, disfigures his human face. As he rises, he looks eerie, threatening, and powerful. His lower body is partially hidden by the beam, but his torso and head bend forward. A shriek like that of a hawk pierces the room, and he disappears behind the beam.

We talk about the significance of the face, and about disfiguration and our fears of demons. Are there demons? What do they look like? How do we confront them? I write into my exegetical journal:

> This work in a microcosm is full of unexpected insights. With the help of embodiment, we discover the richness of individual words. Words are resymbolized; they regain their (almost magic) power. Each *logos* is a myth (remythologizing). I am especially impressed by the depth of just one word: did not Steve's presentation of "arise" contain all the problems of the story? I was reminded of dream analysis which asserts that the first

sentence of our dreams provides the "theme" while the last offers the "message" which the unconscious wants to transmit to the conscious.

Because of time limitations, I cannot conduct some of the "shorter plays," in which three to five participants create a performance based on a combination of their words, such as *arose/house/hide/immediately*, or *children/dogs/yet/gone*.[2] These shorter plays often contain the whole story and represent an intermediate step from solo to ensemble play. They are a good bridge between one-wordplays and the central bibliodramatic play which I call the "grand play."

Bodily Exercise

It is now the morning of the third and final day. We begin again with the already familiar physical exercises—lying, sitting, standing, and walking. Since we are more at home with ourselves and our bodies, we expand those movements. For example, the meditative walk is enriched by the theme "encounter," which prepares us for the coming dramatic play.

We start with an "encounter of the hands." We lie on our backs on blankets and relax the spine. The arms are stretched out and form a straight line with our shoulders, and the palms of the hands look to the ceiling. We raise our hands slowly, with arms outstretched and eyes closed, and draw a semicircle in the air. Our hands meet in the middle of this semicircle above our faces. They will touch briefly and then slowly return to the floor. I have done this exercise frequently, and it is fascinating to observe how tension builds up, as if a magnetic field is created, long before the hands touch.

Our next exercise is an "encounter of the eyes." We pair up and face one another, but we leave the largest possible distance between us. Silently and cautiously, we walk toward one another and stop at an appropriate distance, still looking at one another. Our eyes meet for a brief moment or longer, whatever feels comfortable. Then we return to our original position. Afterwards, we discuss our experiences with the beauty and burden of intimacy and distance.

We find a new partner and line up at a distance of about five to six feet. One of us plays "resistance" while the other plays "insistence." The ensuing struggle between "no" and "yes" relates directly to the Markan story. We again discuss our experiences, and then we change roles.

The Grand Play

Finally, we are prepared to play the whole story. The bibliodramatic centerpiece is based on improvisatory play, or a kind of a "theater of spontaneity." Once again, the group sits in a circle, and as the play director, I ask each participant who or what they want to play. In this play, it is possible to embody any character, object, or even abstract idea (such as "The desire to remain hidden" or "the news that Jesus is there"). Although the roles are prescribed by the text, the players make their own choices. When the players have found their roles, I interview them briefly to facilitate and reinforce the process of identification. "How do you feel—as the house, the sick child, or the dog? Have you thought of a characteristic movement or gesture? Would you care to tell us something about yourself? What is it we should know about you? Find sounds, a particular body posture, or a word or sentence, and look for 'your' place in this space."

In our bibliodrama, we have the following roles:

- The house that lets him enter but cannot hide him (male)
- The house that welcomes him and wants to hide him (male)
- The desire to remain hidden (male)
- The table (female)
- The neighbor (male)
- The neighbor's wife (female)
- The news that Jesus is there (male)
- The woman's house (male)
- The sick child (female and male)
- The woman/mother (two females)
- The grandfather (male)

The players take their places in the room. How we spontaneously place ourselves in this space sheds light on the story and the ensuing dramatic play. The three men who embody various aspects of the house and Jesus' desire to hide there find their place upstage; all of them stand in an upright position. Near the house that welcomes him and wants to hide him, "the neighbor" settles in with "the neighbor's wife." Later in the play, he will introduce himself as a Gentile and sell a calf to "the grandfather" for an offering to the gods. "The table" stands in the middle of the stage and becomes the central symbol. To its left is "the news that Jesus is there." At the front of stage left, diagonally across from "the house that welcomes him and wants to hide him," stands "the woman's house." Under its roof (the player's outstretched arms) lies "the sick child," embodied by both a woman and a man. "The woman/mother," played by two women, sits in front of the house and talks to "the grandfather." The two women sit on the ground, and the grandfather is squatting on a low stool. The entire configuration of high and low, right and left, and male and female is significant for our grand play. It is an image replete with oppositions (see Figure 3.2).

After all players are in place, we freeze the image for a moment. I go from player to player and repeat who they are: "You are the table; you are the sick child; you are the grandfather; and so on." Then the

The desire to remain hidden (male)

The house that lets him enter
but cannot hide him (male)

The house that welcomes him
and wants to hide him (male)

The neighbor (male)
The neighbor's wife (female)

The table
(female)

The news that Jesus
is there (male)

The woman's house
(male)

The grandfather (male)

The sick child
(male and female)

The woman/mother
(two females)

Figure 3.2 *The spatial configuration of roles*

play begins to unfold. Although my description follows a sequential order, the action often occurs simultaneously. "The desire to remain hidden," a partial aspect of Jesus, begins by delivering a lengthy and apologetic speech.

> I want to hide, I want to hide, I want to hide. I have a right to hide. I've already done more than all of you put together. No man can take care of everybody. I'm tired. I must gather new strength for "my own people." That is why I'm here—and that is why nobody should disturb me. I want to remain hidden, and I know why.

He speaks louder now and gesticulates with his arms, his right hand forming a fist as if to defend himself against intruders—if necessary, with violence. "The house that welcomes him and wants to hide him" is barricaded behind chairs. It emphatically agrees with what "the desire to remain hidden" says; it claims to provide the protection Jesus needs and promises to do everything to keep Jesus undisturbed.

Stage left, "the house that lets him enter but cannot hide him" contradicts them. It says that it no longer has a key and that it is open and can never be locked again. With the loss of the key, it has lost its power to lock up and out. A verbal battle ensues: The three men embodying the house and Jesus fight. A crack rips this "house" of Jesus apart.

The woman's house is also full of inner tension. The sick child is embodied by a man and a woman who lie on the floor. They want to touch and lay with one another but an invisible force prevents them from doing so. Whenever they approach one another, it seems that they receive an electric shock. However, they do not give up—it is a truly demonic picture of being torn apart or of a disintegrating person. I spontaneously think of schizophrenia and schism. The woman/mother, in the shape of two women, casts a long and sad look at the sick child and says: "Sometimes I think it is not my child." Then she turns away and quarrels with the grandfather. He declares that something needs to be done to atone the gods, and he suggests buying a calf from the neighbor to give as an offering. The woman/mother disagrees but fails to stop him. The grandfather shuffles along the right edge of the stage and talks to the neighbor about his daughter and her child, and about the power of the gods against which humans are impotent.

Besides the sick child's disintegration and the growing schism between the woman/mother and the grandfather, another tension surfaces. It is a tension between the two sides of the woman/mother, represented by the two female players. One side (player) talks, screams, and argues throughout the play (as, for example, with the grandfather), while the other does not speak but acts. She strongly identifies with the dogs, utters inarticulate sounds, and crawls back and forth on her knees. (I am reminded of brutish strength residing within us.)

The picture I have described so far shows two houses separated from one another and divided within themselves. Each one leads its own life and is involved in its own problems. How can we reconcile these houses? Who can build a bridge? Two players or roles come to mind, "the news that Jesus is there" and "the table." The former is able to cross borders and freely moves around the two houses. Played by a man, he walks to and fro, listens here and there, and repeats softly yet insistently, "Jesus is here. And there. And here. . . ." The table (played by a woman), on the other hand, is centrally located and functions as an integrating symbol.

The simultaneous actions in both the Syrophoenician woman's house and the house in which Jesus tries to hide are, so to speak, Act I of our bibliodramatic play. This phase comes to an end now, and Act II begins in which activities switch to "the news that Jesus is there" and "the table." The news ignores "the desire to remain hidden" and proclaims its message in front of the house of Jesus. At the same time, "the table" forces itself into "the house that welcomes him and wants to hide him," disregarding the barricades. Its mere presence reveals the inherent tension. After "the table" has opened the house of Jesus, it returns to the center, which also is the dividing line between the two houses. The player of "the table" lies down on her back, her arms outstretched (as in the encounter of the hands exercise)—an image of openness which recalls the crucifix. Her words sound like a chant: "All are invited, all at one table!"

At this point in the play (which also introduces the decisive Act III), the woman/mother begins to travel. She hears the message of "the news that Jesus is there" and "the table," and she winds her way across the stage and the line separating the houses. She is a double figure of woman and dog, both pleading with words and radiating with tacit power. The pleading mother (portrayed by one of the two women) is hampered by the resigned comments of the grandfather and the neighbor. She is silenced before she even reaches the house of Jesus. The other mother-figure, however, opens up a path, assumes leadership, and tolerates neither disagreement nor obstacle. She is able to silence both the grandfather and the neighbor with the sheer physical force of her primal, dog-like barking. Encouraged by "the news," "the table," and "the house that lets him enter but cannot hide him," she pushes her way forward to "the desire to remain hidden" and "the house that welcomes him and wants to hide him" and simply brushes them aside. Her brutish, animal-like cry shakes them up and liberates them from their self-imposed prison. They might have been able to resist a verbal confrontation, but such a mother/dog assault of inarticulate sounds and vigorous gestures disarms and overwhelms them. At that very same moment, the behavior of the sick child transforms. The man and woman (the two sides of the child) touch and embrace one another for a long time, then they rise slowly. Their rising is like a resurrection or a rebirth. They leave the house to join the other players at the table for a round dance. The man who plays "the woman's house" (his arms were stretched out over the sick child) finally says: "I am a happy house, for I have been healed." The play ends here.

During the follow-up conversation, we talk about our choice of roles, the unfolding of the improvised performance, and our feelings and insights. The conversation veers from personal-biographical remarks to observations about the biblical text and the play as play (body language, choreography, and libretto).

> I come from a strict Christian home and belong to a free church: I have problems with a Jesus who is available to anybody at any time. You can only belong to Jesus if you truly believe in him. I had to be that house that wants to hide him. I was annoyed that the Gentile neighbor lived directly next to me, as if we had something in common.

> After we had chosen roles I was much disturbed because there was no Jesus. I thought we can't play it this way. During the play, however, I noticed that Jesus is hidden yet present in various roles.

It became clear to me that the house of Jesus (the congregation) is just as much in need of healing as the woman and her house. What we have talked about and what we have played is a double healing. The house of Jesus is healed from its prejudice against Gentiles/dogs/the unclean, while both the child and the woman are liberated from "schizophrenia" and disintegration.

I was so happy that the child's agony had finally subsided. That the embrace and the standing up were possible moved me deeply—a miraculous healing after a long illness.

We allow ourselves plenty of time to think about our play. Not everything must be explained or understood, but it is good to stay with our experiences for a while, as if looking at a painting.

Concluding Discussion

The concluding discussion consists of both a therapeutic-oriented (*seelsorgerlich*) and exegetical part. The former almost organically emerges from the grand play since we were all personally involved. Our choice of roles and our playing have allowed us to learn something about ourselves and the group. Since we talk about our strengths and weaknesses, the therapeutic-oriented conversation requires great sensitivity. What we share is not a matter of right or wrong, or good or bad. Without judgment, we describe what we have witnessed. We are aware that we have been together for only three days; that puts into perspective our statements and makes the encounter with our shadows bearable. Frequently these talks open up new avenues of understanding or even counseling and therapeutic processes. If we truly draw the text into our lives, as Luther suggested, then it can help us to enter new processes of learning and growth which may hurt and heal.

Steve's object, which he had chosen to introduce himself to the group, was, as we recall, a bluff on the seashore where children like to play; the word he later selected from the biblical text was *arise*, reflecting his own story of departure. In the narratio, he identified with the daughter (I entitled the story, "The Anxious Mother"). Perhaps for Steve, the mother is unconsciously Mother Earth, the family farm, and tradition, all of which tried to keep him though he had to leave. Finally, in the grand play, Steve embodied (together with a female coplayer) the sick child who got healed. The New Testament story provided him with images, symbols, and roles of identification which helped Steve in his courageous and determined striving for integration. The story thus had an implicit therapeutic effect. Our bibliodrama is also bibliotherapy.

Dora's object consisted of a stone with a secret. Responding to the exercise "asking for help," she claimed that she cannot ask for help;

later she chose the word *beg* but replaced it with *arise*. Her performance was an organic emergence, a kind of birth, in contrast to Steve's deliberate and forceful separation. In the narratio, Dora recounted her nightmare and her transformation from stone to bird. In the main bibliodramatic play, she portrayed the pleading mother. In Dora's case, too, we notice movement and development toward her secret, inside and outside.

Carl was particularly impressed by the New Testament story. Since he has a sick child at home, we understand why he maintains a certain distance. It is admirable, however, how he has lived with the story in these three days. In the beginning, he spoke about his children but avoided any identification. This is perhaps Carl's challenge: to become the child in the story and to look at the world, the mother, and the father with the eyes of this child. In Carl's *narratio*, the child suffered from epilepsy. Did he suggest an incurable illness? Mark's story of the miraculous healing dates back to biblical times; we, however, must live with the illness today. In the central play, Carl chose the role of the grandfather (albeit no such role existed in the text). He related to the sick child but kept his distance. Would his *anima* be able to help him overcome resignation and to transform his faith to one that can move mountains?

The goal of this therapeutically informed conversation is not psychological interpretation but sensitive perception, not therapeutic confrontation but mutual consolation. In a bibliodramatic setting with a therapist as coleader, it is conceivable to introduce direct intervention and move into the realm of therapy. This, however, would be the exception. Bibliodrama has implicit therapeutic effects because it relies on holistic methods for reenacting healing stories, but it is not therapy itself.

The exegetical part of the concluding talk focuses on the historical dimensions of our story and reminds us that we are not the first to try to understand the text. Now we can work in small groups with our exegetical journal, share questions and insights, and consult exegetical commentaries and sermons. The historical-critical method gives us a certain distance to the text and thus facilitates our parting from our identifications. The commentaries offer additional information which often matches and confirms what we discovered in the play.[3] There is, for example, a long debate about whether or not Mark 7:24–30 is an authentic Jesus-story. Can we interpret the Syrophoenician woman as a biographical story of Jesus who is caught up in a prejudice against Gentiles? Did Jesus consciously and purposefully limit his mission to Israel? For answers we would have to look into other texts; but given the nature of our sources, we will most likely fail to come up with an unambiguous conclusion (cf. Johnson 1986:191f). We have to work on our image of Jesus. Can I imagine the historical

Jesus rejecting a woman asking for help, just as a white physician in an apartheid system might refuse to treat a black child? Can I imagine that in the course of such a story Jesus, too, becomes the subject of a miracle—a miracle healing him from a prejudice? If we read the story biographically, we see a Gentile woman saving Jesus from the prison of a covenantal theology that leaves no room for Gentiles.

Is this a story about testing our faith? Whoever favors this interpretation protects Jesus: "He did not really intend to refuse help; his resistance was merely meant to probe the woman's faith." She demonstrates extreme humility, ignores insults, and maintains exemplary faith against all odds. If we favor this approach, what kind of Jesus would we have? What should we think about the first narrator of this story who depicts Jesus as someone testing people's faith? In our bibliodrama, this interpretation did not apply. The biographical approach, however, was relevant. We did not encounter an omniscient, sovereign Jesus testing our faith; rather, we saw a human being who, under pressure, fell back onto familiar reflexes and prejudices but was eventually liberated by another person, so as to act more humanely.

A third interpretation asserts that the story of the Syrophoenician woman is symbolic of the early church's struggle over the inclusion of Gentiles. The struggle of the Syrophoenician woman would thus have to be read as a reflection of the post-Easter community that retrojected this story into the time of Jesus' ministry. It would be a story within the history of salvation. Our bibliodrama play, among other things, incorporated this symbolic interpretation. We moved the story into the post-Easter situation, or into our situation, where Jesus is absent yet present. He is present in the news (gospel), the house torn apart by infighting (congregation), and, above all, the table (Communion). Jesus is also present in the woman's house in the form of the news and faith. I think that the pleading woman is *anima naturaliter Christiana*, who believes, as Bartimaeus believed, despite the resistance. It is her faith that heals her, the child, and Jesus.

We also look at related texts, such as the Cornelius story (Acts 10–11), and Galatians 2:11ff where Paul recalls the conflict with Peter in Antioch. The issue of fellowship at a communal table threatened to split the congregation into Jewish-Christian and Gentile-Christian parties (Galatians 2:11ff). Was that like apartheid and schism in the church of God who lets the sun rise over all? For Peter (and the James-faction agitating behind his back), Paul became the Syrophoenician woman. There is also Galatians 3:28 and the magnificent text of Ephesians 2:11ff in which Christ united the far and the near; he united Jews and Gentiles, and through his death, he eliminated the dividing wall. He annulled the Law with its commandments and ordinances to melt the two into one new being in his own person and to establish peace and reconcile the two in one single body. These issues became visible in our play, as, for example, in the image of the "schizoid" ailing child or the schism between the house of Jesus and the woman's house. Furthermore, our play, characterized as a post-Easter reenactment, brought a woman on stage who was also *Jesa Christa incognita*, reminding the Christian community, for its own sake, of the word and work of Jesus. In our play, reconciliation did not occur within the closed walls of a church but outside its doors, accessible to all.

Before the group parts, we listen again to Mark's story which has occupied and moved us for three long days. We have not exhausted the text but moved toward greater understanding.

III

Let me end with some hermeneutic reflections that are deliberately suggestive and lead us back to the play.

While historical-critical exegesis consciously keeps biblical texts at a distance and continuously emphasizes the difference between then and now, bibliodrama seeks to relate contemporary experience to the process of understanding. Historical criticism engenders alienation; bibliodrama calls for recognition and intimacy (Schramm and Barth 1987).

Many biblical texts are designed to assist in the task of understanding ourselves. The parables of Jesus are a case in point. They are plays with plots, dialogues, monologues, and leading and supporting roles. Frequently, people who appear in a parable, whether in the past or today, find themselves on stage. We are drawn into the play, whether we like it or not, and we are no longer detached like an ordinary audience. The unique nature of the biblical tradition calls for a comprehensive approach, which bibliodrama is able to offer, whereas historical criticism merely describes one aspect.

Bibliodrama is committed to a pluralistic hermeneutic. It knows and tolerates no exclusive truth claim in contrast to some manifestations of historical criticism. On the contrary, bibliodrama asserts that the biblical tradition is polyvalent. When we play, we discover that not only the text as a whole but also single words are multidetermined. Interpretation is not only explicative but also innovative and creative. In playing, we gain access to the spiritual energy stored up in biblical symbols.

To admit that texts have multiple meanings calls for active participation. Bibliodrama is a collective interpretation of a group of mature individuals. Such interpretation is not arbitrary as is frequently feared. It is true that we play the stories, but the stories also play us. They assert themselves in the playing with a remarkable power (cf. Martin 1985:525f).

Bibliodrama offers a learning environment in which head and heart are as much involved as soul and body. We care about the text as we are equally concerned about ourselves—*nostra res agitur*! The translation of text into body language promotes a holistic process of understanding. Since many (though, by no means, all) biblical texts are healing stories, they have a healing effect as long as we allow them to "do their thing." You cannot enforce healing, but bibliodramatic exegesis and play can foster these processes. Bibliodrama can be described (to paraphrase Ruth Cohn) as "the art to anticipate and replace therapies."

Biblical texts have been (too) often analyzed. In bibliodramatic play, we seek to repeat or reenact them and to meet them on an existential level. When we restrict ourselves to analysis, we remain who we are. Playing, however, offers new experiences and transformations. For playing is "praising the possibilities in our life. In playing we cross boundaries. In playful rehearsals we learn that our reality does not have to remain as it is, but that it can change" (Ernst Lange).

Notes

1. For more information, see R. Hübner, E. Kubitza and F. Rohrer, *Biblische Geschichten erleben* (Hamburg, 1980); ibid., *Spielräume für Gruppen*, 2 vols. (München, 1984, and Hamburg, 1986); Katya Delakova, *Beweglichkeit: Wie wir durch Arbeit mit Körper und Stimme zu kreativer Gestaltung finden* (München, 1984); J. Benthall and T. Polhemus, *The Body as a Medium of Expression* (London, 1977); J. Lawson, *Mime: The Theory and Practice of Expressive Gesture* (London, 1957); and E. Y. Spiegelman, *Metaphor and Meaning in Psychotherapy* (New York/London, 1990): 24ff.

2. In another bibliodramatic workshop, we played, for instance, a drama in four acts with the word combination of *arise-house-hide-go*. In Act I, we were sheltered and hidden in the mother's womb, then born. In Act II, we built a house in which we spent a happy childhood. In Act III, the house turned into a fortress, or a demonic prison, from which we fled in panic (whoever does not shatter the confines of this house becomes a demon—becomes, for example, xenophobic). In Act IV, finally, we discovered and enjoyed our freedom under the open sky and shared a meal with those who had also left. Afterwards, we discussed the dialectic of attachment and freedom and the necessity of shelter and separation. Our experience of individuation (as a result of our growing identity which liberated us to engage in an authentic community) seemed to correspond to Jesus' developing individuation. Leaving his motherland, he entered an "alien nation" (alienation); a foreign (Gentile) woman helped him overcome boundaries, and Jesus learned to appreciate and love the stranger.

3. Compare the splendid essay by Gerd Theissen which provides a brief survey of the history of interpretation and then argues for a social-historical reading of Mark's text. Theissen revives the biographical interpretation: "That Jesus expresses prejudices in this story must shock us at first. . . . But it

is of utmost importance that he overcomes these prejudices. Jesus is changed by this encounter with the woman as much as she is. There is a profound meaning: We only help humanely when we are willing to be changed by those who depend on our help. If Jesus in this story is liberated from an austere and prejudiced attitude, then those who follow him should expect their own kind of prejudices; and they should be willing to give up any resistance which impedes the overcoming of prejudices. To achieve this, even the best among us are dependent on others for opening their hardened hearts" (1984:225).

References

Buber, Martin. 1970. *Tales of the Hasidim.* New York: Schocken Books.

Cohn, Ruth. 1983. *Von der Psychoanalyse zur Themenzentrierten Interaktion.* Stuttgart: Klett-Cotta.

Gordon, Myron, and Norman Liberman. 1972. *Theme-Centered Interaction: An Original Focus on Counseling and Education.* Baltimore: St. Paul Press.

Iser, Wolfgang. 1972. *Der Implizite Leser.* Stuttgart: Ernst-Klett Verlag.

_____. 1985. "Die Appellstruktur der Texte: Unbestimmtheit als Wirkungsbedingung literarischer Prosa." In *Methoden der Interpretation,* ed. C. Schlingmann. Stuttgart: Reclam.

Johnson, Luke Timothy. 1986. *The Writings of the New Testament: An Interpretation.* Philadelphia: Fortress Press.

Kiehn, Antje, et al., eds. 1987. *Bibliodrama.* Stuttgart: Kreuz Verlag.

Martin, Gerhard Marcel. 1985. "Das Bibliodrama und sein Text." *Evangelische Theologie* 45 (November):515–26.

Perls, Frederick S. 1974. *Gestalt-Therapie in Aktion.* Stuttgart: Ernst-Klett Verlag.

Plato. 1933. *Phaedo.* London: Loeb Classical Library.

Schramm, Tim, and Hermann Barth. 1983. *Selbsterfahrung mit der Bibel: Ein Schlüssel zum Lesen und Verstehen.* München/Göttingen: J. Pfeiffer/Vandenhoeck Ruprecht.

_____. 1987. "Bibliodrama und Exegese." In *Bibliodrama,* ed. Antje Kiehn et al. Stuttgart: Kreuz Verlag.

Sternberg, Meir. 1985. *The Poetics of Biblical Narrative: Ideological Literature and the Drama of Reading.* Bloomington: Indiana University Press.

Stevens, John O. 1975. *Die Kunst der Wahrnehmung: Übungen der Gestalttherapie.* München: Chr. Kaiser Verlag.

Theissen, Gerd. 1984. "Lokal- und Sozialkolorit in der Geschichte von der syrophoenikischen Frau (Mark 7:24–30)." *Zeitschrift für die Neutestamentliche Wissenschaft* 75:202–25.

The Origins of Bibliodrama and Its Specific Interest in the Text*

Gerhard Marcel Martin

A Short Definition of Bibliodrama

Many people are looking for new ways and means to approach biblical texts. Bibliodrama is one way. It is an open process of interaction between people (mostly twelve to eighteen participants) and the biblical tradition. Bibliodrama is an experiential and text-oriented approach. The participants learn how to connect their own experiences with those that linger in biblical stories, contexts, and personae, as well as in prayers, meditations, and homiletic passages of the Bible. Experiences residing in biblical stories can also be distorted and buried. The bibliodramatic process, therefore, not only aims at making participants aware of inconsistencies, projections, and inhibitions in biblical texts but also encourages participants to discover the liberating and life-affirming potential of those texts.

With respect to content, these processes consist of plausible and historically conceivable experiences, memories, and expectations that are manifested in biblical texts. Myths, rituals, and historic-biographical material are particularly appropriate for bibliodrama because they possess a dramatic quality. However, even Psalms and the Letters of Paul are a result of experiences and expectations, and are thus accessible to bibliodramatic work. When struggling and empathizing with this material, people encounter themselves in a mediated and indirect way. Group process and self-encounter are legitimate topics of bibliodramatic processes.

*This essay is a revised version based on two articles published in Germany (Martin 1985, 1989). It was translated by Björn Krondorfer.

A complete bibliodramatic process always consists of several units and often lasts for several days. The approach is "holistic," because body-related, aesthetic, and theological work is an indispensable element of bibliodrama. Bibliodrama is based on physical exercises, meditations, and methods borrowed from humanistic psychology and play and theater pedagogy. Depending on the qualification of the instructor and interest of the group, emphasis can be given to playful interactions, depth psychology, religious education, or theological work. The main difference between bibliodrama and a more strictly defined therapeutic work is that the entire process always leads back to biblical material. Hence, individual work within the group is the exception.

My own bibliodramatic work consists of three constitutive stages. It begins with physical exercises and body meditations, continues with playful and imaginative processes, and concludes with an evaluation. During the last stage, a group tries to understand the selected text as well as group process and personal experiences. The evaluation, therefore, has an exegetical and pastoral aim.

Origins of Bibliodrama

During the mid-1970s, bibliodrama developed in Europe as a response to time-specific tensions, crises, and chances. The relevance of biblical traditions and devotional practices was fundamentally questioned, affecting the academic study of theology as well as the work of campus ministries. Only sociopolitical interpretations, and historical and ideological criticism of the Gospels were accepted as legitimate methods. By and large, subjective and devotional dimensions were ignored. As a result, worship services, if they had any value at all, became expressionless, shapeless, and rational. In this climate, even serious attempts to experiment with *"kerygmatic* plays" withered. These *kerygmatic* plays, which were written by Christian authors (but not developed by the participants themselves), intended to transform biblical material into a dramatic plot which laygroups would perform in the context of congregational life.

At the same time, however, a boom of stimuli emerged from the areas of creativity and depth psychology, and influenced theological and church-related endeavors. Even Christian pedagogy discovered—once again—the importance of creative abilities of individuals, as opposed to purely reproductive and intellectual achievements. Both theory and praxis highlighted "festivity" and "play." Although early experiments often degenerated into a sheer battle with materials, colors, fabrics, and paper, they also changed the entire style of communication within the church.

Undoubtedly, this creative period produced great and unrivaled examples. "The Living Theater," the "Bread-and-Puppet Theater," Peter Brook's company, and Jerzy Grotowski's theater laboratory demonstrated effectively how groups can work holistically, use the same kind of material over a period of many years, and make it relevant to the present. All of these groups started with very intense body work, broadened the body's expressive repertoire, and created performances of a material that had entirely "gone through" the actors and was completely "present."

In the same period, the dialogue between theology and depth psychology, which hitherto had only been infrequent and mostly theoretical, became more tangible. Since then, additional training has been offered to ministers with the purpose of enabling them—especially in the field of pastoral care, but also in other areas of parish work—to become more conscious of themselves and their parishioners, and to act accordingly. Through scientific reflection, this training is aiming at revealing and shaping the subjectivity of all participants in any given interaction. Applied to *kerygma*, it means that the white light of the presumably objective Christian message refracts in each existent person and circumstance, and shows the luminous abundance of the sometimes confusing opulence of the colors of the spectrum.

It is in this context that bibliodrama takes on the challenge of a crisis and makes use of new stimuli. Bibliodrama tries to encourage a creative and intellectual process in which a biblical text, carefully delimited in its scope, passes through the participants of a group who, in turn, approach and appropriate the text critically and holistically. As the participants identify with biblical personae and scenes, proximity and distance to biblical traditions become evident. Identification is achieved through the methods of body work, play, talk, and inner imagination, all of which assist in determining one's attachment to and detachment from the material at hand.

Bibliodrama Versus Psychodrama

Any history of bibliodrama would remain incomplete without mentioning psychodrama, despite the fact that there is a definite difference between a psychodramatic and bibliodramatic approach to biblical texts. I would like to present some remarks about the origin of this term.

The first so-called bibliodramas were actually psychodramas with a biblical story.[1] Ward reports that Raber and Warner worked with "the technique of bibliodrama" in seminars for ministers, with religiously interested people, and in Sunday schools (Ward 1967:204f). The report is about Genesis 22, a text that preoccupied one of the female participants. As the protagonist, she played Isaac. The author's brief comment reads: "Needless to say the protagonist gained insights into her relationship with her father" (Ward:205). Apparently, the woman got insights into her relationship with her father with the help of this text which served as a springboard to dive into her biography. Yet there is no mentioning of any further insight into the historical and depth-psychological dimension of the text itself, nor of the potential effect that a reinterpreted text might have on the woman's self-understanding. Ward's laconic conclusion reads: "The psychodrama submethod—'bibliodrama'—was found to be particularly amenable to clergy groups and the often unproductive religious education methods that are perpetuated on weekends throughout this country" (205).

Despite obvious differences between bibliodramatic and psychodramatic work with biblical texts, one cannot ignore the many common assumptions and parallels of their practice. In both bibliodrama and psychodrama, verbal communication is not primary but only one part of a process which includes body work, theater, gestalt, play, and imagination. This distinguishes them from other forms of Bible classes or therapeutic interventions. Structurally, bibliodrama and psychodrama are similar with respect to evaluation, reflection, appropriation, and apprehension. It seems to me, however, that a clear difference remains. After giving feedback concerning identification and role playing—a part that belongs to the final analysis of those processes—bibliodrama always returns to its departure point, which is the interest in the biblical text. This interest, understood as a shared pattern and continuous element of the Christian tradition, can become the central topic of discussion, even if the text sometimes appears to be distant, unfamiliar, and alien. This explains why bibliodrama remains an *indirect* self-encounter. The unique character of bibliodrama is not based on the specific material used to initiate processes (here, psychodrama and bibliodrama are similar), but on the treatment of this material.

Short Examples of Bibliodramatic Work

It might be helpful to pause for a moment and simply list a few bibliodramatic events so that readers, unfamiliar with this work, get a better grasp on the issues at stake.

- Cain kills Abel and, thereafter, lives under the sign of death (Genesis 4). This happens not only in the biblical text but also on the way to a bibliodramatic workshop, passing through the poor neighborhoods of an American city. It also repeatedly happens in the play with constantly changing roles between Cain, Abel, and God (cf. Laeuchli 1987).

- A bibliodramatic meditation of Psalm 139 reveals the trauma of religious education (God as cosmic "cop"). However, it also acknowledges the possibility that trusting God can be experienced as encompassing refuge and security (cf. Martin 1987).
- Students of theology explain to an empty chair, on which Jesus is supposed to sit, why they are not able to play him, until someone, aggravated by the absence, takes on the role of Jesus, trying it on like a new dress.
- At the end of a dialogue between Jesus and Pilate, which lasts for several days, Pilate finally asks every participant, one by one: "What is it that Jesus has that I do not have?" A minister answers after an almost sleepless night: "I do not know what Jesus has that you don't have. Had I to decide between Jesus and you, it might be you I'd consider. After all, you are a human who is guilty and who can become guilty, even if you don't like it. But Jesus . . . "

It should be evident by now that a bibliodramatic approach does not claim to uphold a (seemingly) objective message. Yet, during the unfolding of a bibliodramatic process, the subjectivity of individual insights and experiences transforms it into intersubjectivity. The group shares the internal and external truths of the biblical tradition and acknowledges, if necessary, that not all aspects of the tradition can be contemporized. The participants are no longer in danger of being alienated by imposed theological or ecclesiastical claims; rather, they creatively and critically work together on their mutual interpretations of certain biblical scenes and traditions, and on their own and other's experiences and thoughts. Tim Schramm's assessment seems accurate: "Bibliodrama should be considered as a kind of sermon, a sermon no longer of one individual, but a sermon of the many, a sermon of a mature and responsible congregation" (1987).

Present Fields of Practice in Germany

In the present, and probably near future, bibliodrama takes place in three different areas.

1. Church groups, such as youth groups and councils, have worked with biblical material for long periods of time (in any case, longer than just an evening—sometimes even lasting for months) to reappropriate the Bible through innovative means. Bibliodrama can be one kind of playful, congregational Bible work. It is conceivable to further develop it into Bible theater, refining bibliodramatic scenes to such a degree that they transcend the confines of the original group and can be performed to others (as, for example, during services, celebrations, or

occasions for participatory play). The difference between bibliodrama and traditional *kerygmatic* plays is obvious. Bibliodramatic processes encourage participants to rely on their own theological and aesthetic, personal, and political judgments when appropriating biblical traditions and making them relevant for today.

2. Increasingly and intentionally, bibliodrama is employed in long-term programs for the training and continuing education of church staff, especially of ministers and deacons. The aim of this work is the critical, experiential, and historical interpretation of the biblical tradition. Participants are encouraged to experience, through their own bodies and intellect, the contribution of Christian faith to their personal and professional existence. In addition, they learn the basic methods of bibliodrama, enabling them to apply bibliodramatic principles in their own practice.

3. Finally, there are those therapeutic in-between zones, particularly between bibliodrama and psychodrama, in which, theologically and therapeutically trained people (or trainees) work. This work usually focuses more on personal and social biographies and less on interpreting biblical traditions. It differs from bibliodrama because of the latter's insistence on always returning to the biblical material.

Compared to therapeutic movements, bibliodrama is not strictly organized. In the past, it has only known open forums and unrestrained interchanges, and it ought to keep this freedom in the future. Depending on the qualifications of the leader and the specific interest of the group, either the playful, dramatic, depth-psychological, or theological aspects of bibliodrama can be emphasized. The bibliodramatic movement only remains creative if it is not restricted to the realm of church and religion, art and aesthetics, or therapy and depth psychology. Bibliodrama also does not intend to fill empty spaces, neither for the worshiping community nor for the artistic and therapeutic community. As a holistic approach, bibliodrama keeps in touch with all these disciplines but, if successful, claims its independence while working in between these conventional areas.

Basic Structures and Aims of Bibliodramatic Body Work

I spent a year in New York studying the "art of movement" with Katya Delakova (cf. Delakova 1984; 1991). During that time, I got rid of certain kinds of stiffness, broke taboos of self-perception, learned to send awareness to places where there was no awareness, and enlarged my imaginative sensitivities. I made a surprising discovery: I became alive in those places to which I could send my awareness and where I was able to develop my inner imagination. I performed movement sequences that previously seemed impossible for I could not, in a deep sense, conceive of them.

What you cannot imagine will not take place. This is a basic principle of Moshe Feldenkrais's body work from which Katya Delakova received important stimuli. Delakova was also influenced by other techniques. She started with classical ballet, studied Yugoslavian and Israeli folk dance, and moved on to Chinese and Japanese masters of aikido and T'ai Chi in New York. Her body work has also been considerably influenced by her long-lasting cooperation with her husband's elementary voice, and choir and rhythm exercises that he, Moshe Budmor, developed as a composer, conductor, and musicologist.

Beyond every paramilitary drill are different ways of living in one's body, of familiarizing oneself with it, and of getting to know the body's house or temple, room for room and hallway for hallway, in which one has always been. This is how I live in my body and how I know my home, or my instrument. Breathing therapies, body-oriented meditation schools, *eutony,* music and play therapy, and dance and theater training all offer different methods and techniques. What is to be taught by facilitators of bibliodrama, even if only on a rudimentary level, should be mastered to some degree and understood from within. Different kinds of body work implicitly assist in carrying out different objectives of bibliodramatic processes.

I want to mention four aspects that have proven to be very helpful in my own work.

1. The first is change of focus. People come from various contexts, and they need some distancing before entering a group or a text. They also need distance from the perceptual and behavioral patterns of their daily life, family, job, church, or even therapy group. If a group really wants to encounter a biblical text from a new and original perspective, it must virtually "unlearn" hasty responses and familiar interpretations. Therefore, it is helpful to turn one's attention to what is often ignored: exercises that strengthen one's breathing, movement vocabulary, and sensitivity. Only when a conscious process of unlearning is initiated is it possible to liberate oneself from old patterns and to be open to new experiences, such as a renewed sense of breathing rhythms, movement sequences, and a general sensitivity towards the body.

2. Inspired by Katya Delakova's work, I conduct exercises, as far as possible, with closed eyes because it fosters the possibility of switching tunes, changing one's focus, and unlearning and re-learning. An important side effect of those exercises is the fact that "blind" participants do not compete or correct their own and other people's behavior. Movement sequences are precisely and poetically described by the facilitator, and the participants transform the instructions into movements. Participants also need to be reassured that neither efficiency and control nor right and wrong are important. Thus, a group is able to find its center. At the same time, any dominant behavior, which often prevents quieter participants from becoming active, is discouraged. This method succeeds in soliciting the first interactive responses, emerging from a centered and silent place.

3. During certain stages, physical exercises are a direct preparation for the creative process. Calm breathing, for instance, can lead to meditation or to getting in touch with one's inner images (active imagination). Certain bodily positions, such as open and closed gestures, erect poises, and movements close to the floor, are also directly relevant to the work. In the story of the Temptation of Jesus (Matthew 4:1–11), for example, the devil suggests to the Son of God to pray to him. What would the gesture of such a prayer look like? Physical exercises are always an experimental and experiential discovery of one's vocal and gesticulatory impressions and expressions.

4. Body work is essential for bibliodrama although it differs from traditional athletics, the latter usually following a pattern of effort, exaggerated strain, and relaxation. Bibliodrama, however, also needs to be distinguished from classical bioenergetics and similar methods which aim at exceeding one's present strength and capacities, thus inevitably (though often intentionally) producing stressful situations. By making these distinctions, we arrive at the first "safety valve" of bibliodrama: Since no participant is urged to go beyond her present capacity or to overstep deeply felt personal limits, bibliodrama remains essentially in control of the participant's willingness (or reluctance) to broaden her range of perception and interaction. Bibliodrama produces and provokes as little resistance as possible, and bibliodrama never tries to work against resistance; rather, bibliodrama treats resistance, in the terminology of Ruth Cohn, as "disturbance." This does not imply, of course, that bibliodramatic body work calms people down to such an extent that it impedes the transition to the more active and interactive stage of bibliodrama.

Bibliodrama and Its Interest in the Text

In bibliodrama, a group's initial contact with a text, often characterized by preconscious and capricious interests and imposed meanings, can take on very different forms. It is possible to begin with group improvisations which rely on changing roles and other guidelines. It is also possible to start with active imagination or recitative chants (of Psalms, for example), because they get a text to "sing," bringing it to the group's consciousness. Many publications on alternative Bible work (cf. Wink 1980) and other innovative techniques, exercises, and examples of more or less sophisticated methods are available (cf. Martin 1986). These methods usually (and often successfully) intend to systematically slow down the reader's response and reduce it to its essentials.

It is also conceivable not only to slow down processes that are associative and rely on active and creative reader responses but also to stop them—quite similar to the *epoche* of phenomenology. During these "stops," the text could be perceived *only* as text, or as a web of words and linkages between words. As one step in the bibliodramatic process, this stopping would require a drastic withdrawal from subjectivity and would necessitate a reading that is methodologically reliable and intelligible.

It seems to be that a linguistic-synchronic interpretation is legitimate at this point. Whether it can be effectively and intelligently used needs to be demonstrated for each instance. No method, including this one, can be isolated or taken for granted.

The Use of Linguistic Analysis

When a group stops at a certain point of the bibliodramatic process, it can be helpful to analyze different codes in the biblical text.

Action codes, for instance, can be discovered by asking questions such as: Who are the subjects? What are the actors doing? Topographical codes, on the other hand, can raise the following questions: Which sites are mentioned? Which details about places are given (such as mountains, cities, rivers, and so on). A chronological code could ask: Which details about time does the text present? A sociological code could ask: Which issues about economics, politics, and ideology can be found in the text? A symbolical and mythological code could ask: What symbolic and mythological images and words does the text contain (cf. Clevenot 1978; Füssel 1983, 1987)?

Due to this method, it is possible to study a text even in totally nonhomogeneous groups (as far as their previous theological knowledge is concerned). This deserves mentioning because it is my experience that nonhomogeneous study groups do not appreciate structural or scholarly advice or any other kind of intervention by academic theologians. Advice, in these circumstances, is experienced as oppressive knowledge and denounced accordingly. This discomfort is even present in small work groups and can only be resolved with limited success. A very simple structural analysis, however, allows a reading that starts from an equal and symmetrical basis.

Although the significance of group dynamics and other pedagogical aspects cannot be underestimated, the method of deciphering codes usually increases the awareness of and interest in the text. Participants very often recall that they got a better understanding of subject matter and personae of the text—even though this approach, at first, seemed abstract, impersonal, unpolitical, and void of any emotion.

I would like to describe a specific example for using linguistic analysis in a bibliodramatic setting. This example stems from a rather late phase of a bibliodramatic course on Exodus 32, which I offered in the spring of 1984 at the University of Marburg. The participants, who were familiar with bibliodrama's conscious acknowledgment of subjectivity, showed their sympathy and interest in the *people* (of Israel) and tried to arrive at a positive understanding of the excessive and regressive dance around the golden calf, which they regarded as a positive collective symbol.[2] Interestingly, this group of students (compared to groups that are more differentiated with respect to age and profession, and with which I worked elsewhere on the same text) had trouble identifying with Moses; identifications took place only within an extremely narrow and stereotypical framework. After extensive dramatic work, in which Moses repeatedly descended from the mountain, it became evident that the students actually played out family dramas: Father Moses returns from work, and he is exhausted and easily irritable; the people play the role of children in a quite regressive and anarchic mood; and Aaron, in the role of the mother, tries to appease the conflict.[3]

Theology students who are midway through their education know enough, of course, about exegetical and historical scholarship to recognize their personal preferences and subjective interpretations, but they are not free of them. For example, during the initial encounter with the text, the students were asked to find two particularly appealing words to transform into bodily gestures. Their choice of aggressive and destructive nouns and verbs—*wrath, fire, crushing, smashing, tearing apart*, and so on—was irritating. Furthermore, it was not possible to integrate these words into an emotionally, intellectually, and biographically coherent field. I finally decided to send the students to the mountain with the help of a guided fantasy. Approximately half of them returned from their inner journey with remarkably different images compared to those of the valley with the golden calf, Aaron, and the people. These differences manifested themselves in titles that the students later gave to their (real) paintings of their inner journey. These titles serve as a written record: "Eternal Covenant," "The Weightless Turning to Nothingness," and "Open Redemption." We should not conceal, however, that half of the students had trouble entering the journey and got lost in the midst of fatigue or at the foot of the mountain. Some simply recalled vacation memories though, interestingly, these were often connected to a more archetypal theme: solitude, encounter with animals, mountain lakes, the sky, and the abyss. Experiential processes need time.

Shortly before the end of the semester, I decided to offer a reconstruction of the topographical code of Exodus 32. I wanted to show how this code is animated by assigning personae to different places, or, more accurately, assigning the movement of people *between* different places. I intended to demonstrate the method of linguistic analysis, but I also wanted to evaluate retrospectively what had been achieved in this course and what had for many remained inaccessible and ominous. Figure 4.1 is a drawing of this topographical code which shows a landscape that clearly maps out the whole scene of Exodus 32.

The mountain that Moses ascends is located on the way from the Land of Egypt to the Promised Land. It is Moses alone who goes up and down the mountain (the text does not say whether Joshua accompanies him). The others stay behind in the camp. Moses smashes the tables at the foot of the mountain—and thus, the juxtaposition of God's word from *above* and the people's life in the camp *below* becomes insurmountable. All those who "are on the Lord's side" (Exodus 32:26) are to assemble in the gate of the camp, at this dividing borderline between people and golden calf and Moses and God. This is why the participants could not identify with Moses, why he was "so far away" and "abstract." The participants heard, at best, Moses's call but barely followed him to the gate of the camp, let alone to the mountain.

Such a linguistic-analytical reconstruction of the text's basic structure enabled the group to clearly determine what had been achieved and, more importantly, what had remained inaccessible. The movement within the story itself proved to be more dynamic than the participants' mobility of this bibliodramatic process.

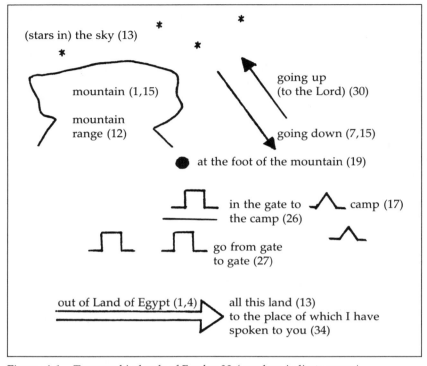

Figure 4.1   *Topographical code of Exodus 32 (numbers indicate verses)*

The Text Is Not Consumed

Keeping the example of Exodus 32 in mind, I would like to move on to a more fundamental question. The above-mentioned examples demonstrate how strongly my bibliodramatic work is determined by the text. It begins and ends with the text. I am emphasizing this because bibliodrama and other new avenues to Bible work are often reprimanded for their allegedly subjective and psychologizing approaches. Because of their projections, transferences, and avoidances (the latter should be understood as defense mechanisms), they lose sight of the text's autonomy. Unfortunately, there are statements—particularly in the dialogue with depth psychology—that seem to reinforce these charges: programmatic statements that profess to explain what happens to individuals or a group when they approach a traditional text or worldview.

The direct and unmediated experience leads humans via the entire, positive-religious potential of humankind to themselves. . . . Human beings,

Protestants, modern humans need for their journey towards humanness the substance of a positive religion, not because they must show it to some kind of authority at the end of their journey, but because they need it as provision for the journey. . . . Because of the analytic process of consumption, the Christian substance is deprived of its objectivity and authority. . . . [In this hermeneutical context], storytelling seizes all religious and non-religious images and figures . . . and, by shaping them, constantly consumes and depletes them—like food whose only purpose is to be consumed; or better, like notes whose only purpose is to be seemingly consumed when being played. (Bernet 1970:39, 129, 137)

Bernet's main point, which cannot be rejected too swiftly, is the radical and personal transposition of an external text to one's own internal and external text and context, a transformation that belongs to the metaphorical realm of "devouring," "consuming," and "depleting." Adopting this framework, I would argue against Bernet (though his last sentence hints at a similar insight) that a musical note remains a musical note and that notes, in contrast to food, are only "seemingly" consumed. It is exactly the nature of not being consumed that allows their continual performance. It seems to me that the symbolic consumption is essential not only to notes but also to religiously solid texts and symbolizations. I would further claim that it is also the fundamental principle of the mainstream of Western, Judeo-Christian religion, which does not call for the dissolution of the cosmos to receive God's revelation. Above the main entrance of the Jewish Theological Seminary in New York, the words of God's revelation at Sinai are inscribed: "And the bush was not consumed" (Exodus 3:2). Whenever God's world appears in the fire of revelation, it will not be consumed!

Let us go back to our starting point—the relationship of bibliodrama to the text. I claim that the interest in reader response and the promotion of interactions between text and reader do not necessarily divert from the interest in and significance of the text. In the course of interpretation and appropriation, the priority does not simply and irreversibly shift from text to reader. This seems to be the main difference between a more theological and a more therapeutical (or depth-psychological) treatment of biblical and other texts. It is essential to bibliodrama.

Each method mentioned so far is determined by the hermeneutic principle that the entire movement always returns to the biblical material. This continuous return to the text, with respect to both method and content, is certainly not unrelated to hermeneutic insights and to assumptions and ramifications of dialectic theology. These connections should not be ignored or denied. Yet the distinctive character of bibliodrama is apparent. It searches for an understanding of revelation and experience which, instead of formulating its own theological hermeneutic, is open to enter a dialogue with other, nontheological epistemologies, especially aesthetics, depth psychology, and the scientific study of communication, media, and texts. We have thus come back to our basic subject, bibliodrama's interest in the text, and I need to take up again the discussion of linguistics and general semiotics.

The Text as Web

Dialectic theology bypasses a question that I have been pursuing in my theoretical work on bibliodrama and on biblical texts in general, which is the question of why and how this material, or this medium, can tolerate, over centuries and millennia, so many reinterpretations, reframings, changes of perspectives, and encroachments without becoming meaningless and irrelevant to the reader, without disintegrating into substance and appearance, and without being "consumed." The text seems to rise like a phoenix from the ashes of interpretation. We could also apply an inverse, yet similar metaphor: The text is like a catalyst that generates extensive transformative processes while, at the same time, the presence of the text is vital, though the text itself cannot change and cannot be consumed. When discussing the question of what constitutes a text, the theories of French structuralism and its metaphors are particularly helpful. The text, they claim, is a web and weave—a starry sky.

> The text, in its mass, is comparable to a sky, at once flat and smooth, deep, without edges and without landmarks; like the soothsayer drawing on it with the tip of his staff an imaginary rectangle wherein to consult, according to certain principles, the flight of birds, the commentator traces through the text certain zones of reading, in order to observe therein the migration of meanings, the outcropping of codes, the passage of citations. (Barthes 1974:14)

How can we read such a "text"? What can be our interest in reading it this way? In any event, what is of interest is not the author's intention but the uncovering of patterns and the exposure of structures, and this is not rehearsed for the purpose of discovering *one* meaning.

> To interpret a text is not to give it a (more or less justified, more or less free) meaning, but on the contrary to appreciate what *plural* constitutes it. . . . It follows that the meaning of a text lies not in this or that interpretation but in the diagrammatic totality of its readings, in their plural system. (Barthes 1974:5, 120)

Structural semantics, considering its basic principles and actual analytical work, displays a loyal and conservative attitude toward the text which, in some respects, corresponds to the bibliodramatic treatment of texts. Barthes explains that, according to such an understanding of structural semantics, "rereading [is] an operation contrary to the commercial and ideological habits of our society." Our society actually suggests to " 'throw away' the story once it has been consumed ('devoured'), so that we can then move on to another story, buy another book." In our society, rereading "is tolerated only in certain marginal categories of readers (children, old people, and professors)" (15, 16).

Admittedly, the above-mentioned semantic theory and praxis are often considered to be overly aesthetic, ahistorical, and apolitical. However, this is not the place to discuss these charges. It must be mentioned, however, that various representatives of structural semantics are trying, with all their might, to counter those arguments and accusations. Belo and Clevenot, for example, do it explicitly in the context of their "materialistic" text analysis; for them, questions of the ideological function of a text, the *cui bono,* and the way it is handed down are of prime importance (Belo 1974; Clevenot 1978). These two scholars refer to the works of (among others) Kristeva and Althusser for whom the text is a form of praxis, and for whom the reconstruction of the written word and the construction of readability and write-ability are central to their work. The title of an anthology edited by Zuma, *Textsemiotik als Ideologiekritik,* is representative of this trend.

What is at stake is nothing more and nothing less than the clarity of the gospel. I think that the above-mentioned approaches to textual understanding do not obscure the gospel—at least not to such a degree that it becomes, in the language of information theory, "white noise," which is the simultaneous presence of an undifferentiated sum of all frequencies (or, as in our case, the undifferentiated sum of all layers of meaning). Indeed, the same text allows different interpretations and readings for different people and worldviews. However, despite this general ambiguity and surplus of meaning, a specific text always remains consistent and reliable. This is why tradition and interpretation are understood as being profoundly historical and biographical.

"Clarity" is a historic category. Psychology of religion, religious education, and pastoral care are able to accept the view that biblical stories, personae, and situations are inevitably contingent on (unstable) historical and biographical processes. However, we are not yet fully aware of the fact that this view also affects our understanding of the text itself and even God's word, for they must be reappropriated as well. Unlike a paved runway or a narrow tube, the text is an open, though confined, field which—like energy fields in physics—has pathways guiding and structuring our reading. The text as an open yet confined field is a cosmos of meaning. As mortal human beings, living in time and space, we are either here or there, or we move from here to there. The reading of a text is not arbitrary but consists of its own changing yet consistent clarity.

I consider the contribution of linguistics and semiotics as important because both theories look at and explain psychological insights, generated in the process of reading, from a very different, almost opposing perspective. Psychology as well as semantic theory are the two foci of an ellipse of an encompassing hermeneutic. It is not as if people simply read uncontrolled by the historical-critical method and dogmatics; rather, the texts themselves, as they are read, are structured in such a way that they seem to solicit an open reading. Theology, therefore, must be in dialogue with other sciences in order to enhance its understanding of text, word, and sign, similar to the way it already integrates its understanding of psychological processes. For if word and Sacrament (text, symbol, and ritual) are, like the psyche, not specifically and exclusively theological realities and media, then they also share communicative potentials and limitations characteristic of those (extratheological) realities.

Notes

1. The term *biblical psychodrama* was already used at a public discussion of the annual meeting of the American Society of Group Psycho-Therapy and Psychodrama in 1962, New York (see Bobroff 1962).

2. The term *collective symbol* has a double meaning: It is a symbol of a collective body which is not only capable of collecting (from the Latin *colligere*, "to gather") groups of people around its symbolic core but also collects the most divergent, sometimes private and preconscious desires, fantasies, and anxieties of individuals.

3. The various titles that students assigned to their role plays are symptomatic: "Sweet home—bitter home," "The helpless Moses," "Down and Out," and "The preventable decline of Moses." In the play, the students have so little respect for Moses that Joshua can say into his face, "Nobody takes you seriously." We would expect from a group of university students that they are capable of acknowledging the function of Moses as superego or paternal authority figure; or that they would recognize the conflict between Moses and Aaron as a mirror image of their professional roles in religion and society. However, such a critical evaluation did not take place.

References

Barthes, Roland. 1974. *S/Z*. Trans. Richard Miller. New York: Hill and Wang.
Belo, Fernando. 1974. *Lecture materialiste de l'evangile de Marc*. Paris: Les Editions du Cerf.

Bernet, Walter. 1970. *Gebet.* Stuttgart: Kreuz.

Bobroff, A. J. 1962. "Biblical Psychodrama." *Group Psychotherapy* 15:129–31.

Clevenot, Michel. 1978. *So kennen wir die Bibel nicht. Anleitung zu einer materialistischen Lektüre biblischer Texte.* München: Kaiser.

Delakova, Katya. 1984. *Beweglichkeit: Wie wir durch die Arbeit mit Körper und Stimme zu kreativer Gestaltung finden.* München: Kösel.

———. 1991. *Das Geheimnis der Katze. Eine Tänzerin und Lehrerin weist Wege zum schöpferischen Üben.* Frankfurt: Brandes and Apsel.

Füssel, Kuno. 1983. *Zeichen und Strukturen. Einführung in Grundbegriffe, Positionen und Tendenzen des Strukturalismus.* Münster: edition liberacion.

———. 1987. *Drei Tage mit Jesus im Tempel. Einführung in die materialistische Lektüre der Bibel für Religionsunterricht, Theologiestudium und Pastoral.* Münster: edition liberacion.

Laeuchli, Samuel. 1987. "Abraham und Isaak. Einführung in eine mimetische Bewältigung." In *Bibliodrama,* ed. Antje Kiehn et al. Stuttgart: Kreuz Verlag.

Martin, Gerhard Marcel. 1985. "Das Bibliodrama und sein Text." *Evangelische Theologie* 45 (November):515–26.

———. 1986. "Mehrdimensionaler Umgang mit der Bibel in Handlungsfeldern der Praktischen Theologie." *Verkündigung und Forschung* 31/2:34–47.

———. 1987. "Bibliodrama—ein Modell wird vorgestellt." In *Bibliodrama,* ed. Antje Kiehn et al. Stuttgart: Kreuz Verlag.

———. 1989. "Kleines Plädoyer fürs Bibliodrama." *Bibel und Liturgie* 62:25,33–35.

Schramm, Tim. 1987. "Bibliodrama und Exegese." In *Bibliodrama,* ed. Antje Kiehn et al. Stuttgart: Kreuz Verlag.

Ward, Jack. 1967. "The Clergy and Psychotherapy." *Group Psychotherapy* 20:204–10.

Wink, Walter. 1980. *Transforming Bible Study.* Nashville: Abingdon Press.

Zima, Peter V., ed. 1977. *Textsemiotik als Ideologiekritik.* Frankfurt: Suhrkamp.

Performing the Gospel of Mark*

David Rhoads

Dissatisfied at length with an analysis centered on the text as object, I realized that narrative could not be satisfactorily explored except as the site of an interaction.

For performance to be successful, it is not enough for it to have purpose; it must also have energy and effect.

Marie Maclean, from the Foreword of
Narrative as Performance

The Gospel of Mark is an amazing story full of action and drama. It was written to be told to an audience in a lively and powerful way. About fifteen years ago, I learned this Gospel in order to present it orally. Since then, I have performed it to a wide variety of audiences. In what follows, I want to share some of what I have learned from this experience. In the first part, I will reflect on my experience of performing—memorizing the Gospel, entering the narrative world, using techniques to tell the story, experiencing the self as medium, and becoming aware of the involvement of the audience. In the second part, I want to show how the demands of performance have led me to a greater understanding of Mark's Gospel. To illustrate this, I will discuss the settings, events, characters, and rhetoric

---

*A video is available of The Dramatic Performance of the Gospel of Mark along with several video courses (SELECT, 2199 East Main Street, Columbus, OH 43209).

of the episode of the Syrophoenician woman. I will conclude with some brief remarks on the implications of this experience for teaching.

The Dynamics of Performance

Learning the Gospel

In the late 1970s, I heard about the British actor Alec McGowen who performed the King James Version of the Gospel of Mark. He learned a verse a day until he committed the whole Gospel to memory, and he played to packed houses in England and the United States. At the time, I was doing my own translation of Mark for a book on that Gospel. I had done a lot of memorizing as a youth and so I decided to learn Mark. A back injury, which kept me laid up for a month, gave me the opportunity. I initially learned Mark to provide an educational experience for my students and to give them a chance to hear the entire Gospel at one sitting and as a story. Soon, I got many chances to perform Mark at churches and educational institutions.

At first, I found it very difficult to retain the whole Gospel of Mark to memory. Modern people are biased toward writing down to remember and are not very practiced in the skills of recall. Initially, I would spend fifteen to twenty hours practicing the memory work before a presentation. In my experience, unless one has the opportunity to perform a narrative over and over, it will be easily forgotten. Each time I recalled it for performance, I committed it more securely to memory. In the last fifteen years, I have performed Mark nearly 200 times. Taking account of practice and memory work, I have probably gone over Mark more than 500 times. Eventually, I got beyond the problem of remembering. I now have the words well in mind, and when I perform, I am no longer trying to remember what words come next.

As this process was taking place, the story came to be liberated from the page. I no longer thought of trying to remember words as they were written on the page; rather, I heard the sounds of the words in my mind as I was recalling them. Now I seldom think in terms of the words themselves so much as the images to which they refer. In the role of narrator of the story, I run pictures through my mind of what I am recounting, and I tell and show the audience what I am seeing in imagination as I perform. I do not think in terms of chapters or verses but about the flow and movement of the story—how it begins, what happens next, and how it turns out. Performing a text is like playing a musical composition. Once the score is committed to memory, neither the artist nor the audience think about notes on a page, but they are caught up in the experience of the music itself; so the storyteller and the hearer of a biblical story are caught up in the story.

Entering the Story World

One of the most interesting aspects of performance is the experience of entering the world of the story. At every point, the storyteller uses imagination to re-create the story. You reenact the world of the story in the space on the stage. The act of performing the whole narrative leads a person to be immersed in this world. It takes two hours to perform the Gospel of Mark. During that time, you have a sense of being inside another world. You enter the whole space and time continuum of this first-century construction of the world. You have a past that goes back through the prophets, David, and the patriarchs to creation and a future that will last only to the end of the generation when the end will come. The cosmos is a flat earth with a canopy over it on which the sun and stars are affixed—a cosmos populated by God and Satan, angels and demons, Jews and Gentiles, and clean and unclean animals. In the midst of this is the drama of Jesus announcing the kingdom, performing healings, calling and struggling with the disciples, engaging in mortal debate with the leaders of Israel, and moving inexorably toward crucifixion.

To enter this space and time is also to realize what is possible and what is not possible in this story. As Coleridge said, when you enter the world of a story, you "suspend disbelief" and accept what is possible and what is not possible in that world. When the protagonist heals the sick, drives out demons, calms a storm, multiplies loaves in the desert, and expects his disciples to be able to do the same, you realize that this is a world in which everything is possible to one who has faith. Yet despite these dramatic possibilities, this world is full of strange paradoxes. While Jesus can heal people, he has no authority to control people. He can drive out a demon, but he cannot successfully command someone to keep quiet about it. He can make a deaf man hear, but he cannot make his disciples comprehend what he is teaching them. Here is a world in which it is easier to get a physically blind man to see than a spiritually blind person to understand. Here too is a world in which someone with authority over illness and demons and nature will come into necessary and violent conflict with the national leaders and be executed—and, of course, there is resurrection from the dead.

Telling the Story

The task of the performer is to re-create this world on stage and to draw the hearers into it. How you tell the story is therefore of utmost importance. After I got beyond the memory problem, I could work on the interaction with the audience—how to tell the story to an audience in an effective way. I do not have training in acting, and I am limited in my capacity to convey the story. I think of my task less as acting and more as storytelling. Yet I did not want simply to stand on stage and recount the Gospel, nor did I want to replicate how the ancient storytellers might have recounted Mark—we are uncertain about that in any case. Therefore, I began to use storytelling techniques drawn from the oral interpretation of literature, and these techniques have helped me to tell Mark's story in a meaningful way.

For example, when I tell the story as narrator, I focus off stage and address the audience. Then, when I play the narrator, I show the audience what a character in the story has said by assuming the role of that character. When I show the character in this way, I focus on stage and address other characters in imagination before me. This helps the audience to distinguish when I use the voice of the narrator and when I assume the voice of a character. When I do a characterization of one of the figures in the story, I try to assume a distinctive posture, voice, gesture, and inflection, meant to be consonant with the traits and dialogue of the character being portrayed (and there are over fifty characters with dialogue in Mark!). I also block my movements by going to different places on the stage to convey intimacy or mystery or action, or to help the audience recall similar episodes that occurred earlier in the story (and the number of scene changes is extraordinary). In addition, I have learned to pace the story with urgency, with deliberateness, or with pauses according to the flow of the story. Finally, in every line, whether speaking as the narrator or as a character, I attend to the subtext. Each line has the meaning content of its words, but when delivered orally it also has a subtext—the message that is conveyed by the "way" a line is delivered. Each decision made by the performer about the subtext leads to a change of inflection, the raising of an eyebrow, a distinct shift in posture, the lowering of the voice, and so on.

In the text, there are explicit and implicit directions for choices about the use of these techniques in performance. When the story says that people were afraid or amazed or alarmed, these are "stage directions" for the performer to signal or express such emotions. When the story says that someone cried out or pleaded, these are guidelines for delivering a line. The change of scene in the story is a guide for movement on stage. The repetition of a word such as *immediately* is an encouragement to pick up the pace of the storytelling. Patterns in the rhetoric, lengths of sentences, the introduction of new information, and the presence of rhetorical questions all affect the pace and rhythm of the storytelling. The consistency of characterization, the intensity of a conflict, and the content of dialogue all become guides to determine subtext. Eventually, a grasp of the whole story also guides the decisions one makes about saying each line and portraying each scene.

These techniques of oral interpretation give the performer a greater repertoire in self-expression with which to tell the story. They also help the performer place in sharper relief so many dimensions of the story. In so doing, the story is made clearer and more interesting for the audience.

Performer as Medium

Through these techniques, I have become aware that all dimensions of the narrative and its rhetoric pass through the performer. The performer *is* the medium. Performance is not just a mental act of memorizing and retelling. In a performance, your whole psychosomatic reality becomes the vehicle for the presentation of the story. At every point, your self—indeed, your body—is an added presence and the medium of the story. In a sense, you try to make yourself transparent to the story. However, that does not happen, because every dimension of the story is enacted in you. You go to Galilee, you heal the leper, you plot to destroy Jesus, you recount the Crucifixion, and so on. In the same way that a text with markings for words on a page mediates a written story, so you become the medium for the story.

A human medium has both limitations and possibilities. In terms of a capacity to tell the story, consider the performer's voice, physical litheness (or lack of it), facial malleability, sense of rhythm, imagination, capacity to mimic, and so on. Even the social location of the performer affects the storytelling. For example, I am a European-American with a graying beard and a noticeable paunch. I am obviously middle class. People know that I am ordained and that I teach at a seminary. Faithfulness to the story can be a problem, for there is no middle class in Mark's narrative world. This Gospel was written from a peasant perspective. Furthermore, Jesus tells people to leave all they have and be prepared for persecution. My social location makes it difficult for me to convey these marginalized positions from which Mark's Gospel was written. All these factors grant both delightful possibilities and the painful awareness of limitations.

Since the performer is a living medium of the word, decisions about interpretation are embodied in the performer—posture and stance, tone and volume, pace of voice and movement, gestures, facial expressions, and location on stage. All sounds and movements become the interpretation. Obviously, the story can be embodied in many different ways. In fact, because the performer changes, no single performance by a player is the same as any other performance by that same player. Performers with different understandings of the story and different gifts for performance will embody the story in a diversity of ways. Some interpretations may be more faithful to Mark's story than others. Nevertheless, within a wide range, there are many legitimate interpretations. Just as every translation is an interpretation, so every performance is an interpretation. Just as every translation captures some aspects of a word or a story and loses other meanings and nuances, so every oral presentation has gains and losses in terms of the meanings and effects of the story. Furthermore, such diversity will enhance and deepen the audience's experience of Mark's Gospel.

Audience as Participant

The performance is the site of an interaction. Therefore, just as a performer enhances and limits the possibilities of a performance, so also does the audience shape a performance.

For example, the life situation of the audience (age, familiarity with Mark, and social location) and the responses of the audience in the course of performance are factors that make every performance unpredictable. Audiences in educational settings are generally more attuned to the humor in Mark and freer in that context to laugh than audiences in churches. On some occasions, I have gotten "on a roll" with the audience in the humor of Mark's Gospel—how the pig herders flee from Jesus's exorcism, how the woman spends all she has on doctors but is only getting worse, and how the disciples are amazed that Jesus asks who touched him in a crowd that is crushing him. On such occasions, I have delivered some lines in ways I had never delivered them before and thereby found new dimensions to Mark's delight in telling his story. In a different vein, the experience of performing Mark at a medium-security prison changed my understanding of Mark's audience and of the nature of Mark's good news. From them, I realized how crucial the miracles were, how important it was for the disciples to succeed, and how much the good news empowers people to be free of "fornications, thefts, murders, adulteries, works of greed, malicious acts . . . " (7:21–22).

In interaction with the performer, the audience participates in the construction of meaning. In some sense, the story will mean what the audience understands it to mean. Yet, even when the performer gets across a faithful portrayal of the Gospel, much commentary would be necessary for a contemporary audience to understand all the meanings of this ancient story. The author of this story took an enormous amount for granted, because he was addressing an audience with whom he shared common meanings and nuances of words, cultural conventions, community life, historical experiences, and an ancient worldview. Hearing Mark today, without the aid of explanations, is like hearing a joke from another culture. You have to know the shared assumptions about life in order to "get it." Such gaps in understanding may involve knowledge of the Sabbath laws or the dynamics of purity and pollution or the pattern of telling episodes in a chiastic series. The performer will seek to use various means of self-expression to convey these meanings without in any way adding to the words of the story or seeking to provide an explanation. Yet, given a contemporary audience, this is often difficult or impossible. Nevertheless, much of this story can be understood very well without having to fill in these gaps.

Yet the interaction between performer and audience is much more than communication. The audience participates in more ways than understanding. Words and stories do not just have denotations of meaning. They also have an impact on people. We are not dealing simply with the notion of conveying information about events to an audience. The narrative is much less a vehicle for an idea, as if we could get the idea or the theology and then no longer need the story. The story is not just a vehicle, or a component added to an idea. The story itself has energy and power. The story affects the whole person—heart, soul, mind, and body. Words do not just have meaning; they create effects. Words and stories are "speech acts." Something happens to the audience as a result of experiencing the story. The story can confront the hearer, evoke sadness or delight, lead one to identify with some characters and be repelled by others, engender wonder or hope, change one's values, empower for love, or lead one through a catharsis purging fear and pity. Mark's narrative seeks nothing less than to liberate people from lives of anxious self-concern to be prepared to follow Jesus in a life for others, even to death.

By the sheer force of the words and the impact of the interaction, the performer seeks to draw hearers into the story world—as, in a darkened theater, the audience may be drawn into the world of a film. Emerging from a powerful film, you may be a different person or you may be empowered to change your life. The performer of Mark seeks to bring the audience through the whole story so that they are not the same people at the end as they were at the beginning. Yet the performer never controls the outcome. The performer may encounter resistance or indifference or sleepiness. There are hearers who simply do not accept the point of view of the story. The performance may simply be for many people an evening of good or bad entertainment. On the other hand, people may be changed or affirmed or empowered or forgiven or healed in ways you might never have expected. Regardless of the actual reactions, the performer has a sense of what people could experience—given her interpretation of the story—and seeks to foster that experience.

Performance and Interpretation

There is a relationship between performance and interpretation that has enabled me to learn more about the Gospel of Mark. As we have indicated, the experience of assuming the role of the narrator and actually telling the story is different from the experience of reading or hearing the Gospel. The demands of performance impress upon one the need to make choices about the meaning and rhetoric of the story that a reader or a hearer of the Gospel might not make. For this reason, I find it helpful to make my own translations for performance. Translations are not often made with the idea of storytelling in mind. Translations have been made primarily to convey meaning to a reading audience. Few translations have taken into consideration the oral impact of the rhetoric on an audience. The experience of telling the story assists in this very process of translation, because I often change and adjust the translation in light of the experience of performance.

The Syrophoenician Woman

To illustrate the interaction between performance and interpretation, I would like to reflect on a single episode from the Gospel of Mark. I have chosen the episode of Jesus's encounter with the Syrophoenician woman. I do not thereby mean to isolate this episode from the story as a whole. Indeed, the episode comes forty minutes or so into the story, and the episode follows and precedes other episodes that are closely related to it. I have begun the translation a few lines before the episode commences and continued a few lines after it ends.

> And summoning the crowd again, he said to them "Hear me everyone and understand. There is nothing from outside people that by going into them is able to defile them. Rather, the things which go out from people are the things that defile people."
>
> And when he entered into a house from the crowd, his disciples asked him about the parable. And he says to them, "Do you too lack understanding like this? Don't you perceive that everything which enters into people from the outside is not able to defile them because it does not enter into their hearts but into their stomachs and goes on out into the latrine"—thereby rendering clean all foods.
>
> He said, "What comes out from people is what defiles people. For from inside from the hearts of people come the evil designs: fornications, thefts, murders, adulteries, acts of greed, malicious deeds, deceit, amorality, en-

vious eye, blasphemy, arrogance, reckless folly. All these wicked things come from inside and defile people."

Now from there arising he went off to the territory of Tyre, and entering a house he wanted no one to know about him and he was not able to escape notice. Instead a woman whose little daughter had an unclean spirit at once heard about him, came and fell before him.

Now the woman was Greek, a Syrophoenician by birth and she asked Jesus to drive out the demon from her daughter.

And he said to her, "Let first the children be satisfied, for it is not good to take the bread for the children and throw it to the little dogs."

But she answers and says to him, "Lord, even the little dogs down under the table eat of the little children's crumbs."

And he said to her, "Because of this word, go on off. The demon has gone out from your daughter."

And going off to her house, she found the little girl thrown on the bed and the demon gone out.

And coming back out from the territory of Tyre, he went through Sidon to the Sea of Galilee up the middle of the territory of the Decapolis.

And people bring to him a deaf and tongue-tied man and plead with Jesus to lay his hand on him.

And taking him apart from the crowd privately, he thrust his fingers into his ears and spitting touched the man's tongue. And looking up to heaven, he groaned and he says to him, "Ephphatha!" which means "Be opened!"

And at once his ears were opened and the binding of his tongue was released and he began speaking clearly.

(7:14–35)

This is a wonderful story full of conflict, drama, surprises, and puzzles, and with interesting characters and a strange setting. As we unpack the dynamics of this episode, we will look at both the story world and the rhetoric of the story.

The Story: Settings

Decisions about movement on stage lead the performer to interpret carefully every spatial detail of Mark's story. You become acutely aware of every place—how it relates to people and events as well as what else happens there in the rest of the story. In this episode, I move all the way across the stage to go to Tyre, because it is a distance away. Jesus goes a long way off to seclude himself. Earlier in the story, people came from Tyre to Galilee because they had heard of Jesus and wanted to see him (3:3–7). That is why Jesus cannot remain hidden for long in Tyre—because his reputation precedes him. As I perform, I enter a house that I imagine to be a typical first-century house. Because it has a gate open to the courtyard, passersby have access to it. After the encounter between Jesus and the woman in the house, I see the woman going home to her daughter. After that, I pass through Sidon (across the stage) "to the Sea of Galilee up the middle of the territory of the Decapolis." Now I have stayed in Gentile territory, gone around the Sea of Galilee from the north, and returned to the place where Jesus had earlier exorcized a "Legion" of demons and had been asked to leave the territory (5:1–20).

In this episode, the physical movements on stage also make me aware of crossing boundaries: Jesus crosses into "the borders" of Tyre into Gentile territory; the woman crosses the boundary to the house; Jesus goes to Sidon and the Decapolis. Jesus's movements into the Gentile territory of Tyre, Sidon, and the Decapolis are significant. If the protagonist of a story were traveling in the United States and then went into Canada or Mexico, the hearer would be very aware of this boundary crossing, and would remember the events there and recall them when the protagonist returned to Canada or Mexico. There are also social boundaries—a Jewish holy man entering impure territory, a female talking to a strange man, and a demon leaving. In addition, the preceding episode involved the overcoming of a bodily boundary when Jesus declared all foods clean. This sequence of episodes is similar to episodes in Acts when Peter's vision of all foods being declared clean led Peter to cross the boundary of the unclean house of Cornelius in Caesarea and convert the first Gentile (Acts 10:1–48). In both cases, the boundary crossing is a breakthrough in the story. Jesus's encounter with the Syrophoenician woman overcomes the last barrier to Gentiles in a whole series of boundary-crossing episodes in Mark's narrative.

The Story: Events

Mark does not often make explicit the connections between events. It is up to the listener to infer the relationships. Mark may not be thinking of cause and effect between events as we might. Yet the performer needs to press the questions of relationship: Is an event contingent upon earlier events? Does an event fulfill an earlier prophecy? Are two events connected by comparison or contrast? Are two events connected by thematic development? Is there a series of events in which a conflict escalates?

About this episode, for example, I wonder: Why does Jesus go to Tyre in Gentile territory and hide in a house? As a result of performing, it has become clear to me that Mark may be making many connections at once. Based on the whole story, Jesus may be withdrawing after conflict with the Pharisees (earlier, he withdrew after a conflict) or to seek rest from a frantic pace (he did this also) or to escape the disciples and their failure to understand his parable (his impatience with them is growing) or all of the above. Perhaps the narrator is suggesting that Jesus was hiding to avoid Gentiles, since he does tell the Syrophoenician woman that he will not give bread to Gentiles. The performer searches the whole story, especially the immediate context, for causes and connections. The lack of explanation and explicit connections by Mark leaves the story open to different legitimate interpretations. In any case, the performer's decision about this event will bear directly upon performance, whether, for example, in the brief account of Jesus's movement to Tyre, the performer should convey an attitude of eagerness, weariness, or secrecy.

The act of narration makes one aware not only of connections between episodes but also of the sequence of action and dialogue within an episode. At every line, the performer asks: Why does this happen next? Why does she say this in response to that? Why does he do that after she says this? You can see the sequence here:

- He goes off and hides (to rest, to escape disciples, to avoid Gentiles?).
- She hears about him and falls at his feet (because of those who had gone from Tyre to see Jesus in Galilee).
- She is a Greek, yet she asks Jesus to exorcize the demon (this is new information and creates suspense).
- He refuses her request (a surprise, yet he explains).
- She understands the riddle (a surprise, because even the disciples do not understand; she is clever and persistent).
- He declares the child freed of the demon (again he explains that it is because of her word).
- The woman goes off and finds the daughter healed (the words of Jesus were effective).
- Jesus goes off to the Decapolis (to try again where he had been rejected in Gentile territory).

At every point, therefore, the performer is acutely aware of the flow of the story. Each decision will affect the telling of the story. Sometimes in the middle of a perfomance, I will see a connection I had not seen before. For example, I know that Jesus calls the woman a dog because Jews sometimes referred to Gentiles as dogs. In that time, dogs were not treated as pets, but roamed around scavenging for scraps. Dogs were considered unclean, as were Gentiles. Suddenly, in a performance, I (as Jesus) see this woman begging at my feet for what is not rightfully hers—acting like a scavenger dog! In my mind, I am saying "Oh, now I see why he says that to her. It's a response to what she is doing. No wonder they exchange proverbs about dogs." At times, the connections leap across the story. When Jesus says, "Because of this word, go on off. The demon has gone out from your daughter," it has the same feel as an earlier line of Jesus's to a woman healed of a flow of blood: "Your faith has restored you. Go in peace, and be free of your ailment" (5:34).

As oral narrator, one also attends to the pace of events. Here, there is an awareness of the relation between story time and plotted time. How long does an event take in the story world (story time), and how long does it take to narrate the event (plotted time)? In this episode, there is an acceleration of time when a day's journey to Tyre (story time) takes about two seconds to narrate (plotted time). This statement introduces setting. Then there is a deceleration of time as the woman hears about Jesus and falls at his feet. This introduces a character. Then there is a descriptive pause: No action takes place while the narrator tells us that the woman was a Greek and a Syrophoenician by birth. Descriptive pauses are unusual in Mark and signal the introduction of important information. The narration needs to slow down to let this new information sink in before we go on. What follows in the story will not be understood unless we slow down. Then the pace becomes equivalent to dialogue in a dramatic scene, in which the recounting of the scene takes about the same time as it takes for the scene to occur in story time. Such scenes signal the heart of an episode. Finally, time accelerates again as the woman goes off to her house and Jesus goes off to the Decapolis. These are the consequences of the action and the dialogue. Then a new episode commences.

The Story: Characters

Characters are a key dimension of the Markan narration. Some are ongoing characters, such as Jesus, the disciples, and the Pharisees. Most characters simply make cameo appearances and then are gone. Yet many of these characters are memorable—the leper, the man with the withered hand, Jairus and his daughter, the woman with the flow of blood, the Syrophoenician woman, blind Bartimaeus, and so on. In the course of telling and retelling the Gospel of Mark, I have come to think that each of these minor characters appears at a strategic place in the narrative and is not interchangeable with any other. The episode of the Syrophoenician woman may seem to be just one more miracle story. Yet the Syrophoenician woman appears just after Jesus has declared all foods clean and just before Jesus gives bread to Gentiles. Jesus' encounter with her is the hinge event that leads to his mission in Gentile territory.

As a performer, you get to know each character well. In the role of narrator, you tell about her in introductions and descriptions. You assume the role of that character in the course of showing what she said or did. You also talk with and react to that character in the roles you play as other characters in the story. With regard to the Syrophoenician woman, for example, the performer tells about her as narrator, pleads with Jesus as the woman herself, and reacts to her request in the role of Jesus.

From performing this episode, I have concluded that the woman is the driving force of the whole scene. This woman is determined to get her daughter restored. Despite Jesus' efforts to hide, she finds him. Despite her origins, she asks him. Despite his refusal, she persists. She goes home only when her request is met. The question for the performer is: How do you display her actions or say her lines? To decide this, one has to think through the text. When she falls at his feet, is she kneeling or prostrate? What is her attitude in speaking? What is the subtext? Is she a person pleading rather pathetically for her daughter, or is she a feisty inferior who persists and cleverly gets her way? How do you express her attitude by gesture and posture? How can the characterization convey the way she upstages Jesus with her proverbial response to his cryptic allegory?

The characterization of Jesus in this episode is also very interesting. At every point, the demands of performance press upon one the need to make decisions that exegetes might not otherwise make. A performer will want to answer the following questions:

- Why does Jesus go to Tyre and hide?
- Why does he reject the Syrophoenician woman's request?
- What is Jesus' time scheme for Jews and Gentiles?
- Why does he speak here in a parabolic allegory?
- What does he mean by this allegory?
- Does he change his mind or has he only been testing the woman?
- Did Jesus heal the woman? Or was it her faith? Or God?
- Why does he immediately go back to the Decapolis?

Each of these questions can be answered in different ways. However, all of the decisions about them will be reflected in the gestures, inflections, facial expressions, posture, pace, volume, and tone presented in each line.

As performer, I find there is one key question to the characterization of Jesus in this episode: Does he reject the woman's request as a test, or does he really mean it? In other words, does he change his mind? If I perform it one way, Jesus will be playful and coy. If I perform it another way, Jesus will be serious and then surprised. I find the story makes better sense when we assume that Jesus is not just testing her but really does initially reject her request. This interpretation is consistent with the integrity of Jesus' words throughout the story. Also, according to Jesus' explanation, he rejects the woman's request because he will not give bread to the Gentiles (the dogs) before the Jews (the children) are satisfied. After all, when he went in Gentile territory before (the Decapolis), the people asked him to leave. This interpretation also explains why he was hiding in Tyre—because he was not intending to heal Gentiles. Furthermore, in what follows this episode, Jesus seems to have changed his mind about not giving bread to the Gentiles before the Jews are satisfied, because he stays in Gentile territory (returning to the Decapolis) and performs healings and provides bread in the desert to Gentiles. Then the question arises: What does it say about Mark's overall characterization that Jesus changes his mind as well as the strategy of his mission as a result of the intelligence and persistent faith of this Gentile woman?

In characterization, it is also important to provide continuity through the story. This one vignette takes only about sixty seconds to perform. It passes quickly as part of the flow of the story. The character of Jesus should be consistent with what the audience has seen and heard, even if new insights come. Regarding the role of the woman, it is important to reflect how similar she is to all the other suppliants with faith who come to Jesus for healing. They appear in a recurring type of scene with characters who respond favorably to his proclamation of the Kingdom.

The Rhetoric

The performer attends especially to the rhetoric of the story, or how the story is told—style, word order, choice of words, grammar, and so on—in order to create certain effects on the audience. Because the Gospel of Mark was written to be read aloud, it contains many sophisticated features of oral storytelling. I have learned a great deal about Mark by using these features to enhance performance.

One such feature for oral storytelling is Mark's spare style. Mark says an enormous amount in few words. His descriptions are suggestive rather than exhaustive: ". . . and entering a house he wanted no one to know about him," "Now the woman was Greek," ". . . she found the little girl thrown on the bed and the demon gone out." Mark does not write with a flourish, varying his vocabulary and seeking dramatic figures of speech or fancy turns of phrase. His choice of words is simple, and he repeats the same words and phrases in many contexts. Repetition is the lifeblood of oral narration, and our narrator employs repetition to great effect. The narrator of this story also seldom tells us what people are like—he does not say explicitly that the woman has faith or that Jesus changes his mind. The narrator does not tell us the meaning of events—he does not say overtly that this episode is a breakthrough to Gentiles or that the words of the woman will change Jesus's subsequent actions—rather, the narator *shows* us the actions and the words of the characters, and simply depicts the course of events. The listeners must infer the rest. The listeners are left to experience the traits of the characters in their behavior, the meaning of the events in their recounting, and the effects of the narrative in its telling.

Another feature of Mark's oral storytelling is word order. In Greek, nouns are identified by case endings rather than by their place in the sentence. As such, the Greek writer can put the nominative subject almost anywhere in the sentence and the reader will know it is the subject. Word placement can indicate emphasis, pace, repetition, parallelism, and so on. When we try to be faithful in English to the Greek word order, the sentence is often awkward or unintelligible. Here, the performer of an English text is at an advantage, since it is possible in spoken English to employ a greater variety of word order than in written English (although in written English poetry uses word order freely). Take the different effect of "Let the children be satisfied first" and "Let first the children be satisfied." In the former example, the word *first* is in the background and is less important than the feeding of the children. In the second example, the word *first* is foregrounded and emphasizes the temporal order as the reason for Jesus's rejection of the woman's request. In written English, the first example seems most natural and the second seems awkward. However, in spoken English, as part of a performance, either one may be said naturally. The second example, in which the performer stresses the word *first*, renders faithfully Mark's word order in Greek and conveys the desired impact.

Word order often expreses parallelism. In the Greek text of this episode, the last words of Jesus parallel the subsequent results of his words.

a. "*. . . go on off.*
b. has gone out from *your daughter.*"
c. *The demon*

a. And *going off* to her house,
b. she found *the little girl* thrown on the bed
c. and *the demon* gone out.

Such parallelism can often be rendered faithfully in the word order of an oral narration, even when it cannot be so rendered in a written style for reading—although in this example from our episode, it is too awkward even for oral narration. The content and order reveal a one-to-one correlation between what Jesus says and what happens as a result. The parallelism emphasizes the authority of Jesus and the power and reliability of his words, as well as the faithful response of a suppliant. When such parallelism recurs after many of Jesus' healings, the accumulative effect is considerable.

Another feature of oral narration in Mark's Gospel is the historical present, or the use of the Greek present tense to narrate events of the past. In English, we often use the present tense in popular speech to make an anecdote more vivid and immediate. Yet, in written English, it is awkward to go back and forth between the present and past tenses. As a result, most English translations render the historical present in the simple past. Yet historical presents are an important part of Mark's storytelling and occur in most episodes of the narrative. Historical presents can often be rendered in oral performance without any awkwardness at all. There is one historical present in the episode of the Syrophoenician woman: "But she answers and says to him . . ." Several occur in the next episode cited above: "And people bring to him a deaf and tongue-tied man and plead with Jesus to lay his hands on him." These are limited examples. The historical present occurs more extensively in other episodes, such as the raising of Jairus's daughter (Reynolds Price 1978). In performance, the historical present makes the narrative much more vivid and intensifies the reader's involvement with the story.

Repetition is a key technique of Mark's oral narration. The repetition of words, lines, types of episodes, structures of episodes, and so on are central to oral narration. One of the most pervasive stylistic elements of Mark's narrative is repetition in two-step progressions. First, a word or phrase occurs, and then the same thing is repeated in other, more specific terms. The first element makes a point, and the second element nails it down with greater specificity. In our episode, the two-step progression is evident in the words: "Now the woman was Greek, a Syrophoenician by birth. . . ." This two-step progression, occurring as it does in a descriptive pause, signals important information. She was a Greek (probably not a Jew), a Syrophoenician by birth (definitely not a Jew). The pace at which one narrates this line conveys the two steps with the surprise and the suspense involved.

Another stylistic feature that is evident in this episode is Mark's careful use of diminutives. I do not think I would ever have noticed the number of diminutives in this episode but for the need in performance to imagine the little girl and the little dogs and the little children's crumbs under the table and the woman on the ground at Jesus' feet. There are six diminutives in this episode: little daughter (1), little pieces (crumbs—1), little dogs (2), little ones (2). In our episode, there is a play on these diminutives. In Jesus' reference to little dogs (puppies), the woman found an opening in Jesus' rejection of her request, because puppies were allowed to scavenge under the table when the children ate. Also, in the last line, the narrator includes the little girl as one of the children of God by depicting her as one of the "little ones." The repetition of diminutives leads the performer to accent this feature just enough to alert the hearer to this delightful motif.

Patterns Through the Story

The recurrence of these and many other techniques of oral narration give coherence to Mark's narrative. Other grammatical features of the Markan style also bind the narrative together. *Asyndeton* is the interruption of a sentence so the narrator can make an aside (a descriptive pause addressed to the audience). *Parataxis* is the habit of stringing lines together, usually with the Greek word *kai* (and). It looks strange in written English to begin every sentence with the word *and*. Yet this is Mark's style. In oral narration, this stylistic feature is usually not noticed unless pointed out. Yet the overall effect of such narration is to make the story flow and to make more natural connections from line to line and from episode to episode. The author of Mark also strings participles together in such a way as to create an almost breathless narration (see Reynolds Price 1978).

Finally, there are many structural elements of Mark's overall story that connect episodes to one another. There is the series of three episodes (three call scenes, three boat scenes, and three passion predictions), episodes in a chiastic pattern (the five conflict stories in Galilee), similar episodes that frame a section (stories of blind men being healed frame the journey to Jerusalem), the sandwiching of one story between the beginning and ending of another (the woman with the flow wedged inside the story of Jairus's daughter and the denial of Peter within the trial of Jesus), the use of type scenes (healings, exorcisms, and conflict stories), and the repetition of verbal motifs running through the story like threads ("handed over," "the way," "put to death," and "good news"). It is because these structures overlap and interlace the whole story that Joanna Dewey referred to Mark's Gospel as "a seamless interwoven tapestry." The use of verbal threads from previous episodes ("went off," "unclean spirit," "fell at his feet," "bread," "satisfied," and "house") and the presence of a type scene (the healing of a suppliant with faith) both weave the episode of the Syrophoenician woman into the Markan tapestry.

All these features figure in the translation and narration of one sixty-second episode in the context of a two-hour performance. Yet the demands of performing it lead one to know the story well so as to convey it faithfully, both in content and form.

Implications

Because of my experience with Mark's narrative, I have learned and performed other narratives as a way to understand a text better. The practice enhances my research in the biblical writings and also meets devotional needs. In churches and classes, I often present the Sermon on the Mount from Matthew's Gospel and Paul's Letter to the Galatians. I also engage students in the process of learning and performing biblical texts. In a course on Paul, students present to classmates Paul's Letter to Philemon. I have found no better way for students to understand the dynamics of a letter—form, content, rhetoric, and historical context—than to learn and perform one brief letter. In courses on the Gospels, students usually perform three or four episodes throughout the semester. In retreats and workshops with pastors and laypeople, participants engage in learning and telling stories. The experience of performing and listening is delightful. It promotes a faithful interpretation of the stories and makes the learning experience more meaningful at a personal level. Telling biblical stories thus provides a communal experience in which together we can encounter the word in ever fresh and transforming ways.

References

Boomershine, Thomas. 1988. *Story Journey: An Invitation to the Gospel as Storytelling*. Nashville: Abingdon Press.

Chatman, Seymour. 1987. *Story and Discourse: Narrative Structure in Fiction and Film*. Ithaca, N.Y.: Cornell University.

Dewey, Joanna. 1991. "Mark as Interwoven Tapestry: Forecasts and Echoes for a Listening Audience." *Catholic Biblical Quarterly* 53:221–236.

Kort, Wesley. 1988. *Story, Text, and Scripture: Literary Interests in Biblical Narratives*. University Park: Pennsylvania State University.

Lee, Charlotte and Timothy Gura. 1992. *Oral Interpretation*. 8th ed. Boston: Houghton Mifflin.

Maclean, Marie. 1988. *Narrative as Performance: The Baudelairean Experiment*. London: Routledge, Chapman & Hall.

McGowen, Alec. 1985. *Personal Mark: An Actor's Proclamation of St. Mark's Gospel*. New York: Crossroad.

Moore, Stephen. 1989. *Literary Criticism of the Gospels: The Theoretical Challenge*. New Haven, Conn.: Yale University Press.

Powell, Mark. 1990. *What is Narrative Criticism?* Minneapolis: Fortress Press.

Price, Reynolds. 1978. *A Palpable God: Thirty Stories Translated from the Bible With an Essay on the Origins and Life of Narrative*. New York: Atheneum.

Rhoads, David and Donald Michie. 1982. *Mark as Story: An Introduction to the Narrative of a Gospel*. Phildelphia: Fortress Press.

Rimmon-Kenan, Shlomith. 1983. *Narrative Fiction: Contemporary Poetics*. New York: Methuen.

Bible Study and Movement
for Human Transformation

Walter Wink

It was 1954, and I was only nineteen when I first discovered that there is a somatic approach to Scripture. I was in a spiritual crisis and had found my way, providentially, to Camp Farthest Out, a pious but profound retreat program focusing on prayer. At one point, they put on Beethoven's "Moonlight Sonata" and asked us to express ourselves with pastels. Grabbing a large chunk of charcoal, I drew a scene more appropriate to *Night on Bald Mountain*. Looking at my creation, I suddenly realized that I was a wreck.

Later they put on a musical rendition of the Lord's Prayer and asked us to express the prayer with our bodies. I was tall, skinny, awkward, and embarrassed, but I got to my feet and tried to move. My mind said "Move!" but my body, like Balaam's ass, balked. I ordered it. It sneered. It was in that moment that I discovered that, notwithstanding my intellectual belief in God, my body was an atheist.

My body had taught me two things. My hand somehow knew what my conscious mind had no inkling of: that I was in the thick of a spiritual crisis that would result in a profound reorganization of my life. My body also knew that my mind's rational deliberations about God had in no sense become incarnate. I was split, head and body, spirituality and sexuality, and reason and emotions. An ecstatic experience of God soon after not only did nothing to heal that split but also widened it. Now at last I knew I had a problem, and I knew what it was. I have spent my life since then trying to resolve it.

Why did my body have access to a wisdom of which my conscious mind knew nothing? How was it that Jesus's prayer, which I had

120

been praying all my life, had not penetrated below my neck, as it were? I had been reading the Gospels devotionally for a long time; I had heard them weekly in church. What was so different about trying (and failing!) to "read" them with my flesh? I had always regarded my body as a slave and had subjected it to strict disciplines. Now it was staging a slave revolt, and nothing in my experience prepared me for it.

I once forced myself to sit down and read five books by Rudolf Steiner. I only understood one sentence: "Physiologically speaking, it is Lucifer's constant endeavor to send the life forces out of the rest of our organism into our head" (1961:40). Seen in that light, one could indict the entire development of the body-mind split as a Luciferian victory, in which rational lucidity divorced from the body and emotions reigned supreme. In the words of William H. Poteat, Cartesianism (the philosophy of Descartes which legitimated Western splitness) has left us "culturally insane" (1985:6).

It is vain to attempt to defeat the body-mind split by Cartesian reasoning, however. For that we need a new way of thinking: thinkfeeling, or mindbodily thinking. That requires the entire being, what the Hebrews called *nephesh*, "the animated, ensouled body," or "the integrated totality of the incarnate self."

It was not until 1971, however, that I found a method that actually took these concerns about body-mind-spirit integration seriously and made them operational. I attended a seminar titled "The Records of the Life of Jesus" with the Guild for Psychological Studies at Four Springs in Middletown, California. Here, I found the Bible being studied by means of Socratic dialogue and a rich variety of exercises and experiments that sought to embody or incarnate the insights of Scripture into one's life. We studied the baptism of Jesus, and then we did a picture of it. We mimed all the characters in the parable of the Prodigal Son. We walked wooded mountain trails reciting mantras drawn from the Lord's Prayer. We surrounded Bible study with hours of meditative silence. We tried to locate our own inner paralytics by fashioning them with clay. I found this strange, exhilarating, and immensely profitable, as one part of my being after another responded, as if found for the first time by means of these imaginative exercises.

However, that was not all. We did play readings, we moved spontaneously to music, we meditated before selected pieces of art, we danced, we built altars and fashioned impromptu rituals, we mimed poetry, we studied the stars, we practiced contemplation, and we reflected on myths from the world's religions, especially Native American. It was a rich spread centered on incarnating in our own bodies the life of God incarnated by Jesus. We were, in effect, asking ourselves what would happen if we stopped thinking of Jesus as the sole incarnation of God and saw him rather as the guide who showed us how to incarnate God ourselves.

I had always wanted to be able to dance freely and with abandon. I had even taken a class in jazz dancing in college (I was the only male in the class; my fraternity brothers, who worked off their physical education requirement by playing Ping-Pong, watched me, leering and laughing, from the balcony); not surprisingly, that did not take. I had been attending movement classes for several years, but I still regarded it as an athletic challenge, a matter of making my body do what I told it. Though I was a fairly good athlete, I was still awkward and basically afraid that if I started cavorting around, I would simply fall flat on my face.

One afternoon, during that first seminar at Four Springs, the leaders put on Sibelius's "The Oceanides" and invited us to move to it in the swimming pool. This was a major breakthrough for me. No matter what I did—if I lost my balance—the water would catch me. I could simply continue the movement under water. More important yet, the music somehow seemed to know my own heart perfectly. It was as if the music was no longer coming into me from outside, but from my own depths; it was as if the music were being played by my own heart. After it was over, I lay by the pool, astonished that someone from a different country and a different time could know so precisely the innermost feelings of my heart. For the first time, I had a clear sense that we are not isolated monads discretely separated from one another, but that we are actually linked together by mysterious connections I scarcely understood but could no longer deny.

Clearly, all of this could have been done without the Bible as the focus of our task. Later, I attended other seminars at Four Springs with different themes: the ring trilogies of Tolkien and Wagner, the Iroquois myth of the Secret of No-Face, the Navaho myth of Changing Woman. However, none was as powerful for me as the encounter with Scripture. The process of freeing my body up had taken place in the context of the symbol system in which I found my meaning and identity. In some ways, the prohibitions that had led to my personal and physical rigidities appeared to come from the Bible, and it was essential that the transformations I was experiencing were not only "licensed" by Scripture but also provoked by it. The Bible was giving me new insights about my body, my being, and my destiny, and I was gaining a new way of regarding the Bible.

When I returned to teach New Testament at Union Theological Seminary in New York the next fall, I began to incorporate the more holistic approach I had learned from the Guild for Psychological Studies. In the first session of a class on the Gospel of Mark, I had the students do a picture of the baptism of Jesus without consulting any commentaries, just as we had done at Four Springs. Only this was taking place in an academic setting, and I was under pressure to do rigorous graduate-level teaching. As a doctoral student, I had done an exhaustive exegesis of Jesus's baptism, so I was pretty sure I was on top of the literature. I wanted to see if drawing the picture might provide an alternative route to knowledge, or a different way of knowing. In their pictures, the students collectively scored every significant exegetical point it had taken me four months in the library to discover! It was not my intention to substitute art for exegesis; but the point had been made. There is more than one avenue to exegetical insight. "The heart has its reasons the mind knows not of" (Pascal). How much richer the return if we would use both together!

It would be a half dozen years before I came upon split brain research and was able to use it as a conceptual framework for understanding what was happening. The left brain, specialized for analytical, logical, and abstract thinking, had seized control of the academy. It demanded that all thinking be done in a cause-and-effect mode, using language and a sequential sense of time (*chronos*). What we had been neglecting was the other side of the brain, the right hemisphere, which does not have the capacity for speech but is capable of knowing in unique ways to which the left hemisphere is not privy. The right brain is specialized in spatial relations and in synthetic, imaginative, a-causal, metaphorical kinds of thinking. Its sense of time is the present, or now (*kairos*). It is the side most involved in music, designing, perception of wholes, complex visual patterns (like the recognition of faces), voice recognition, gestalts, shapes, sizes, colors, textures, and forms. However, since it cannot use direct speech, we must allow it to speak in the only ways it can: through clay, paints, movement, mime, and music. An educative mode that draws on both sides of the brain would, then, be optimal. (For a more complete discussion of the application of split-brain theory to biblical study, see my *Transforming Bible Study*, chapter 1.)

It does not require much effort from either side of the brain to figure out what kind of a reception this approach received from my academic colleagues. The students, for their part, loved it; for once, their whole beings were being engaged in an encounter with Scripture, with reality and with God. Powerful things were happening to them as a result of encountering Scripture. We built a weekend retreat into the course, with time for movement and silence. Teaching became midwifery in the transformation of those who felt called to become enablers of transformation. They were learning, not only a content, but a method—one that they could use in many different contexts (churches, prisons, retirement homes, social change struggles, and nontraditional ministries).

One of my biggest complaints with theological education is that teaching through the lecture mode, while sometimes necessary and even effective, is almost totally untransferable to a parish setting. Except in very few churches where the membership is heavily laced with holders of graduate degrees, lectures are ineffective and usually unwanted in the parish setting. Here was a method, however, that could serve as the medium for graduate education and, at the same, be learned in the process of imbibing information. It could be used in virtually any conceivable small group setting, and some not so small. The professor, rather than modeling a methodology largely irrelevant to the needs of Christian workers (except future seminary teachers— and not even these, if they were to use this method), would be modeling an approach immediately transferable to other situations.

It all made so much sense to me. However, it was apparently unsettling when laughter emanated from my classes as students presented Jesus's resurrection appearance in John 21 as a farce (including Peter's dressing to spring into the water and the disciples counting all 153 of the fish). The use of oil pastels in a graduate seminary seemed puerile, and the shouting of the Lord's Prayer at the top of our lungs to get a physiological sense of the importance and meaning of the imperative construction of each of its petitions was understandably disturbing. Besides, there was a fiscal crisis. Therefore, it was not really surprising, though still painful, when I was denied tenure.

I had written a little tract in 1973, *The Bible in Human Transformation*, which began with the attention-getting statement that biblical critical scholarship was bankrupt. It was not dead, only bankrupt—unable to achieve the purposes for which it had been created. It was caught in objectivism, or the illusion that the exegete could operate in a detached, value-neutral, ahistorical manner, as if the exegete were not very much attached to a powerful institution—seeking tenure, promotion, and recognition—in a specific historical time that laid on the scholar certain demands. This objectivistic approach brought with it a vested interest in undermining the Bible's authority and demystifying the religious tradition. It required functional atheism for its practice and created an unbridgeable gulf between the past and today. The outcome of biblical studies in the academy, I remarked, was a trained incapacity to deal with the real problems of actual living persons in their daily lives.

Furthermore, biblical studies increasingly fell prey to a form of technologism which regarded as legitimate only those questions that the historical-critical method could answer. Biblical scholarship had become cut off from any community for whose life its results might be significant. In its objectivist mode, it was irrelevant to the teaching of those students who did not need to be weaned from Fundamentalism, but had no faith at all.

I was not trumpeting the demise of a critical approach to Scripture in the least, but only its getting "stuck" in an alienated distance. I wanted to see the text rebound on the exegete and call the exegete's life into question. It seemed to me that the approach developed by the Guild for Psychological Studies was just what was needed to move us *through* criticism and out the other side, into what Paul Ricoeur calls a "second naïveté," where we can once again hear the question that first brought the text to speech. Now we would read the text, not to dominate it by means of our technical skill but to be changed.

That is what I thought. Despite the great amount of interest—furor, rather—that the book caused, it seemed to bear little fruit in seminary teaching. Biblical scholars, with very few exceptions, continued to use the lecture mode. It was easier to remove the threat. Therefore, I entered a period of exile, to all effects blacklisted by other biblical scholars from teaching in other academic seminaries. Through the good offices of Professor Robert Lynn, who was then doubling up at Union Seminary and as the head of Auburn Seminary, I began to work at Auburn doing continuing education.

Auburn fully supported my approach. Perhaps I should explain that Auburn had been a Presbyterian seminary in Auburn, New York, until it closed in 1939 and moved down to Union Seminary, where it continued a shadow existence, funding endowed chairs at Union, providing scholarships for Presbyterian students, and operating a summer program for clergy. Under Bob Lynn's leadership, Auburn launched a full-scale continuing education program for clergy and laity. It has no academic classes, offers no degrees, and has no student body. In practical terms, this means that I spend a great deal of time on the road, doing workshops and retreats all over the United States and Canada.

Something was still missing, however. Though I was doing many exercises that involved art, mime, and role playing, I was not using movement or music—and that had been one of the most decisively important elements in my own transformation. I had taken many movement classes, but quite honestly felt no vocation for leading movement—and no clear idea how to do so. However, my wife, June Keener-Wink, had also taken these movement classes, had been in a movement leadership group, and had been teaching movement to children for almost a decade. What we lacked was a model for integrating Bible study with body movement. With great trepidation, we experimented by leading a few weekend retreats together. People responded affirmatively even though we were largely unable to explain how Scripture and movement integrate. It was clear that the participants were doing the integration themselves. We have been trying ever since to make connections between Scripture, movement, and life. I wish I could tell you that we have, after eight years of working together, completed that task, but we are far from doing so. As I reflect on it now, I am not even sure it is necessary to make this connection consciously.

There is no intrinsic connection between body work and Scripture. They can each be profitably done separately. What we have discovered, however, is that when we work alone, the results are greatly diminished. There is something that happens when the central symbol system of the Christian faith is experienced both intellectually and organismically.

Perhaps I should try to give some idea of what June does in the body movement session. To introduce the movement session she sometimes makes a statement like this:

> The body of Christ is made up of bodies. We cannot be a part of the body of Christ except in our bodies. The notion of the "body of Christ" was Paul's way of naming the new reality that had come about in the events triggered by Jesus. The early church had experienced a new mutation in human evolution. Human evolution, as scientists have pointed out, is no longer physical but social. The new human possibility emerging, which Paul called the "new creation," is a corporate reality in which the individual is not swallowed up by the collective, but each person is on a journey to authentic being-in-community. This new experience involved neither the tyranny of the group over the individual, nor the rugged individualism that rejects all group relationship or accountability. It represents a new potential, possible only after people have fought free of the dominance of the group and have found their own path through responding to the guidance of God.
>
> This new corporate body is made up of bodies. And our freedom to relate to one another and to respond to the promptings of the Holy Spirit depends on the way we relate to our own bodies. Our availability to God is to a great extent determined by how free we are spontaneously to respond to what God presents to us as bodies.
>
> Historically, the church has denied the body and has split body from soul, nurturing only the soul and repressing, ignoring, or disciplining the body. Such an attitude is unbiblical. There are no separate words for "soul" or "body" in Hebrew. There is, rather, one word that combines them both—*nephesh*, "animated body, living being." The Hebrews simply could not regard the human person as split into separate parts, but as an integral being. This view is now being reaffirmed by modern medicine.
>
> We do movement therefore as a way of integrating physical and spiri-

tual, outer and inner, and the substance of our flesh and the substance of faith. The movement is explicitly an attempt to heal the ancient split that fractures our beings and sets us at odds with our bodies. Our goal is to recover a sense of our bodies as temples of the Holy Spirit within us.

As with any art, one cannot always make direct correlations between the movement and Bible study. But we trust from experience that these correlations are being made nonetheless at the core of the self. Bible study cannot be holistic if it deals only with the intellect. Only when the whole person is involved with Scripture can we hope to heal the split between body and spirit and enable people to become more authentic human beings-in-community.

We are not interested in using body movement to understand the Bible better. The goal is rather to use both Bible and body movement as means of facilitating the transformation of participants. The Bible, despite its explicitly emancipatory aims, has for a great many people been an instrument of domination and destruction in their lives. The guilt and inadequacies that people associate with their bodies are often reinforced by injunctions from Scripture: "be perfect," "do not be angry," and "judge not." Touching ourselves, especially in masturbation, was for many children a no-no.

Some people, having left the church, find themselves in secular self-help workshops which encourage them to express their emotions. They bang on a bed with a tennis racquet or a baseball bat and finally get in touch with the rage they had never felt free to express. As salutary and indispensable a stage in healing as this is, this step alone is not enough. For whereas before they had repressed their *anger*, now they have repressed the *injunction* against anger. Healing will not be complete until the injunction has itself been reexamined and the person freed from a false reading of Scripture. (The New English Bible shows the way when it translates Matthew 5:22, "Anyone who *nurses anger* against his brother [or sister] must be brought to judgment." The word *nurses* is an active verb, indicating action continuous in the present). The issue is not being angry, but what we do with it.

New insights never strike us as really true or truly real until they can be related to the symbol system that most profoundly informs our lives. For those of us who identify ourselves as Christians, intellectual and emotional transformation is not complete until fresh insights can be brought into some kind of congruence with our central religious text. All the more powerful, then, are those insights whose very genesis lies in Scripture.

As we have worked with people in groups, we have discovered that their capacity to recover the freedom to move is associated with a new self-image. They discover self-acceptance despite not being perfect according to cultural norms of beauty. The ability to respond spontaneously in one's body means that a person is overcoming inhibitions and terrors often dating back to childhood. What is being enacted is precisely the healing that Scripture itself describes. When we become capable of organismic spontaneity—that is, when we are able to respond appropriately to the everlasting goodness of life in the moment—we find that we are living in the presence of God. We are more supple, more vulnerable, and freed from frozen bodies incapable of dancing to the occasion. We are available to God in a new way, more attentive to what the Spirit wants done, and more willing to do it, even if it requires doing something with our bodies that would previously have embarrassed us and thus prevented our response.

The movement is not a tool for deepening our understanding of Scripture; it is a way of bringing about in our bodies the new possibilities for living that the gospel proclaims have now, in Jesus, broken into the world. We are not trying simply to grasp what the Bible means but to become the people that the Bible proclaims. We are not just learning about the Bible but attempting to incarnate the God revealed by Jesus, who incarnated that God. We are not merely examining the doctrine of the Holy Spirit but opening our bodies, quite literally, to become the temples of the Holy Spirit within us.

I should add that we work with laity and clergy, the vast majority of whom have never been exposed to movement work previously. Therefore, we are always beginning from scratch. June has had to develop an approach to movement in which everyone can participate, regardless of their shape, age, or physical condition. (She encourages even those in wheelchairs to move as much as they are able.) The task is to awaken people to their embodiedness, to make them aware that they are a *nephesh*, to move from "I *have* a body" to "I am a nephesh capable of incarnating God."

In the first movement session, June typically invites us (and no one is obliged to do anything more than they want) to do stretching and bending to limber up our bodies. Then she has the group lie on the floor and breathe. She relaxes us into the Everlasting Arms. We let God breathe in us. This is a time for meditation, with perhaps the reading of a poem. Then, slowly and gently, we begin to move, still on the floor, not so much moving ourselves but joining the movement already going on within us. At last we come to our feet, using movement to express the prayer of each of us, as if there were no other way to pray but through our bodies. Throughout this session and all the sessions she does with the group, her focus is on those most anxious and afraid of expressing themselves through movement in a group setting. Therefore, she places heavy stress on getting a sense of groundedness in the earth, Mother Earth, God's earth. She also emphasizes the sense of flow in our breathing and movement, noting that flow is the physiological manifestation of trust, that trust is love, and that love unites us with God.

In another session, she might introduce the "planes," a concept taken from Rudolf Laban's theory of movement. First, she has us draw with our fingers in the air, extending from the spine, our "Front Door." After defining it, we turn it into a large oval, then we paint it top to bottom, then horizontally, and then we just play with its surface. Next, we locate the "Table Plane," in which we are standing, reaching out to draw its four corners, then rendering it as a circle, then a figure eight, and then exploring the whole table plane any way we like. To the sides we describe the "Wheel Planes," making a large oval to the one side, which then becomes a figure eight standing, then a figure eight on its side, then spokes; then we play with the wheel any way we like. We repeat the same steps on the other side. Last, there is the "Rear Door." We cannot entirely inscribe it, but we do the best we can.

Having accomplished all these very simple movements, we have now defined our "kinesphere." This is an orbit that we take with us everywhere we go. It is our own inalienable space. No matter where we move, or how, our entire orbit goes with us. No one can take it from us. The very act of drawing the orbit's dimensions is both a reclaiming and a recognition of its existence. Our drawing is a rudimentary dance. Without being aware of it, everyone in the room has accomplished our first dance together.

Next we begin to move our orbits through the room, daring to take a few steps and then a few more, as we reach out into our orbits with the hand leading, always watching our fingers (and therefore no one is watching anyone else!) and returning our hand to our center— opening and closing as we gradually explore the room.

In subsequent sessions (each interspersed with Bible studies), June adds more and more action to our orbits. We may play with the different qualities of space: quick and slow, bound and free, direct and indirect, or light and forceful. Together these provide a vocabulary of movement—virtually a "Myers-Briggs" of our use of space. We may find a partner and begin moving, without touching, in and out of their orbit. Having surmounted this obstacle—the introduction of another person into what has until now been a wholly private affair— she might ask us to get another partner and join hands, moving together in harmony. Then, without words, one of us will begin leading and the other following; then the reverse and then back to harmony.

With these and a large repertoire of other movements, she brings us imperceptibly to the point where we are moving freely, perhaps even unself-consciously.

When she puts on a piece of music and asks us to respond to it with our bodies, using the planes of our orbits, it is merely the next small step in a progression that has prepared us, without our thinking of it in those terms, to dance. We are, of course, not dancing—that would be too hard, or next to impossible! We are just moving in our orbits as we have been doing before. All we are adding is music and the desire to respond to it appropriately and spontaneously. Yet, lo and behold, we *are* dancing, some of us for the first time in our lives, without "steps" and without any kind of norms or judgments or criticism. We are free from the censure and inhibitions that have bound us all our lives (if this is indeed for us a "first"). All this can take place in only two days, and how much richer it becomes in a longer workshop!

There is also important work to be done with our body images. Many people hate their bodies, feel betrayed by them, or have betrayed them. To be in dialogue with our bodies, to do a "Touch Dance" in which we simply move to music, touching and claiming our own *nephesh*, can be a tremendously liberating thing for those who have lived alienated from their own physical beings.

How did we get alienated from our own substantial beings in the first place? As Emilie Conrad-Da'oud points out, what we call our body is, to a large extent, a cultural construction. Each culture imposes on its members a definition of the human form and prescribes the manner of movement (compare, for example, the typical movements of natives of Haiti and Evanston, Illinois). "I saw that what I called 'my body'—how I moved, talked, even how I thought—was a cultural imprint." The notion that we consist of solid bodies with fixed forms that move from here to there through space is, she says, a cultural construct that served us well when our main concern was physical survival, but today, when we no longer have to fight off woolly mammoths or bears, such cultural fixations are a threat to our continued existence.

Having separated ourselves from our environment to gain control over it, she continues, we became alienated from the nature with which we continued to be indissolubly connected. Even the concept of the central nervous system is a cultural construct, developed on analogy from centralized, hierarchical political systems. "The notion of a body governed by a central nervous system and a single ego matches that of a country ruled by a central government and a single leader." Both images stress separation, boundaries, hierarchy, and control.

Anything that looks or acts unusual—a wiggling movement in the upper back, a person of a different skin color—becomes a threat. To this mentality, appearance and performance are everything, and one dare not sink beneath the surface into feeling and relating to the other for fear boundaries melt and, in communion, one will lose control. (Shaffer 1987:94)

To renounce this profound need for control means recognizing that there is already a dance going on in our cells or our structures—a dance of myriad movement forms beyond anything we can imagine.

The body, too, is the victim of a system of dominations that has characterized human societies at least since the rise of the conquest empires. It is not enough, then, to seek deliverance for individuals, but to seek it for communities, for cultures, for nations, and for the planet itself. The suppression of the body is one with the suppression of peoples. The fetishism of control operates against minorities, women, the poor, and the gospel in precisely the same way that it operates against the *nephesh:* divide and rule. The body-mind split is the spawn of the "domination system" and a useful tool in the preservation of injustice imposed on ourselves and our social order.

The biblical injunction, "So glorify God in your (plural) body (singular)" in 1 Corinthians 6:20 is of a piece, then, with the vision of our redemption in Romans 8:23—"we wait for adoption, the redemption of our (plural) body (singular)" and 1 Corinthians 6:19—"your (plural) body (singular) is a temple of the Holy Spirit within you (plural)." Apparently, Paul cannot conceive of redemption in individualistic terms, as the purveyors of narcissistic salvation would have it, whether it be in heaven or an upper-middle class heaven on earth. He can only imagine a new *community*—the body of Christ—in which the former victims of the alienated and alienating system of domination are gradually becoming free from habituation to their splitness and obeisance to the powers that be. He can only conceive of our being liberated *together*, in our bodies (he is surely thinking of the Hebrew term *nephesh* when he uses the Greek word *soma* here). Biblical, mindbodily thinking will inevitably lead, therefore, to political action aimed at liberating the victims of the domination system.

It is impossible to convey an experiential approach with mere words. I have, I hope, been able to indicate something of what we do. Ours is a society in which people are still split off from their bodies, regarding them as the devil's own carcass, the seat of sin, or a seething volcano of lusts and passions that must be repressed; or, at the other extreme, regarding their bodies as indifferent to the soul (if they even think about their souls), a playground for any and all pleasures, and a hedonist's palace. The task of integrating body and soul, mind and emotions, and sexuality and spirituality—of reclaiming our *neph-*

esh—is overwhelmingly difficult in our pathological society. The union of Bible study and body movement alone is obviously not adequate to the healing of that split, but it can make an important contribution.

References

Poteat, William H. 1985. *Polanyian Meditations: In Search of a Post-Critical Logic.* Durham, N.C.: Duke University Press.

Shaffer, Carolyn. 1987. "Dancing in the Dark." *Somatics* 5 (November/December):49–55, 94, 98.

Steiner, Rudolf. 1961. *The Mission of the Archangel Michael.* Hudson, N. Y.: Anthroposophic Press.

Wink, Walter. 1973. *The Bible in Human Transformation: Toward a New Paradigm for Biblical Studies.* Philadelphia: Fortress Press.

_____. 1980. *Transforming Bible Study.* Nashville: Abingdon Press.

God's Body, the Midrashic Process, and the Embodiment of Torah

Arthur Waskow

If we *davven* in a circle, where is God? God is not somewhere else. God is not in the ark, across many rows of heads and past an empty gulf of no-man's-land. God is not in Jerusalem, thousands of miles away. God is not high above, reigning in royal splendor. As we davven in a circle, God begins to appear in the faces around the circle—and in the vibrations between them—and in our own hearts and minds.

Unbidden, unintended, and undeliberated, the choice of the *havurah* movement—the Jewish movement to create small, intimate, face-to-face congregations—twenty-five years ago to davven in circles has come round to affecting the process of Torah study, the practice of prayer, and images of God. This is no longer only among the *havurot* but in the wider and wider circles of the movement for Jewish renewal that grew out of and beyond the *havurot*.

Part of what the *havurot* are doing is what Judaism has been doing for a long time—to make *midrash,* the profoundly playful discovery of meaning between the lines of a tale or a text. However, the Jewish renewal movement has also experimented with new forms of midrash-making and has included encounter, dance, drama, and other forms of embodiment in its practice of Torah. It thus seeks to deepen our understanding of the world, of ourselves, and of our relationship to Jewish culture.

To make midrash has a long tradition within Jewish culture. In the biblical era of Jewish thought and history, passages of what to a modern, critical eye look like midrashim on previous texts were interwoven with those texts so as to appear within and as part of broader texts—all of which became canonized as Revelation. In the rabbinic era, the midrashic process was understood as the discovery (uncovering) of previously hidden aspects of God's revelation at Mount Sinai. Thus, the midrashic wrestle within and with Torah was truly a wrestle with God.

In the modern era, many Jews have not viewed Torah as the revelation of divine truth and have therefore not seen the midrashic process as a guide to thought or action. The "scientific" paradigm—including the "scientific" politics of Machiavelli, Mill, and Marx; and the "scientific" psychologies of Freud, Pavlov, and Piaget—has turned many away from wrestling with a text to analyzing data as a path to profound truth.

However, we are no longer unambiguously convinced by or living within the paradigm of science. In recent years, both practical and philosophical doubts have grown about the efficacy of the scientific method as the sole path to truth. Some philosophers have suggested that science is itself a text with all the problems of truthfulness that arise in any text. At the same time, literary philosophers have begun to re-create a sense that truths about the world and about the self can emerge from a reader's engagement with a literary text. In a new sense, therefore, it begins to seem possible for the midrashic process to put the midrash-maker in touch with God—if by God is meant in part the rest of reality, the ground of truth, and the mystery beneath and within mastery.

Out of these and other currents of what may begin to be understood as a postmodern era, there has emerged new interest in the midrashic process—not only in analyzing its place in history but also in taking part in the process, in the present and the future. This beginning of a shift in approach from the modern, scientific worldview to a postmodern one offers an opportunity not only to learn about a characteristically Jewish path of thought but also to join in it and enrich it. The midrashic process is a particularly apt one to renew in this way because within itself is the assumption of open-endedness, unveiling, and enrichment. This process (perhaps unlike some other elements of biblical and rabbinic life paths) can be rejoined by renewing and reinventing Judaism—instead of by restoring Judaism to what it was before the modern era.

The midrashic process of "wrestling" with the text can change both the text and the reader. Even the most ancient and well-known texts can take on new meaning when looked at under new light, and even the most modern and enlightened reader can change his behavior and worldview by opening up to texts that have been reread in many different times and cultures.

The Embodiment of Torah

The basic approach to midrash-making is very simple: A group of people read together a passage from the Torah and respond to it. (*Torah* should be broadly understood: The Torah might be a passage from the Bible, the Talmud, the Zohar, a Hasidic tale or sermon, or a modern Jewish philosopher such as Buber, Heschel, or Plaskow.) Responses to the Torah can rely on and employ forms of embodiment. Among the fullest examples of such embodiment are drushodrama, drushodance, medium as message, and aliyadrush.

Drushodrama

Coined from *drusho*, the root of *midrash* (*d'rash*, or seeking, means to search deep into a text for its inner essence or to search into the "empty" spaces around it for their unspoken hints of meaning), *drushodrama* is an improvised drama that reinterprets Torah. It is a powerful technique for evoking responses. It usually begins with reading aloud together a dramatic tale of Torah, then stopping at some climactic moment and asking the group to choose roles in the story (human, animal, inanimate, and divine). The group then acts out what happens next instead of talking about it.

For example, in the story of the binding of Isaac (Genesis 22), read until God has completed the command to Abraham or until Abraham sacrifices the ram. Then stop. Ask for volunteers to act out Abraham, Isaac, the ram, the wood, the donkey, the boys down the mountain, Sarah, and God. Give the volunteers a limited amount of time to share a sense of what they want to do; then press them to begin. (They will often be mildly embarrassed and reluctant.) More interesting midrash usually emerges from the flow of action than from the talk of "getting ready." As an example of what can happen, a 10-year-old boy, playing Isaac on his way down the mountain after the binding, begins to stumble. "Wait!" says the teacher, "What are you doing?" "Mmmm . . ." says the boy, "I'm broken." "Of course," say the others, "just because Abraham didn't kill him doesn't mean that everything is okay." Then the teacher weaves this response together with the classical rabbinic midrash that the aged Isaac of the Jacob-Esau story had been blinded not by old age but by the flash of the knife above him at the binding.

For another example, choose the story of Jacob's intended marriage to Rachel, when Leah is substituted. Read until the verse that says, "Look! In the morning, it was Leah!" Ask people to play Jacob, Laban, Leah, Rachel, and God.

This last example suggests an important element to take into account when planning drushodrama and other midrashic processes—

that one of the most intense, buried energies within the Jewish people is that of women seeking to link their own spiritual experience to that of Jewish women in the past by uncovering the hidden experience of the women in the Bible and of rabbinic history. Focusing on stories of such women as Sarah, Rebekah, Rachel, Leah, Dina, Shifra, and Miriam opens up new areas for midrash that have been little explored by the male-dominated tradition. Indeed, one experience with drushodrama paints the moral.

The passage addressed was Genesis 34, the rape of Dina. After the group read the story together, the teachers (Phyllis Berman and myself at the National Havurah Summer Institute in 1984) asked for an open discussion. Slowly there emerged a sense that the most puzzling aspect of the story was the silence of Dina. The teachers asked whether someone would come forward to be the voice of Dina. A man volunteered, but the teachers asked him to wait until at least two women had spoken for Dina. A silence gathered in the room, and finally one woman took a deep breath, rose, shut her eyes, and said:

Raped.
I have been raped three times in the story.
Once. I was raped by Sh'chem.
Twice. I was raped when my brothers ignored me, refused to ask
   me what I wanted—and murdered all the men of Sh'chem.
Three times. The Torah itself is raping me. Still raping me.
Because it does not speak my voice.

Then she sat down, in tears. The room was deathly silent. After several minutes, the teachers asked whether any other women wanted to speak in Dina's voice. Again there was silence. Finally one of the teachers asked, "Do I take it that all of the women here think that Dina's voice has already spoken—that there are no other words they want Dina to say?" The women nodded. Afterward, the woman who spoke as Dina said that she lost all consciousness of being herself and really became Dina.

It is this process of "becoming" a character in the story that most powerfully breaks through both personal embarrassment and the cultural distance from biblical life. The becoming seems to be accomplished more easily by drushodrama than by more verbal midrash-making, because the physical and the emotional as well as the intellectual aspects of the reader are engaged.

Drushodance

In another version of this approach (which might be called drusho-dancing or drushodreaming), the teacher, Liz Lerman, a professional dancer and choreographer, had the group read together the biblical portion of Korah (Numbers 16–17) concerning the rebellion of Korah and others against Moses, and the affirmation of Aaron's priesthood through the blossoming of an almond branch.

After the reading, the teacher moved the group outdoors onto a small open field, led some simple movement exercises, and then asked everyone in the group to become some character from the Korah portion (human, animate, or inanimate—the almond branch, Moses, the mouth of the earth that swallowed Korah, and so on). Each person was to find a comfortable place in the field and begin through any combination of mime, gesture, dance, chant, and words to express the character she had chosen, intermittently chanting the character's name: "Korah! Korah!" "Almond branch! Almond branch!" and so on. Whenever the actor had "had enough" of one character, she was to move to a different place and become a different character. Actors could, if they chose, interconnect with one another—Korah with the mouth of the earth, for example—but they were not required to do so.

Then the enactment of the portion began and went on for about thirty minutes. Since there was no time sequence—all and any part of the portion was enacted in any order or simultaneously according to the individual desires of the actors—the reenactment was more like a collective dream than a drama. After about thirty minutes, the teacher ended the reenactment and led a discussion of what had just happened. Individuals reported an extraordinary sense of more deeply understanding various aspects of the portion, and the group as a whole noticed and reported a sense that out of the seeming disorder of the reenactment emerged a different order—one governed not by the chronology of the portion but by a recorded "psychological chronology." For example, the group found itself moving together, late in the reenactment, to become a forest of blossoming almond branches—an effort, the individuals reported, that affirmed life and fruitfulness after a searing set of encounters with frustration, pain, and death.

In this enactment, as well as in a number of others, actors who chose to become God reported afterward that their previous semi-stated theological assumptions were shaken by the experience. God often came to seem almost powerless, unable to reshape and channel the intense interactions of other participants—sometimes reduced only to the role of comforter, as in rubbing the shoulders of a Leah deeply pained by Jacob's rejection and Laban's manipulation. "The pain of God" was often reported—arising from God's witnessing of people's creation of injustice, hunger, and so on, and God's inability to change the situation—even by direct intervention and exhortation.

Medium as Message

Another way to embody the life experience of the Torah readers in the Torah itself is to understand the readers' own emotional responses to the texts they are reading as a reflection of the inner meaning of the texts themselves.

One example of a powerful text to approach this way is the Sotah chapter (Numbers 5) on how to respond to the jealousy of a husband who, without evidence, accuses his wife of adultery. Many groups will explode—some readers out of a scornful sense that the passage is sexist, superstitious, magical, and irrational, and others from a sense that the text is holy, truthful at some deeper level, and not to be ignored or scorned. Let the explosion gather force. Then ask the group to reexamine these explosive reactions in light of the text. Were they becoming "part of the story"—quarreling, like the Sotah and her spouse, over jealousies and angers that no evidence could resolve? Is the next passage—on Nazirite status—or the next—on the identical gifts of the twelve tribal leaders to the Mishkan—written to soothe the turmoil? What is the relationship between message and medium in Torah? Can Torah reach out to create the effects in its readers that it wishes or is Torah "self-re-created" in readers' responses?

This approach to midrashic processes bears some analogies to a classical kabbalistic understanding of the relations between human action and Torah. Primordially, said some Kabbalists, the Torah was encoded in a steady stream of letters (perhaps even arranged in an order different from the Torah that we know). This primordial Torah underwent a reshaping when Adam and Eve ate from the Tree of Knowing Good and Evil. Not only did the Torah itself then begin to describe that very choice in the Garden, but only then does it come to describe all the *mitzvot* (commandment, connective act, good deed) that human beings must obey to walk a holy path in the world outside Eden. If the Torah can be conceived as shifting its form and word in response to the choices and actions of human beings, then the meaning of Torah can be understood to grow in part from the responses of human beings to its texts.

Aliyadrush

In traditional synagogues, the *sidra* (Torah portion) is divided into seven sections, and seven individuals are honored by being called up to bless God for the Torah. In Hebrew, the word *aliyah* means "going up" or "being called up to the Torah." For the most part, Jewish renewal communities do not read the entire weekly *sidra* but rather choose a particular narrative or section of laws from the *sidra*. *Aliyadrush*, then, would be an innovative way of doing *sidra*, a fusing of individual life path, Torah study, and prayer.

Jewish renewal communities have developed a variety of customs for reading Torah. This example was developed by the P'nai Or Religious Fellowship in its practice and then encoded in its innovative guide to Shabbat-morning prayer, *Or Chadash* (New Light).

The Torah reader (or community) may chant the *sidra* section aloud or read it dramatically from the Torah scroll, and he decides how many *aliyot* there will be (usually three on an ordinary Shabbat in which the entire *sidra* is not read) and for what each *aliyah* is. Generally, three passages are chosen that bear themes that speak to the group. Then the group connects the *aliyah* to the message of those verses.

For example, in reading the *sidra* on crossing the Red Sea, one might call for one *aliyah* all who are hesitating on whether to choose a major change in their lives and need a blessing of discernment and courage to choose; for a second *aliyah*, those who are in stormy mid-passage and need a blessing of strength and perseverance; for a third, those who have crossed and need a blessing of fulfillment and joy. People, then, choose themselves to come for each *aliyah* as it connects to them—once, twice, three times, or not at all. After each *aliyah*, the leader makes a *mi-sheh-beyrach* (special blessing) beginning with the traditional Hebrew formula and continuing *ex tempore* in English to evoke the blessings that seem needed. The ancient Torah text thus becomes embodied in the present life experience of the congregants.

The Embodiment of Prayer

The embodiment of God through new forms of prayer—somewhat more radical in feeling and in theology than the embodiment of Torah—is being explored chiefly by the above mentioned P'nai Or Religious Fellowship, following a path first charted by Rabbi Zalman Schachter. Their guide to Shabbat-morning prayer (*Or Chadash*) begins with a passage loosely translated from the work of Rebbe Menachem Nahum of Chernobyl:

> What is the world?
> The world is God,
> Wrapped in robes of God
> So as to appear to be material.
> And who are we?
> We too are God,
> Wrapped in robes of God,
> And our task is to unveil the robes
> And so dis-cover
> That we and all the world are
> God.

Or Chadash emerged from the discovery that many members of our generation can respond to the One with much more ease and passion by using "immanent" images of God, such as Breath of Life, or *Ruach ha-Olam*, rather than "transcendent" images like King (*Melech ha-Olam*), Father, Lord, or even Mother.

In regular synagogues, many Jews who have been using older images of God and older ways of praying because they knew of no alternative, feel new life in themselves and their community when they experiment with approaches offered by the Jewish renewal movement. Some find it especially helpful to address God in English or Hebrew as Wellspring, Source of Life, Life of the Worlds, *Chai ha-Olamim*, and especially as Breath of Life or with the actual breathing of a wordless name, "Yyyyhhhwwwhhh" or "Yahh." In congregations where the traditional melodies and rhythms are well known, some people prefer to treat them more or less as lulling mantras. In congregations where Hebrew is fairly unfamiliar, the desire for more acceptable cognitive meaning and the desire for mantra have sometimes found a successful synthesis in the chanting of English.

Dance as Part of Prayer

This need and desire for experiencing God as immanent goes deeper—as one might imagine—than specific words into the very embodiment of those words. The use of the body to express words of prayer is not new in Jewish life. When the Temple stood, the Levites danced on such occasions as *simchat beit ha-shoevah*, the first day of Sukkot. The sacrifices involved a good deal of bodily exertion, of which the shaking of the *lulav* (palm branch) on Sukkot still survives.

Several parts of a traditional Jewish service lend themselves to using dance and gesture to embody the meaning of the words. Most obvious is *birkot hashachar*, the blessings of dawn. Originally these were said at home—when the cockcrow was first heard, the eyes opened, and the feet set upon the solid floor. In the synagogue, these are usually said with little effort to reexperience the body's reawakening.

One way to embody these prayers is to ask each congregant in the davvening circle to create a gesture on the spot that expresses each of the blessings, and then for the whole congregation to imitate this gesture. These gestures can be repeated—first one, then two, then three, and so on—until the congregation has in effect created a unique dance for that one morning.

In other parts of the service, preplanned simple line or circle dances can be guided by the *shlichat tzibbur* in ways that encourage spiritual opening. Passages whose words cognitively celebrate the renewal of breath in the morning can become actual bodily breathing exercises by slowly chanting the words with emphasis on their long "ahhh" vowel sounds.

Dialogue/Encounter as Part of Prayer

Traditional Jewish prayer has included the chanting of Psalms at various points in the different services. Since the Psalms are addressed directly to God, they offer an important opportunity to affirm the embodiment of God in the community of davveners.

P'nai Or has taken this opportunity by arranging that, once or twice in each service, a psalm is read in dialogue by pairs of people within the *minyan*.

- Typically, the leader of services will choose one of the Psalms and ask the community to divide quickly into dyads of people sitting near each other.
- The leader will suggest that one person in each pair read the first verse of the Psalm silently, absorb it, and think how she wishes to express something close to this thought in her own words.
- Then she will face the "spark of God" in the other partner to say the new thought aloud. (In effect, the new thought is a midrash on the written content of the Psalm.)
- The second partner pays full attention to what the first one says and then turns back to the printed page to absorb the second verse of the Psalm and do the same work of midrashic transmutation—taking into account both what he has already heard and what the text says. Now he in turn addresses the first partner.
- This process continues until the Psalm is completed.

For many participants, the Psalm comes alive with meaning in the present, and the movement of thought and feeling that is characteristic of most Psalms becomes far more intelligible than emerges from a more or less rote reading. In addition, by addressing a human partner as God and being addressed as God, many participants find themselves spiritually moved in new ways.

Politics as Part of Prayer

The Shalom Center (a Jewish renewal center in Philadelphia) has been exploring the creation of public liturgies that address public policy—especially the protection of the earth from the dangers of nuclear holocaust, global warming, or other major catastrophes. Because these questions address the unity of the interrelated web of life more obviously than many others, addressing them through prayer has seemed less of a transgression into the nakedly and narrowly political sphere.

What is the relationship between prayer and public action, between real connection with God and real transformation of the world, and between true davvening and true *tikkun olam* (healing the world)? Two comments of Rabbenu Abraham Joshua Heschel follow.

He said the first at a conference on liturgical renewal: "Prayer is meaningless unless it is subversive, unless it seeks to overthrow and to ruin the pyramids of callousness, hatred, opportunism, and falsehood. The liturgical movement must become a revolutionary movement, seeking to overthrow the forces that continue to destroy the promise, the hope, the vision."

He said the second when he came home from taking part in a civil rights march in Selma, Alabama, alongside Martin Luther King, Jr., Catholic nuns, Protestant church leaders, and secular civil rights activists: "I felt that my feet were praying."

These are the two sides of the question: Is it possible to shape liturgies that subvert the injustice, war, tyranny, and exploitation of the earth around us while also subverting the callousness, hatred, opportunism, and falsehood within us? Is it possible to shape public "political" acts in such a way that we are praying?

So far, efforts at these fusions have included the following.

- Creating a pre-Pesach Seder against "the ultimate Pharaoh" at the U. S. government's H-bomb testing facility in Nevada, ending with a walk-on in which a number of the Seder celebrants were arrested.
- Using, at the base of the U.S. Capitol building during the Gulf War, a basically traditional liturgy for the calling of a *taanit tzibbur*, a public fast, in time of such calamities as war. The ceremony included draping the Sefer Torah in sackcloth and ashes, blowing the shofar, and reading from Torah, Prophets, and modern Jewish poets.
- Celebrating *Hoshanna Rabbah*, the beating of willows on the earth and the chanting of prayers for the protection of the earth from plague and famine, on the banks of a river endangered by pollution.

In these events, the medium and the message fused. As one participant said, "If earth is spirit, politics is prayer." It became clear in such actions that the divine intervention the prayers were imploring would have to include human action. God was no longer totally separate from human beings.

Problems with the Embodiment of God

One main objection to these approaches is that the new methods and symbols are not Jewish—either because they are too new and break with accepted Jewish practice or because they echo other traditions too much—especially that they seem too pantheist or panentheist, too Buddhist, or even too incarnational and therefore too Christian.

There do not seem to have been many public dialogues around these questions. Informally, as these issues arise, people in the Jewish renewal movement tend to respond to these concerns at three levels.

First, some people claim that these images are not as new as many assume. In the Kabbala and Hassidut especially, Jews have explored such ideas and used such metaphors before. To many, they seem like an unexpected but reasonable fusion of Mordechai Kaplan's "trans-naturalist" Reconstructionism, with images from the days of Hasidic upheaval in the eighteenth century and one new element: feminist spirituality.

Second, some people suggest that the Jewish people and Judaism are going through an upheaval and transformation as profound as the one that shaped and was shaped by the Talmud, as the rabbis tried to digest Hellenism into Torah rather than either rejecting or surrendering to Hellenism. According to this model, modernity has played in the last few centuries the role Hellenism played then. On these assumptions, it would be neither surprising nor outrageous to find new approaches being explored as Jews sought new names and ways of connecting with God. As for those who dismiss such ways of thinking as historicism that itself denigrates the Eternal, some people in the Jewish renewal movement answer that it is God who has veiled Itself from our access in the old ways, God who is working in the world to bring about these changes, and therefore God who is calling us to create new forms of contact.

Third, some people simply say that it is not surprising that the new forms might remind people of other traditions, because God is after all one and universal. Although there are and will continue to be many differences in the ways Jews approach that one God from the ways Christians, Buddhists, and Native Americans do, there are also likely to be some similarities as different communities try to overhear and approach the one truth.

Critics often raise another major concern—perhaps the most important—that a God "embodied" in the universe is less likely to demand of us a constant transcendence of the present state of things. If whatever is, is divine, then who will need to change it?

However, the notion of *tikkun olam* (healing the world) in the Kabbala is not so static. Even those who said God, Israel, and Torah were one did not think we could forget about doing the *mitzvot* that would repair the shattered vessel. They simply said that God, Torah, and Israel were all shattered and needed healing.

The main question, in the model of the movement for Jewish renewal, is what these *mitzvot* are—in principle and in practice. If God is embodied in the world, then in principle the *mitzvot* are not commands issued by a Commander, but *connections* that heal the shattered world. (The Aramaic usage of *tzi-vui*, the root beneath *mitzvah*, points in this direction.)

In practice, we must today reexamine whatever have in the past traditionally been understood as *mitzvot*. When we reexamine them in the light of our own generation, some practices that once seemed to heal and connect may today seem to divide more than they connect—making unbridgeable chasms between human beings and the earth, women and men, gay and lesbian Jews and heterosexual Jews, or Jews and non-Jews. After looking with great care, we may conclude that some specific practices harm the unity more than they heal the unity. If so, then with respect we must decide that in our own day these specifics are not *mitzvot*, whatever they were before. They have instead become *aveirot*, transgressions against, or fragmentations of, the Holy One.

From this standpoint, there are "lower" and "fuller" versions of immanence. Although it is true that whatever exists is divinity, it may be divinity in its reduced and shattered state. It remains our task through conscious action to lift this divinity from merely being All (*ha-kol*) to its fuller level of conscious harmony (*shalom*).

In this way, God's Body—which we are all part of—becomes most fully God's Body only when we seek to know and act as part of it.

EIGHT

Cain and Abel:
A Case for Family Therapy?*

Alix Pirani

The story of Cain and Abel is the first biblical account of fatal conflict between brothers. It is frequently referred to but commonly misread, and I have often asked myself why Cain and Abel's parents did nothing to avert the tragedy. In particular, where was Eve when all this was happening? It reflects for me our present-day situation: We are everywhere imperiled by wars between men who cannot make good brotherhood, and the women's influence and what are thought of as feminine qualities are apparently powerless to prevent meaningless murder and destruction. This story of the first family seems very much the story of the "family of man"—and I note the gender designated there.

Bible stories have, I believe, a far greater influence on the Western psyche than is often acknowledged. I have explored episodes from Genesis in psychodrama groups and participants have found in them profound meaning and relevance—which surprised them—as well as an urge to change the story for our contemporary context: to re-vise, or re-vision. When I consider the dynamic of the Cain and Abel conflict and wonder whether family therapy might have altered the course of events, I too am endeavoring to change the story. Therefore, I have decided to borrow the approach of psychodrama and write what is my own psychodrama: the female family therapist working with the Bible's first family.

*This is a revised version of an article first published in *European Judaism*.

The immediate paradoxes are obvious, and they are crucial. I have to put the family in a modern setting while preserving the timelessness of their predicament; I have to provide mundane versions of spiritual events and deities in human form. I am looking at the origins of a family, which has been conceived as the original family. In effect, I am looking at the way creation led to destruction—and I am seeking a means to re-creation, which is the task of any therapist.

I need to say that as an eclectic practitioner I have no one particular therapeutic stance or specialism in one way of working, though my main orientations are in humanistic and transpersonal psychology. As a writer, I enjoy making free with my imagination, and have allowed myself the writer's licence to rework the myth while holding to the essential questions at its heart.

So here is the family therapist's story and case study:

It was Cain who first consulted me, but I had met him already with his family—his parents Eve and Adam, and his younger brother Abel. They were all at a friend's garden party in the country district I had just moved into. I gathered they were well known and respected locally and worked a farm which Cain's grandfather had settled them on. My friend said they were a happy family who kept rather to themselves. The parents were in a good partnership, and both sons were hardworking, which was necessary because the land they had been given was very hard to work. When I chatted with them, however, I was not comfortable. There was an anxious compulsiveness that made me uneasy. Eve had that knitted brow you often see in mothers—a focus of the family's tensions. When they discovered I was a therapist, they smiled politely and changed the subject, but Cain looked at me thoughtfully. He seemed troubled.

It was no surprise when some time later he asked to come and see me. He looked worried, morose, and even hunted. His eyes were angry, and he was afraid to look at me directly; his color was very red, and his breathing was short and restricted. In a man of his father's age, one would have guessed high blood pressure, and I wondered what his father was currently experiencing. However, Cain was around twenty and a strong broad-shouldered farmer, and I felt apprehensive as he sat crouched forward in his chair, very tense and glancing at me cautiously.

He said he was depressed—finding it hard to be with people or make social contact—listless, and reluctant to work. He found getting up in the morning increasingly difficult. He could not tell his parents how he was feeling—such things were not spoken of. "We're supposed to be the model family," he said cynically. I questioned him about the loss of interest in his work. The apathy had been developing for some time but had come to a crisis a few weeks back. His grandfather, who lived on a nearby estate, had upset him by failing to appreciate the product of his labors. Cain worked the land and had proudly brought him some very fine vegetables he had grown, but the old man was unimpressed. Yet when Abel, who looked after the livestock, brought the grandfather a side of lamb, it was received with pleasure and praise for the farm's flock of sheep. Cain had been furious and had said so. "The old boy told me to try harder. And to beware of anger, and sinful thoughts. He must have known what was coming . . ." What had come, I asked, and Cain said he had been having nightmares full of violence and had become so angry with Abel and so jealous that he frightened himself. At times, he was devoured by obsessive envy and hatred, and he could hardly bear to be in his brother's carefree presence. "I've tried to talk with him—but he's basking in being the favorite, and he doesn't want to know."

I said it was not unnatural for someone to be envious of a younger brother. Hadn't he always been?

"According to my parents, I adored my baby brother from the word *go*. . . . They were always careful not to favor one of us above the other."

"Jealousy is not on . . . ," I observed. "Did you not tell your parents what happened with your grandfather?"

"Good Lord, no," Cain said. "You can't complain about the old man to them. They wouldn't hear of it. His word is law."

"Does your father not see what's happening between his sons?"

"He wouldn't notice. Wouldn't understand either. Too busy doing the farm accounts."

"Your mother?"

A glint came into his eye: rage. "He'd be nowhere without her. She's his main support."

I noted that he had not answered my question.

"His," I said. "Does she support you?"

The question puzzled him. "Should I expect her to? I think in a way I support her."

He said suddenly, looking at me with a grin, "If they only knew what goes through my imagination—how I've thought of getting rid of Abel—fascinating, all the ways you can dispose of someone."

Then his face fell, and he said hollowly, "I dreamed the other night he'd disappeared, and I was afraid I'd killed him, and I was supposed to be looking after him, and I went to find my parents, but they were nowhere to be seen . . . hidden away together somewhere." He frowned, and I saw a three-year-old boy and his guilty feelings. Then he said gleefully, darkly, "Imagine all that blood, eh?" and now I had a thirteen-year-old perhaps before me, insinuating, snake-like, telling me of his hidden dangerous power—his penis, exposing his guilty secret in order to impress me. It raised questions in my mind about his relationship with his mother and the Oedipal triangle he was involved in as the firstborn son. I already had the uncomfortable conviction that were we to work together for any length of time, though much of his anger was about the men, all the sexual rage and hatred would ultimately be directed at me, the mother-figure, and to tease Cain in any way would be to invite mayhem. I asked if he had had any girlfriends or contemplated marriage. There was a brief history of mistrust, the need for love, sexual frustration, hurt pride, and disdain.

He came to see me twice more. He got some relief from his guilty distress by talking with me, but he was still driven by fits of desperate destructiveness. I felt increasingly that there was little I could do. If there was real danger to Abel, it could not be averted unless it were openly acknowledged. Cain was, I was sure, carrying the suppressed anger and frustration of the whole family, and unless one could work with the family he would continue to bear the burden of its unresolved problems. These were gradually being revealed to me: Adam's denied impotence and midlife depression, Eve's frustrated creativity, Abel's defensive insouciance. The family was efficient and adequate to its tasks, but joyless. The parents' relationship lacked vitality, and behind them the old man, the patriarch, seemed to exert an unalterable controlling authority.

The colleagues with whom I discussed the case in our supervision group could only guess at the origins of this imbalance of power. There were doubtless many secrets, and Cain was manifesting something that had been carefully concealed. It did not surprise me when his mother contacted me and said he would not be coming again, as he found the sessions too disturbing.

Nor did it surprise me a few weeks later when I heard that Abel had been tragically killed in a farm accident caused by a machine his brother had been operating. There were comments and gossip, since Cain's tendency to belligerence was well known, but the inquest exonerated him from blame, and the old man, who was quite feared and respected in the neighborhood, came out that day and walked at Cain's side down the high street with a dignity that defied anyone to condemn or harm the young man.

In all the concern to deal with the guilt and unspoken accusations, one heard little of the loss of Abel, whom I had supposed to be the potential golden boy. When I contemplated the family structure, I concluded that they had killed off the youngest because they could not kill off the oldest, and the hapless Abel had received all the negative feelings that were meant for his grandfather.

About a month after the inquest Cain came to see me again. He looked very different—more upright and clearer, but with a frown and a cleft in the brow that would now always mark him. It reminded me of his mother's anxious frown. The bioenergetic analyst in our supervision group saw that frown as sexual guilt; another colleague believed it related to birth trauma—the desperation of the baby violently pushing its way out of its mother's womb. Both interpretations seemed relevant. Cain's eyes were clouded, and he blinked involuntarily now and again, but he avoided my gaze less than before, and said, "I presume you heard what happened—" He was telling me almost as though it would satisfy and ease me. Which it did, for I no longer felt afraid in his presence. It seemed he had acted out his destiny, and most of the pent-up violence was gone. The moral distress and the guilt, of course, had not gone and I foresaw that once the initial shock of bereavement had passed, he would be left with an acute identity crisis, for he had become a murderer, and where could he go from there?

He came regularly to sessions, with the tacit agreement of his parents. He had become the family's "referred patient." They had closed ranks socially and closed completely on their feelings also. Little had been said among the three; I could get no impression of any discussion of the accident, any grief, mourning, or mutual comforting. The shock had made them go silent. Cain, though, immediately after the tragedy had been summoned by his grandfather, who had berated him angrily, pouring imprecations on his head and predicting dreadful retribution for his crime. Under this onslaught, Cain had broken down and wept, protesting that he could not take such terrible punishment. The old man had relented a little and had promised to protect him, as he subsequently did.

I was struck by the powerful intimacy of the connection between these two, and I probed into their relationship. "We were very close when I was small," said Cain. "It sometimes seemed like he was more my father than Adam."

"So why," I asked, "do you suppose he rejected your produce and preferred Abel's?"

"Well," said Cain, "he was very odd about the land he'd given us. Superstitious. I never quite understood. He knew it wasn't good land, and he sometimes cursed it. He said it would curse me. I sometimes think he envies the earth and its produce—hates it. Doesn't like me to enjoy working it. I know that sounds odd . . . He condemned me for my jealousy, but he's the one who's jealous . . . And there's always been some mystery about the way he came to give my parents this land."

I said there seemed to be many mysteries in the family. He said the only one he knew, that he was not supposed to tell anyone, was that the old man was not in fact Adam's father. He had adopted Adam, and then Eve, when they were babies. "They're not brother and sister," said Cain, "but their marriage still seems incestuous even so, doesn't it . . . ? And how do we know they weren't his illegitimate children?"

Over the next weeks, as the horror of what he had done came to Cain, it became clear that the love and hatred and guilt he felt for his dead brother could never be integrated by him unless the whole family's pain came into the open. Communication between all four had seized up, and there were signs of strain; so I suggested a series of sessions for the whole family together. Cain was happy with this, and after a while the parents agreed. The old man resisted a great deal at first, but when he saw they intended to go ahead he obviously reckoned he had better be there and make sure I did not usurp his position. Cain reported his comment that psychotherapy was a load of nonsense invented by a Viennese atheist . . . "And as for a woman doing it . . . !"

When the family first met together in my consulting room, the old man's position was obvious. They all always deferred to him and hardly ever revealed how much his control irked them. He was like an odd mixture of Godfather, Mafia-style, and a moral philosophy don. He was paternal, stern, rarely genial, and, in this situation, rattled. He started saying defensively that he saw no need for all this— he had settled the whole issue with Cain himself. Nobody was to condemn the boy; or had they brought him here to accuse *him* of having caused the tragedy by his discrimination between the two brothers? He spoke evenly, as one accustomed to being the sole authority, but reproach was in the air. Abel seemed more present than absent, and it was immediately apparent that this family had been quite unable to mourn his death.

I said that this was not a law court—no one was on trial—and I was there not as Cain's advocate but to help the whole family. Each one would have my understanding and support. As time went on, it became difficult for me to maintain this position. I had to work hard in the supervision group to deal with my countertransference, especially my reactions to the old man's high-handed and dismissive attitude toward me, trying to undermine my authority from his fear of losing his own. I had to examine and question my own need to compete and to undermine *his* authority. Aware that he was projecting on to me his fears of impotence, I judged that the impotence I was feeling must be what he was feeling. In a later session, I was able to tell him that I appreciated how exposed and alone he must feel, wielding so much power, and perhaps the family was giving him more power than was healthy and the burden on him to make discriminations and judgments might be shifted and shared, just as the burden of guilt Cain carried might be shifted and shared. At that, I saw for the first time some respect and even gratitude, albeit grudging, from him. He understood; he had, after all, a formidable intelligence and respect for wisdom.

It remained to unearth the secret of his power over them. It clearly had to do with some guilt from the past, and I was sure it had a sexual element. There were still many unresolved tensions between Adam and Eve, who seemed never to speak directly to one another. They agreed to be interviewed separately and then together as a couple. My supervision group colleagues were interested in the generational patterns. We sensed there was an Oedipal situation for Cain and his parents; we suspected something similar must have operated with Eve and Adam and their parent. We also believed that Cain and Abel had been acting out in different ways Adam's and Eve's relationship. The Kleinian in our group saw immediately how much envy played a part in their dynamic—envy acknowledged and unacknowledged. As the powerful breast, the philanthropist, the old man would be feared and hated by his dependants, but that was superficially denied by them. Why, I asked, did he, as Cain suggested, seem to envy the earth, the land itself. My colleague pointed out that Mother Earth was herself the breast—unpredictable, capable of cursing us, to be feared and hated—and the old man was trying to deny his dependence on her, though he was in awe of her. Nevertheless he had annexed a piece of her, I said, and given it to Adam as his patrimony. He had also appropriated the maternal role in his adoption and raising of the two children—where was their mother? When I had asked Cain about this he said no one knew, and the family joke was that Adam had been made out of the dust of the earth. The earth, note, not "found under a gooseberry bush." The bioenergetic analyst in our group asked about the family's body structure. I reported that, sure enough, their grounding was poor. They did not walk well on the earth, which denoted an ambivalent relationship to mother and an uncertainty of support. They had relatively locked pelvises and rigid bodies; raised shoulders and short breathing denoted the fear that dominated Cain's parents. He and his grandfather had them too, with the seductiveness and manipulative power seen in the eyes that go with Lowen's psychopathic character structure.

My meetings with Eve were not easy. She was obviously mistrustful of me as another woman. Most of her replies to my questions were off the point or were about Adam—not herself—or were replies that Adam or their father would have given. She was very afraid I might be judging or accusing her. The sympathy I felt for the pain she must be suffering seemed not to be getting through. I wanted to know why she had not seen the enmity developing between her sons, and, if she had, why she had done nothing to mediate or to help keep the peace, but I saw that my asking her would be taken as blaming. I soon found that she was someone who was so chock-full of guilt that she could not bear to be criticized at all. She had therefore lost her discrimination and sense of responsibility. No, she had not noticed the trouble between her sons, she had always taught them it was childish to quarrel. She had not seen Cain's anger and frustration, nor that Abel was despised by his brother. It was clear that Eve refused to see those aspects of her sons that both she and Adam were feeling but denying—anger, frustration, humiliation, and envy—what they had felt perhaps most strongly at the age their sons were approaching. Whatever Eve and Adam had learned to suppress in themselves when they were coming up to twenty, they certainly would not want to see now—particularly if the agent of repression, their parent, was still the authority on whom they were dependent.

I was certain Eve must have been tacitly approving Cain's anger, which she pretended not to see; she must surely be resenting her subordinate position in this family, the endless devotion to her menfolk's needs, the silence and ineffectuality of Adam, the ignoring of her opinions, and her father's persistent, subtly despising comments about her.

She gave herself away then by saying, "Of course Cain was always an aggressive child. I think he was born with a chip on his shoulder." This enabled me to explore with her the crucial origins of Cain's personality and family role. Much was revealed as she looked back to the time of his birth. It had been a wearying, difficult pregnancy and a horrifying labor, she said. She had felt dreadfully alone. She was twenty, not long married, had no mother to turn to, and at the time had not been getting on too well with her father; he had filled her with dire predictions of the pain of childbirth, made her terrified, and told her it was what a woman had to suffer—one of her curses. She was paying, he had said, for her sins. Adam had not been present at the birth; he was intimidated by it all and by their father, who had dominated the whole procedure. In the postnatal period, Eve had been acutely depressed.

"But that's all in the past now," she said.

"No," I replied, "I think it's very much in the present." She did not catch on, but I felt she had been able to speak freely about something that had hurt her so badly she had never forgotten it. She must unconsciously have recognized that Cain's behavior now had some relation to the violence and distress of his birth and early days, and the unhappy womb in which he had been nurtured, feeding off his mother's in-turned fear and anger. By the time she and I met again, I had been pondering the nature of the triangle she had been caught in and the way she had almost been more married to father than to husband, perhaps still was, and bound to father by ties of guilt. "What sins," I asked her, "did your father think you were paying for?"

"Disobeying him, of course," she said, as though that were reason enough for the lonely agony she had endured. "I had been very foolish. We grew up on his estate—a beautiful place, Eden—and I think we would have had it as ours when we married. But there was trouble between the three of us, mostly my fault, and he told us to leave and gave us this place to live in and work instead. I don't think Adam has ever forgiven me for that, and I always feel I'm to blame for the unhappiness we've had since." A note of self-satisfaction had set in. I tried putting it to her that perhaps the men had something to answer for, but she would not see that. She enjoyed being the weak and bad one, the repentant sinner, and there was still concealment about the sin itself. I guessed that whatever it was, she must be protecting Adam and the old man and preserving their blameless image. This might be done out of devotion, but it had become for her, of course, a powerful role. They had come to rely on her to prop them up and keep them blameless. Cain, in this family, would know how phony that was. Yet he too would be trapped by his mother's power to define his potency—prop him up. He mistrusted her and despised his father. Caught in this double bind, he would inevitably see his seemingly irreproachable lightweight brother as a reason for his own torment. The favored one must be phony also and could not be trusted.

There was no overt sexual problem, but the fact that sex was never mentioned was, of course, the problem. The background of adoption was significant. Often when children are adopted, the unknown natural parents become the focus for sexual fantasy, anger, and guilt, while the adoptive parents are idealized as nonsexual progenitors.

I could sense the dark connection between Eve and Cain. She had probably been more openly and comfortably affectionate with Abel, thus increasing the rivalry. Thoughtlessly teasing her growing sons into an exciting rivalry was a sure way of getting back at Adam and at men generally, and having them act out her aggressiveness for her.

I had only one short meeting with Adam on his own—short because of his taciturnity and his disinclination to make any movement for himself or look beneath the surface of things. I wanted to understand the pattern of father-son relationships in the family, and how it was he had so little authority, but hard as I tried I could get no inkling of his feelings. "I'm a farmer and a businessman and I'm not good at understanding all this sort of thing—haven't time for it . . . I've often thought Cain would come to no good; his grandfather and his mother spoil him . . . spoiled both of them. These youngsters all want too much. Hard work is what it comes down to in this life." It seemed pointless to try and get beneath this defensive façade of clichés; however, as he was on his way out of the room, he said more thoughtfully, "You work and sweat for your family and your children's future and what do they do . . . ? Are they grateful?" He had let me see a little of his depression . . . and perhaps revealed why *I* felt I had to work and sweat to get anywhere with him.

When I saw the couple together, the lack of communication was painful. Their suppressed anxiety at first made me anxious also. As we talked over what had happened, they did manage to own up to some of the rivalries and resentments they felt about their father and their sons, but these were spoken of with a dismissive lightness, as though insignificant. I imagined Abel had got that cynical want of seriousness from them, and it had become a naïveté and blindness to danger that had proved fatal. About their own relationship, the two seemingly could not speak, and when I pointed this out, they generalized about marriages, each talking into the air. From what they said, I heard hints of disappointed expectation, impatience, and accusations of sexual impotence and frigidity. I asked if they enjoyed much leisure time together; it seemed they did not. Adam was virtually a workaholic, and, when Eve was not busy in the house, she helped him with secretarial tasks. They were slaves to the farm. Had they ever had any fun together? Oh yes, said Adam bitterly, when they lived in Eden before they married, but that was all in the past—you did not expect that in later life.

When all four met with me again together, I said that I felt there were secrets and mysteries from the past that still plagued this family, and this was making it difficult for me and for them to deal with their crisis in the present. There seemed to be a collusion to conceal the circumstances of the birth and adoption of Adam and Eve, and also events around the time of their marriage. The suppression of unacceptable truths and unwelcome feelings was damaging everyone.

There was a long silence. Then Cain said, "It's all to do with that Lilith, isn't it?"

The old man immediately snapped, "What do you know about her?"

"I've heard rumors," Cain said.

"You know nothing about her," the old man said.

"I've heard rumors," Cain repeated. He eyed his father and grandfather scornfully and said, "Is it true she had it off with both of you?"

Well, then, as they say, the shit hit the fan. The mention of this woman, of whom I had never heard, caused absolute havoc, as it later transpired she had once done in person. Eve berated Cain for his disrespect; the old man began a long diatribe on the evil nature of the unmentionable Lilith; Adam grew impatient with him and moaned that he had heard all that before; Eve then turned on Adam and said he was hardly the one to speak, considering his secret involvement with Lilith, at which Adam retorted that Eve was no better than Lilith's underhand accomplice in mischief and what had that done for them?

Within five minutes the room was transformed and so was Cain, as he saw revealed all the hurt, hatred, sexual anger, viciousness, and jealousy that had lain under the surface for twenty or more years. I saw in that moment that he would no longer need to carry it; and it had taken the death of Abel to release it.

As far as I could piece it together—for almost everything anyone said was denied or contradicted by someone else—Lilith's mother was Adamah (in Hebrew, "earth," "ground"), who had originally owned the land that had been appropriated by the old man, who cultivated his beautiful Eden there. Through his alliance with Lilith, he had taken possession of Adamah's domain—an extensive area largely uncultivated. When I heard that, I realized why he had his paranoid superstitions about the land. Lilith was, by all accounts, a wise and subtle woman, spirited, full of lively vitality, sexually powerful, ruthless at times, passionate in loving, and devilishly cunning—a sort of Cleopatra-figure, but with a knowledge of corruption, both human and natural, that gave her great depth and a realistic ability to live and love without high expectations of perfection. That the old man might have experienced this woman's love and then lost her or rejected her, opened up a whole new view of his situation to me. He had lost something irreplaceable, was bitter and vindictive, had banished her from his goodwill, and spoke nothing but ill of her. Yet for all anyone would ever know, she might be the mother of Adam and Eve. Adam, it seemed, did have a relationship with her, but she would not stay with him and submit to the men's regime. She fled— was in effect discarded. She had apparently also led Eve astray in some way.

The secret was out—the secret of this family's disowned sexuality and rebellious creativity. It was a classic case of scapegoating. Lilith had been cast out, taking with her all the disgraced, unacceptable, or shadow feelings of the family, who could vilify her and avoid experiencing their own inner chaos, greed, and darkness. However, she had also taken with her their ability to love deeply and realistically without debilitating superego expectations, so they had all been bereft of a potentially wise mother. The scapegoating had rebounded with a vengeance. In pretending she was dead to them and concealing her very existence, they could not even speak their enmity and fear of her, which would have left the sons free to judge for themselves. Cain embodied all the shadow in himself and acted it out un-awarely. The unspoken fear, loathing, sexual guilt, and rage, stored up for twenty years, drove him mad enough to kill; and, insofar as the dispossessed Lilith wanted vengefully to kill the men and their offspring, as they feared, so Cain had become possessed by her.

In later discussion with my colleagues, the Kleinian said the old man's reaction to the loss of Lilith showed the classic manic defences against depression: control, triumph, and contempt. The Jungian ob-served that Cain had become Eve's animus and was himself anima-ridden. The pattern of scapegoating interested us. This family was particularly adept at displacing its feelings of inferiority on one an-other and playing victim. Abel was seemingly the innocent scape-goat, sacrificed like the slaughtered lamb, perhaps willingly, to the grandfather. Cain was branded and ostracized for having manifested the family's destructiveness. Eve had been scapegoated long ago by the men for being allied to the sexually seductive Lilith—which was what they had been.

In an individual interview I had with Eve, she recalled Lilith's im-pact on her. She had come to see Eve when she heard of her impend-ing marriage to Adam. Their father had been telling them how the ideal marriage should be, but had left them very innocent. Lilith's ap-proach was different. "She was like an older sister, or mother," Eve said. "She told me a lot about being a woman—about birth, death, and masturbation; and that menstruation was not a curse; and about sexual love between women, our right to independence, and our right to own land, as her mother had. She talked about sexual matu-rity between men and women, and about pain. And witchcraft . . . I knew it was scandalous, yet it wasn't. She was very loving and open-eyed and wise. She said the life we led in Eden was all a con. Nothing could be so perfect and I shouldn't let the men dominate me. And my father had as good as stolen Adamah's land and had wanted to steal and possess Lilith also. She said Adam ought to marry her, because if he married me we would neither of us ever grow up. But she was so much older than him that was unlikely. I was amazed by it all. I told Adam everything she told me. He didn't say much. I'm sure he did have a relationship with her—had already or did later. But he never told me about it."

"You haven't forgotten her," I observed.

"No," she said, "I haven't. How could I? As soon as *he* discovered what had happened, he was livid. He said she was wicked, a snake in the grass, and I was a fool to be taken in by her, and Adam had been led astray. Adam blamed me, and said she was a temptress and so was I. And we were turned out of Eden and put here in the unculti-vated part of the estate. I was very upset and mortified. He had brought us up, after all. I felt so guilty. I let Adam put me in my place, and we knuckled down to work."

"Were neither of you angry with him?" I asked. "Defiant? He must have been afraid of you to want to turn you out."

"No, we weren't as strong as Lilith. And we didn't understand him like she did. And we were too spoiled to want to risk financial independence. Eden spoiled us."

The pattern of power and feeling in the family began to change. As Adam was openly spoken of as a sexual being, his energy and self-confidence revived visibly, and Cain and the grandfather had to respect that, instead of colluding to disempower him. The increase in vitality, which even led to some quite risqué jokes being shared between Adam and Cain and Eve, was a pleasure to see; and it outfaced the old man's killjoy control. He wisely then kept his silence and in subsequent meetings managed to listen to their expressions of resentment toward him without retaliation. He began to look more sad than stern.

In the end, they were able to mourn the loss of the son and grandson and brother they loved, and with that came relief, gradually, from the guilt that had so much ruled their lives. It took time . . . Eve had to work through much repressed negative material and relinquish her power as the submissive sinner. Cain was able, finally, to forgive himself and feel released. He quite soon found a wife and left home. Adam and Eve were released also. She became pregnant and had another son. Seth; this one, I felt, would know who his father was. I had hopes, and still do, that having allowed themselves to mourn the loss of Abel, they might be able to mourn the loss of those blissful days of innocence in Eden and move forward from the guilt about that. However, behind that was a much greater loss, and I do not know whether the old man will ever come to terms with that and stop denying what he lost by casting her out. Eve tells me, when we meet now, that she feels more and more that Lilith was the mother she never had, who came to her almost disguised and unrecognized, and left again. Recently Eve has been trying to discover where she is. The old man let on that she has another name, Shekhinah (feminine aspect of God), and this may help Eve to get in touch with her. "I haven't found her yet," Eve wrote to me not long ago, "but I conjure her up when I need her. During Seth's birth, I imagined she was with me. She understood everything I was going through and her patience and realism helped us both—him and me. I was not being punished for my sins. And even if in my extremity I felt I wanted to kill the baby who seemed to want to kill me, she understood that too. The men once said she's the sort who'd want to kill her own child. Well, maybe we all are."

When I reviewed the case recently with my supervision group, I was able to report that Adam has slowed down, accepted that they do not have to have everything perfect, and is no longer trying to prove and punish himself. He leads a more leisurely and pleasurable life with Eve and Seth. She has grown in confidence as lover and mother, and has begun to concern herself with conservation and ecology, different ways of managing the land that is theirs without exploiting it. The realization that their patriarch could be sexual and fallible has made a difference to them all.

My Kleinian colleague observed that I had helped the family get beyond the paranoid-schizoid position and work through the depressive position toward ambivalence, which of course involves mourning. The Freudian's view was that we solved Cain's Oedipal conflict by restoring his father's sexual potency and claim on Eve. The bioenergeticist confirmed my observation that the family body, in a literal, metaphorical, and structural sense, had become far more grounded, less top-heavy. By releasing the tightly held pelvis—held by sexual and anal repression—the vital energy, which previously had been directed upwards and lodged in the head and shoulders (a manic tendency, precariously held in Adam and Eve but unbounded in Cain, where it went, so to speak, over the top) had been able to flow downwards to the earth again.

A family therapy specialist in our group says that for a time I provided the missing mother for the family that had so much suffered from her absence, so that they were able to realize what had been missing and use me to re-create her for themselves. When I see how this family moved through a process of transformation to new ways of respecting one another and that it was the spirit of the scapegoated woman, of Lilith-Shekhinah, that returned to them when they needed her and helped them come to terms with their mutual destructiveness, I feel confident that there is a process we may call love, or therapy, working in our universe. If we have faith in it, it is always available to us.

References

Bible. Genesis 2; 3; 4:1–15; 4:16–17, 25–6; 5:1–4.
Cooper, H. 1987–1988. "Persecution and Silence: The Myth of Cain and Abel." *Harvest* (Journal of Jungian Studies, Analytical Psychology Club) 33:7–27.
Koltuv, B. B. 1986. *The Book of Lilith*. York Beach, Maine: Nicolas-Hays.
Patai, R. 1990. *The Hebrew Goddess*. Detroit: Wayne State University Press.
Pirani, A., ed. 1991. *The Absent Mother: Restoring the Goddess to Judaism and Christianity*. San Francisco: Harper Collins.

NINE

Performance and Biblical Reading: Its Power and Hazard

Tom F. Driver

The example I have to give of a somatic approach to the Bible is so deceptively simple that it may be described in one sentence: Readers sit in a circle, passing a Bible from hand to hand for each participant to read a verse or two of a chosen passage, then each one comments upon what she read before offering the text to the next person.

That is the simple technique, which I think is employed with some frequency in Bible study groups. In this article, I will describe the context in which I have used it with the most significant results, then discuss the theory of performance that throws light on the power of the technique, and finally describe a particular class session that was especially dramatic.

Experience in Theology

I teach a course entitled "The Experiential Basis of Theological Thinking," which aims to assist seminary students in finding links between their life experiences and their theological convictions. If, as in many cases, the latter are not yet very strong or clear, the aim is to encourage their formation by reflecting upon intersections between the student's prior experiences and the material being studied in seminary. We also ponder what the concept "experience" has meant to differing philosophers and the role that experience is assigned in various approaches to theological method.

The idea for the course came to me long ago when I noticed that

159

my students, many of whom brought with them to seminary rich personal histories full of quite significant experiences, did not tend to call upon this resource when writing theological papers. Their written work sounded as if theology had nothing to learn from what people actually underwent in their lives but owed all its inspiration to the Bible and the theological tradition in libraries. Having noticed this in my students, I then noticed it in myself and recognized it as a deception (not consciously chosen) through which I kept hidden much of what determined the way I read theology, thought about it, and wrote about it. Deciding to do something about this, I designed the course. This took place in about 1971.

Shortly after I started the course, the importance of experience in theological formation received powerful statement in the burgeoning black and feminist theologies. The insistent appeal that these theologies make to experience in their method, plus the testimony that their particular kinds of experience had long been ignored and delegitimated by "male-stream" theology helped me to see that the deception in which I and other theologians so frequently engaged by concealing the experiential roots of our theologies was in fact a power play, cultivating an illusion of neutrality and universality that has been very advantageous in helping white, male Western theologians maintain hegemony over their profession. In 1977, when I published *Patterns of Grace*, which grew out of the course, Delores Williams, a feminist theologian, told me that I had written the first liberation theology by a North American white man. Surprised by the remark, I asked what she meant. "Well," she replied, "you have used experience as the basis for what you do, instead of hiding it; and I mean your own experience and not somebody else's."

In 1991, Francis Schüssler Fiorenza pointed out that feminist theology interprets experience in a radically different way from the liberal theological tradition. Fiorenza's early interest had been in the transcendental theology of Karl Rahner, Bernard Lonergan, and Friedrich Schleiermacher, which "sought to ground theology not in confessional particularity but in anthropological universality" (Fiorenza 1991, 96). Feminism posed a serious challenge to this approach, because it claimed that what passed for anthropological universality was in fact a particular view of humanity stemming from male experience and the consistent exclusion of women's experiences. "The feminist appeal to experience, in my view," writes Fiorenza

> is functionally different from the liberal appeal to experience. Feminist theology explores the particularity of women's experience as part of a critical as well as constructive task. It is critical insofar as it questions false pretensions to universality; it is constructive insofar as it seeks to elaborate religious symbols and categories adequate to women's experiences. (1991:96)

Later he adds that

> the appeal to experience should not be taken as an appeal to a founda-
> tional experience, but rather as an appeal to particular experiences that are
> overloaded with particular interpretations. (1991:97)

The discrimination Fiorenza makes between these quite different
appeals to experience is important for understanding what I have
hoped to achieve in my course. Although I have called it "The Experiential Basis of Theological Thinking," I have not supposed that all human experience is somehow the same, nor have I thought that an
individual's religion, faith, or theology is likely to be based upon a
single foundational experience. Even where a strong conversion experience is present, this gains its meaning from the personal history
that preceded and has followed it. The tasks are to heighten awareness of the particular experiences that are of greatest importance to an
individual, to see how these have been interpreted in the person's ongoing history, to find out whether other persons have similar experiences with similar interpretations, to see connections between the
experiences and the interpretation given to theological matters, and
perhaps to submit the whole to reinterpretation as a result of the
process.

Essentially, the work to be done is that of storytelling. This is why
interpretation looms so large. However, the interpretations yielded
by the process are not as likely to be generalized principles as to be
stories refashioned and told once more from a shifted point of view.

The telling of one's own story is difficult: So many things have
happened; there are in one life so many different phases, places, and
periods that one may almost seem to have been many different
selves; or at present there may be so many conflicting desires and
projects that there appear to be a host of competing selves all using
the same name.

Interpretation of experience poses a narrative challenge, that is, a
moral one. A narrative not only consists of factual and aesthetic con-
siderations but also has a moral dimension, which means that a storyteller must either examine or imply some moral responsibility for the
narrated events. Even if responsibility turns out to rest with fate or
sheer luck, the decision to represent it so belongs to the story's moral
dimension. In telling one's own story, the narrator and the protagonist coincide, and what is required (or should I say revealed?) is a
point of view. Whose point of view is required? Mine is required.
What if I do not want or cannot find a way to adopt a point of view?
Then I am less than me, and I experience myself as divided or vague.

Depth psychology has taught us that not all our experiences are
available to memory. Some have been repressed. I am not trained as

a clinical psychologist, and I am distrustful of some of depth psychology's principles and methods; but I take seriously the insight that there are unconscious processes hiding from consciousness certain experiences we have had that are too painful to think about or too shameful or (as I think true in many cases) have moral implications we do not wish to face. Everyone, I like to say, has experience, but not everyone knows or wants to know what experience they have had.

Personal identity is not an ontological given but a moral achievement, more fully realized by some individuals than by others and never entirely finished. The task is made simpler when one has a strong group identification, something more likely to happen with members of minority, oppressed, and new immigrant groups than with most others.

Liberation movements are motivated by increasing awareness of experiences of oppression. These experiences may have gone on for generations during which awareness of them has been so discouraged and discouraging that the awareness recedes into a dull area, like a chronic pain. The experience of oppression, like mortality itself, comes to seem one's fate and the fate of one's children, and so the awareness of it dims. Leaders of liberation movements—like Nat Turner, Susan B. Anthony, Augusto Sandino, Che Guevera, and Martin Luther King, Jr.—assume the task of awakening awareness of experience, otherwise known as "stirring up the people." What is stirred up is memory, awareness, recognition, and concomitantly a hope for change.

Appeals to experience, then—be they for political, therapeutical, artistic, or pedagogical purposes—require not simply the consulting of a known repository of memories and the fitting of them together like pieces of a jigsaw puzzle (the ideal form of which is predetermined) but instead the gradual increase in awareness of what has happened. This project is inseparable from a project of interpretation. If something is lost to my consciousness, I cannot interpret it. Conversely, without interpretation I cannot be conscious of anything. Awareness and interpretation go hand in hand.

Body Selves

It may be asked what all this has to do with body. The answer depends a great deal on how the body itself is interpreted, that is, experienced. It makes all the difference whether "body" is thought of and experienced as object or as subject. For the most part, our culture fosters experience of objectified bodies. Advertising, fiction, health clubs, video, film, and the cult of athleticism all include powerful inducements to regard human bodies from the outside, as objects to be seen, possessed, or imitated.

In this milieu, many people are induced to measure their bodies, almost daily, against ideal images of health, fitness, and beauty. To a point, this is inevitable, but in our society body objectification has risen to a pathological point. Unfortunately, a number of religious and philosophical traditions contribute to this, having insisted historically upon a separation between spirit and flesh, or mind and body. Their moral message is to identify oneself with the "higher" half of the dualism, with spirit or mind, not with flesh or body. When the body is no longer the self, it has no other fate than to become a kind of half-living object. In a poem of that name, Delmore Schwartz called it a "heavy bear" that he had to lug around. Had he been a youth of today he would doubtless have sent the heavy bear to a fitness center to get trim, but he would not thereby have turned the object into a subject.

The purchase of a moral and spiritual identity at the price of alienating and objectifying the body may be called "cheap transcendence." Love of the body, even in sickness and the decay of old age, as an experiencing self is required for a genuine transcendence. By this, I mean a transcendence that is achieved not by division but by integration.

To summarize the argument so far, I am saying that the contemporary (some would say postmodern) appeal to experience as a source of theological reflection entails a project of awareness and interpretation of present and past experiences. This cannot well be undertaken as long as one's body is viewed as an object rather than as the locus or, as I would prefer to say, the dedicated ground of one's own experiencing. It is no accident that the slogan of black liberation in the 1960s was "black is beautiful," because that was an act of reclaiming subjective identity for body selves that had long been objectified by slavery and other humiliations. The women's movement has also insisted on the irreducible ethical importance of body rights and has sought to reveal the long history of injustices perpetrated upon the bodies of women. The antidote is the affirmation expressed in the title of a popular book, *Our Bodies, Our Selves* (1984).[1]

If, as the saying goes, beauty is as beauty does, then we may also say that a body self is as a body self does. Whereas an objectified body is something to be looked at and done to, an embodied subject expresses itself through action. When Jesus said, "This is my body," he did not mean, "This is how I look." He meant, "This is how I express and give myself in the world."

Performance

As every actor knows, there is a world of difference between a performance generated by attention to its effect upon an audience and another motivated by the search for a hidden truth. My interest in drawing upon experience in the teaching of theology, which led me to acknowledge the epistemological primacy of the subjective body, led to awareness of a necessary link between learning and doing.

The genuinely human, or moral, quality in performance is adumbrated in the word's ambiguity. *To perform* means both "to do" and "to pretend." The same is true of the verb *to act*. If I pretend something, I make a show of it. I put on an act, as we say. I make an outward display, different from reality, designed to deceive or to entertain. Although this is acting, even in the theater it is not considered the best, for it avoids the level of truth-disclosure that is felt to be necessary in all endeavors deserving the name "art."

To be very good, let alone great, acting must go beyond pretense, taking the actor and the audience to a level in which something is risked and accomplished—a level in which the performance does not only pretend and show but actually does something valuable for both the performer and the spectator in the moment of its realization. I like to call this a moment of transformation. Its occurrence moves theater close to ritual, that is, to performance having transcendent quality and import.[2]

Outside the theater—let us say in a therapy session or a classroom—performance does not start from the side of pretending and showing, since there is no demand to prepare a show for an audience. Instead, the emphasis falls upon an existential doing, the "getting at" something true, real, and liberating (as it also does, for that matter, in some of the best theater workshops). One is asked to speak of what one knows, perhaps in body language or with paints, clay, or music as well as with words. The teacher, therapist, or colearner may challenge or supplement what is said, prodding the learner onward, creating a dialogue that can lead to greater disclosures.

In this process, which, if done well, is a genuine dialectic, the participants become, sooner or later, aware that they are performers; that is, to do what they are doing, they must go beyond what they know, or know that they know, into a realm of imagining. They must also keep this imagined reality connected with the already known. They must attempt to fuse what they are doing with what they are imagining, and thus to create a new reality that did not exist before. They edge toward moments of transformation. Anyone who has taken part in excellent teaching and learning sessions has experienced such moments.

Within the learning process I have just described, there is a second sense in which the learner and doer becomes a learner and performer.

Learning requires expression, which is why so many academic assignments take the form of oral or written reports. In the classroom, provided the students are not simply an audience "absorbing" a presentation, the learners express themselves, and this creates for each one a momentary stage and audience. At the same time, the individual learner is aware of himself as both performer and spectator, trying to notice what he himself is experiencing, what he is saying, where his difficulty lies, where the pleasure or excitement is, and thus to anticipate where his present path of discovery will take him. Actually working (at the pursuit of some truth), he is also observing himself work, and he is granting permission for the others in the room to observe him also as he moves from one state of knowledge to another. This requires a high degree of trust, which it is the instructor's business to foster.

In the measure in which learning fails to occur, the performance will turn bad. Sometimes it will stall: The learner and performer will fall silent, withdraw, or end with a resigning gesture. In the worst-case scenario, the learner will sulk, turning her frustration or embarrassment into passive aggression. (An active hostility would indicate that she was still engaged, and the learning was still in process.)

At other times, the performance may become shallow. The learner and performer starts playing to the gallery. He makes long, rambling speeches. He changes the subject. He parades erudition as a substitute for inquiry. He displays a diversionary, perhaps seductive, humor. The ambiguity in performance between doing and showing is tilted toward showing off. The performer needs to get on track again or to stop, because in the learning situation, life is not a cabaret.

I am suggesting, then, that learning requires performance—even more, that learning *is* performance of a certain kind. It is not performance in the sense of *mimesis* or the reproduction of an already-known state of affairs. It is performance of a creative kind, in which the self is extended beyond itself through acts of recollection, synthesis, imagination, and communication.

If learning were passive, we would not speak of it as performative. To call it performance is to say that it is active, reality-based, creative, and social. Even when we study in solitude, we have to internalize the social audience, often writing, talking, or "playing" to ourselves. The learner may do without applause but not without the affirming or challenging response of other learning selves.

Monday Seminar and Friday Workshop

My experiential course, as I call it, meets twice a week. On Monday afternoons, we spend two hours in seminar, sitting around a table discussing assigned readings. Whereas in the lecture hall one person is given virtual monopoly over performance rights, in a seminar these rights and responsibilities are shared. All are encouraged to take turns having their say. In the lecture hall, it is not expected that the performer will learn during the lecture, although on some rare and wonderful occasions this happens. The expectation in a seminar, however, is that every participant, including instructor, is a learner and that all are performers in the creative, exploratory sense I have been describing, doing their learning in public and showing (revealing) it for the benefit of others present.

The Monday sessions in my course are thus given to performance in a way long sanctioned in the academy. On Friday mornings, we perform more intensively and with greater risk.

The Friday sessions, also two hours long, are called workshops. The ideal number of participants is about twelve.[3] We use a room some thirty feet square from which all furniture has been removed.

The floor, partly bare and partly carpeted, is our great leveler and springboard. It offers our bodies "grounding" so that we can sit, lie, sprawl, stand, jump, or run. In seminar chairs, people are apt to forget what their bodies are doing, but not on an open floor, where adjustments of the body within the gravity field must frequently be made as long as one does not lie down and go to sleep.

We begin every workshop with physical activity—usually gentle kinds of standing, stretching, centering, body-tapping, partner-touching, and so on—designed to awaken the senses and focus attention upon here and now existence within a physical world. The immediate reality—this room, these people, and my body self, all as experienced right now—becomes the stage on which the morning's scenes will be played.

Next, we usually sit on the floor in a circle for the "check-in." We want to find out whether anyone has a preoccupation so urgent that it will get in the way. If so, we must give it some attention before we go on, or our performing will be dominated by a pretending from the start, an avoidance of here and now reality that can only foster illusion. Sometimes the check-in period lasts all morning. Sometimes it causes a complete change of agenda from what I had planned ahead; but usually we are able to clear the decks and turn to my suggested starting point.

The first few weeks of the course are given over to what I call "stories and sensibilities." We read fictional and nonfictional stories, and some essays in which the writers communicate how they feel and think. Authors used in recent years have included Bell Hooks, Augustine of Hippo, James Baldwin, Alice Walker, Annie Dillard, and Malcolm Boyd. I also like to include Phyllis Trible's *Texts of Terror* (1984), with its close textual analyses of four biblical passages that tell stories of women who were brutally abused. Trible's meticulous, methodical approach to the stories' literary structures helps readers to linger over their experience of the Bible's word-textures as well as its manifest meanings, while Trible's coolly indignant commentary evokes the reader's emotional reactions to the gruesome content of the stories. Here, we are a long, long way from Sunday school.

A Quiet Performance

On one occasion, we had read Trible's book and discussed it in the Monday seminar. The session had been a good one, yet I sensed that the material was stirring up many unexpressed thoughts and feelings. Vaguely aware of unfinished business, I decided to return to it on Friday.

I brought the Bible to the workshop, not Trible's book. It was my own frayed copy of the Revised Standard Version, acquired years ago when I was a student and now held together with red tape to reinforce a disintegrating cover. After the check-in, I sat cross-legged in the circle with this old volume in front of me and spoke of what I proposed we do next.

I said that one of the four stories analyzed in *Texts of Terror* is so terrible that I was having a hard time either thinking or not thinking about it. It is a story I do not want to find in the Bible (or anywhere else) and do not know what to do with. In fact, I must have been repressing my memory of the story, because I did not even recall its existence until a few years ago when feminists began pointing to it with justifiable outrage. Even then, I did not go back and reread the story until I got interested in Trible's book. She has helped a lot, but I am still troubled and would like more help. I ask: Could we read the story together and see where it takes us?

Thank God we were sitting on the floor. There were no chairs to shape us into conventional postures, no table to hide our bodies from the waist down, no table to lean upon using a pose of studiousness to mask embarrassment, and no table to form a barricade between ourselves and the people facing us. I felt I wanted such protection now in the worst way, yet knew it would blunt my learning. Suddenly the room seemed terribly empty, and we, though not naked, were somehow defenseless people exposed in it with little way to hide.[4] I learned later that some participants did not want to proceed, but they did not say so.

I explained the method: I would begin by reading aloud. I would read slowly, so that I could think as I read. My reading would be like biting off a chunk of the text to chew on. As soon as I had enough to chew over, I would stop reading, think a bit, and share my thoughts. Commentary from other persons was not invited at this time. It would be better to let each person have a go at the text and to finish reading through the whole story, after which we could engage in discussion. When I finished sharing my thoughts about the bit I had read, I would hand the Bible to the person on my right, and we would proceed around the circle, reading, thinking, sharing, and listening.

I paused to see whether it was right to go on. Clearly, there was tension but no one said to stop, and I interpreted the silence to mean assent coupled with a certain dread. Later, I wondered if I should have turned back.

The violent story I chose is found in Judges 19. I opened the Bible to this place and began to read:

> In those days, when there was no king in Israel, a certain Levite was sojourning in the remote parts of the hill country of Ephraim, who took to himself a concubine from Bethlehem in Judah. And his concubine became angry with him [or played the harlot against him], and she went away from him to her father's house at Bethlehem in Judah, and was there some four months.

Here I stopped. My mind was already full. Furthermore, the method required not taking bites too big, but small ones that can be better chewed over. I put the book in my lap and attended to my feelings.

I am a seminary professor with only rudimentary training in biblical scholarship. I do not, and could not, teach courses in the Bible, nor could most of my colleagues in the theological field, a realm largely and unfortunately cut off from the biblical field. I know a little Greek and less Hebrew. My biblical history is rusty. So having rashly decided to look closely at this biblical text and having deliberately decided that neither I nor the students should make exegetical preparation, I am flooded with shame when I realize that I am ignorant of things that a little homework would inform me about: What, at this stage of history, was a Levite? Does this man, like the Levite in the parable of the Good Samaritan, belong to a priestly order, or is it only his tribal affinity that is being mentioned? I recognize Ephraim as another Israelite tribe, named for another of the sons of Jacob, but where is Mount Ephraim? Why is the Levite living there? Does he dwell in a region not his own?

Suddenly my shame is compounded. I cannot remember whether Phyllis Trible's book discussed any of these points, although I reread it only the week before. What is happening here? Am I blocking? Do I really prefer the ignorance I have about details in this story? Would I rather think about my academic embarrassment than about the story's import?

Then there is the concubine, who is said to be "his." I suppose I know close enough what a concubine is (was), but how did he get her? What exactly is she supposed to have done to merit the description that she played the harlot? Did she wink at another man? Did she sleep with him? How many men? Did she get pregnant and run away from home?

The Revised Standard Version's preferred reading of verse 2a avoids mention of her playing the harlot, saying simply that she "became angry" with the Levite. Why is she angry? Is she, by the time the story begins, already the victim of abuse? Did she run away because the Levite beat her?

In any case, what these few words seem to make clear is that she is not her own person. She belongs to this man, and if she "plays the harlot," it is "against him." When she runs away, it is to her father's house—not her mother's. Who is her mother? Where is her mother? The nameless daughter of the absent mother makes a swift appearance and disappearance in these two verses, like a frightened doe fleeing through the landscape. . . .

I share these feelings and thoughts aloud as they become clear to me. However, there is something I do not share, something signaled in my words, but signaled, I hope, only to myself. I do not know whether I will speak of it later. I had better not.

After a short pause, I hand the Bible to the next person, and so it goes, around the circle. I could not reconstruct, even if there were time and space for it, the particular comments of every reader, but the reader of this article needs to have the biblical passage in mind. It continues like this:

> Then her husband arose and went after her, to speak kindly to her and bring her back. He had with him his servant and a couple of asses. And he came [she brought him] to her father's house: and when the girl's father saw him, he came with joy to meet him. And his father-in-law, the girl's father, made him stay, and he remained with him three days; so they ate and drank, and lodged there. And on the fourth day they arose early in the morning, and he prepared to go; but the girl's father said to his son-in-law, "Strengthen your heart with a morsel of bread, and after that you may go." So the two men sat and ate and drank together; and the girl's father said to the man, "Be pleased to spend the night, and let your heart be merry." And when the man rose up to go, his father-in-law urged him, till he lodged there again. And on the fifth day he arose early in the morning to depart; and the girl's father said, "Strengthen your heart, and tarry until the day declines." So they ate, both of them. And when the man and his concubine and his servant rose up to depart his father-in-law, the girl's father, said to him, "Behold, now the day has waned toward evening; pray tarry all night. Behold, the day draws to its close; lodge here and let your heart be merry; and tomorrow you shall arise early in the morning for your journey, and go home."

I have set a trap for you, good reader. If you are tempted, as many of us are in the haste of our reading these days, to skip quickly over the long biblical quotations I now put in front of you, because you know (or are supposed to know) the Bible already, and all you want is to find out what Mr. Driver's two cents worth is—if this is your temptation, you prove my point about performance. For what we were doing in that room, encamped in a circle on the floor, the dog-eared text making its way slowly around, was to take the text out of the domain of sight-reading and place it firmly in the domain of per-formance. To read hurriedly for "content," with eye sweeping down the page, is one thing. To read aloud while others wait to read after you, letting your thoughts clear so you can speak about the text on the spot—in a situation in which any attempt to show off will imme-diately be recognized for what it is—this is quite another thing. If you, good reader, now wish to perceive something of our experience performing the text that day, you must slow down, read in small bits, and chew.

One effect of our method was to put us in touch with the oral tell-ing of the story in days before it was ever written down. Our ears can hear the artful use of repetition to pace the story, which in this case instills a growing sense of unease. Tension within our group mounts. We go on, breaking the text into bite sizes:

> But the man would not spend the night; he rose up and departed, and ar-rived opposite Jebus (that is, Jerusalem). He had with him a couple of sad-dled asses, and his concubine was with him.

> When they were near Jebus, the day was far spent, and the servant said to his master, "Come now, let us turn aside to this city of the Jebusites, and spend the night in it." And his master said to him, "We will not turn aside into the city of foreigners, who do not belong to the people of Israel; but we will pass on to Gibeah." And he said to his servant, "Come and let us draw near to one of these places, and spend the night at Gibeah or at Ramah."

> So they passed on and went their way; and the sun went down on them near Gibeah, which belongs to Benjamin, and they turned aside there, to go in and spend the night at Gibeah. And he went in and sat down in the open square of the city; for no man took them into his house to spend the night.

Here I can skip a little, although again reminding you that part of the force of our method lay in its ponderous pace. The text is a te-dious one with an explosive ending. Our reading intensified both the tedium and the explosion.

Thus, we read of the travelers finally being taken in for the night by an old Ephraimite man, not a native of the Benjaminite town of Gi-beah where they were. He brought them to his house, washed their feet, and gave them food and drink. Now we must return to the text:

As they were making their hearts merry, behold, the men of the city, base fellows, beset the house round about, beating on the door; and they said to the old man, the master of the house, "Bring out the man who came into your house, that we may know him."

And the man, the master of the house, went out to them and said to them, "No, my brethren, do not act so wickedly; seeing that this man has come into my house, do not do this vile thing.

Behold, here are my virgin daughter and his concubine; let me bring them out now. Ravish them and do with them what seems good to you; but against this man do not do so vile a thing."

But the men would not listen to him. So the man seized his concubine, and put her out to them; and they knew her, and abused her all night until the morning.

And as the dawn began to break, they let her go. And as morning appeared, the woman came and fell down at the door of the man's house where her master was, till it was light.

And her master rose up in the morning, and when he opened the door of the house and went out to go on his way, behold there was his concubine lying at the door of the house, with her hands on the threshold.

He said to her, "Get up, let us be going." But there was no answer.

Then he put her upon the ass; and the man rose up and went away to his home.

And when he entered his house, he took a knife, and laying hold of his concubine he divided her, limb by limb, into twelve pieces, and sent her throughout all the territory of Israel.

And all who saw it said, "Such a thing has never happened or been seen from the day that the people of Israel came up out of the land of Egypt until this day; consider it, take counsel, and speak."

For a time, we were speechless. The text, plus the things we had said about it in each other's hearing, had shocked us.

Anguish in the Bones

Reading this story aloud, using the method I have described, became terribly painful. The anguish could be felt in one's bones. It expressed itself in faltering, quavering voices. It could be seen in the twisting of bodies, many of them wrenched in contorted poses, and in the tears that welled up in some readers' eyes. The reading seemed interminable. We went from one excruciating detail to another, and when the woman, after her night's ordeal of rape, is discovered to have crawled back to the door of the house from which she had been turned out and put her dying hand upon the threshold, I heard moans.

When the story was done, we looked at each other in silence. It was as if we sat in a pile of wreckage. The story itself was one of devastation, but now we had, in addition to it, some present catastrophes. During the go-round of reading and commentary, four persons out of the thirteen—two women and two men—informed us that as children they had suffered sexual abuse by members of their own families. In all four cases, the abusers were men.

We sat mute for a time, not sure, in our pain and bewilderment, whether to look at one another. Refusing to be ancient history, the biblical story had come like an earthquake into our midst. Structures of illusion and cover-up collapsed. The planet seemed to open in giant crevices all around us. We did not know into what depths we might fall.

How many persons in this little circle, I silently wondered, are like me in having secret memories—memories that hurt but are not to be talked about now—stirred up by the story? We were a circle of refugees sitting in a broken landscape, wondering where to go and what to do.

There was nothing to do but to keep going. Turning to one of the women who had spoken of being abused in childhood, I asked if she wished to tell us more about it. She did, and we began the difficult, pain-ridden work of sharing things long unspoken, comparing personal histories, seeing what they tell us of patriarchal society, and how they have influenced our understanding of God.[5]

Let the reader beware. We did not entirely "recover" from that day's earthquake. It generated fear in some students that lasted all semester. Some felt that I handled the situation badly. Some said I should never have proposed reading that text aloud together. I would say that for the next eight weeks we were negotiating a crisis, most of us trying as best we could to learn from adversity, and I would say that the results were mixed.

My story about storytelling is not a success story. Frankly, I do not know what the long-term results of this experiment have been. For that reason, I have not again used any of the "texts of terror" in the classroom. To recall the nameless, dismembered concubine is for me as troubling as ever.

I am convinced, however, that the method is a powerful one, particularly when a group has an extended life together and when furniture can be moved out of the way, leaving people to deal with themselves, each other, the text, and little else. In those circumstances, the method is likely to generate a great deal of involvement.

However, the nature and content of that involvement is unpredictable, because it depends upon the text chosen, the individuals who participate, and the interactions among them.

The power of the Bible to wound is very great—and so is that of the family. These two potentials came together in a way I had not anticipated—holy Scripture, holy family, and holy terror. What shall we say of a God of love when the force of evil in sanctified places is so strong?

There is one thing that may be said. For those who have experienced the wounding power of Scripture and of the family, the structure of patriarchal theology cracks and crumbles. That theology has always depended on the denigration of bodies, their abuse, and their exploitation for sex, reproduction, and labor. To read the Bible with a strong sense of body presence is a challenge to the rule of fathers. I see this more clearly since that day that my students and I passed a biblical text from hand to hand and came, to our dismay, upon the sickening reality of incest.

Notes

1. See also Harrison 1985, especially 129–30.

2. For a more extended discussion of performance, including its confessional, ethical, and theatrical modes, see Driver 1991, Chapters 5 and 6.

3. Larger numbers can be accommodated in subgroups if the room is of adequate size. I have occasionally worked with up to fifty persons in workshop sessions, subdividing them into units of four, six, eight, or twelve individuals for various activities. In a room with several such small groups working, each creates its own environment, paying no attention to others that are similarly engaged.

4. Voids, which can be frightening, are often the starting points for creativity. The actor's bare stage, like the artist's empty canvas or the poet's blank piece of paper, can symbolize an inner vacuity not unlike that of a religious person's sudden, devastating awareness of the nothingness of self and of God. (See Driver <1977> 1990; and Brook 1968.) This is the nothingness that makes creation possible. It is an existential or imaginative nothingness, recognizable by the dread or terror it carries. Unfortunately, it has not been well understood in the theological doctrine of *creatio ex nihilo*, which has more often been used to emphasize God's alleged patriarchal omnipotence than to illuminate divine creativity.

5. This classroom session took place in March of 1990. This account of it was written in the summer of 1991, about two months before Professor Anita Hill came before Congress and a shocked public to tell of the sexual harassment she had experienced from Supreme Court nominee Clarence Thomas when she worked for him ten years earlier. In the wake of her testimony, women throughout America of all races and social classes have told long-

hidden stories of their sexual harassment and abuse. For breaking silence, many women have, like Professor Hill, found themselves abused yet again by people who attack their character and credibility. The land is full of terror generated by the deadly power that men are still able to exercise over women.

References

Boston Women's Health Book Collective. [1973.] 1984. *The New Our Bodies, Our Selves: A Book By and For Women.* New York: Simon and Schuster (Touchstone Books).

Brook, Peter. 1968. *The Empty Space.* New York: Atheneum.

Driver, Tom F. [1977.] 1990. *Patterns of Grace: The Word of God as Human Experience.* New York: Union Theological Seminary.

———. 1991. *The Magic of Ritual: Our Need for Liberating Rites that Transform Our Lives and Our Communities.* San Francisco: Harper Collins.

Fiorenza, Francis. S. 1991. "The Influence of Feminist Theory on My Theological Work." *Journal of Feminist Studies in Religion,* 7(1):95–105.

Harrison, B. W. 1985. *Making the Connections: Essays in Feminist Social Ethics.* Ed. Carol S. Robb. Boston: Beacon Press.

Trible, Phyllis. 1984. *Texts of Terror.* Philadelphia: Fortress Press.

Jacob, Esau, and the Crisis of Male Identity: Investigations into the Seriousness of Play

Björn Krondorfer

What I Assume When I Enter a Play Process

My training in religious studies and experimental drama has helped me to conduct and reflect upon creative and improvisatory play processes that use biblical narratives as the starting place, mirror, and amplifier for exploring the predicament of our cultural, social, and biographical existence. In my nomenclature, a "play process" is defined as the conscious reliance on the body for interpreting (or reinterpreting) and expressing reality. I, therefore, sometimes speak of body-centered play processes, indicating that I neither pursue the task of biblical exegesis nor liturgical play (the latter is, in most instances, restricted to parameters set by a particular belief system). My praxis of entering a play process is informed by ritual and performance studies as well as by my experience with a certain style of experimental drama (the movement-oriented poor theater of Grotowski, Chaikin, et al.) and improvisatory dance.

Play processes are enjoyable; but far from being mere entertainment, they require serious work. They are liminal activities, and they generate transformations (cf. Turner 1982a, 1986; Schechner 1977). Something needs to "happen" during play processes, either to the players, to a theme (topic or text), or to the dynamics between player and theme. Whether transformation happens depends largely on how much attention has been paid to the interaction of certain ritual qualities and to the observance of certain hermeneutic principles. Since these qualities and principles are an integral part of my practice, a few theoretical remarks are necessary before I describe and reflect upon a workshop on the story of Jacob and Esau.

Of numerous ritual qualities, I consider ambiguity, transgression, resistance, and condensation indispensable and of critical import.

"Ambiguity," for example, is a necessary component of spontaneous, improvisatory play. We know, of course, that experiences of ambiguity are often circumvented, because ambiguous speech, images, figures, events, and appearances threaten the structure by which we order our lives. Ambiguity is perceived as dangerous because, as anthropologist Mary Douglas writes, it resists our attempts "to force experience into logical categories of noncontradiction" (1984:162). Despite this threat, ambiguities and paradoxes are imbued in our existence. When we play, and especially when we play biblical narratives, we will experience ambiguity—not only because play, in general, is a liminal activity but also because biblical narratives themselves are characterized by ambiguity. Literary theory points out that complexity and ambiguity linger behind the apparent simplicity of many biblical stories, and that the narrative structure itself plays with multiple meanings (cf. Auerbach 1953; Alter 1981; Sternberg 1987). When we enact those narratives, their structure provides a protective framework within which we can temporarily, but fully, explore and tolerate ambiguity. The presence or absence of ambiguity can actually serve as an indicator of a play's openness. If players do not experience ambiguity, they might be subject to a hidden, unconscious, or deliberate agenda. Play, then, is no longer an open-ended process.

"Transgression" is another essential ritual quality of play.[1] Transgression occurs in the form of inverting daily rules, violating taboos, ridiculing social and sacred order, permitting bodily excess, or generating new perspectives and interpretations. (Ritual) play, Abrahams writes, gives "license to depict and explore motives that we are not permitted to examine" otherwise; they are "exempted from full judgment on moral grounds" and "become the embodiment of the dark side of a culture's vocabulary" (1986:30).

In body-centered play processes, we can explore and express transgression through our bodies. When reenacting biblical narratives, I am always struck by the vitality of such embodied transgressions. Players discover freedom from physical, emotional, and mental restraints, which enables them to reevaluate their understanding of text and themselves. It becomes easier to tolerate troublesome interpretations, inconsistencies, and gaps, and to recover, reimagine, and voice dangerous and painful memories encoded in biblical narratives.

Inevitably, various forms of "resistance" will arise in play processes, often in response to ambiguity, transgression, pain, and anxiety (cf. Laeuchli 1987:171–77). Resistance, whether caused by existential anxieties (cf. Tillich 1952) or defenses against self-comprehension (Freud 1904, 1917, 1926), is often an acting out of old "scripted experiences" (Rardin 1979:183). Unfortunately, there are many playful and ritualistic experimentations that are not invested in discovering new scripts; rather, they simply use play as an alternate method for confirming an already established worldview. I call this kind of play "self-referential." Liturgical dance, naïve bibliodramas, or poorly conducted New Age workshops are often self-referential. They shy away from ambiguity and transgression, and are likely to discontinue a play process whenever resistance becomes too vigorous. However, if signs of resistance are ignored, play is at risk of repeating interpretive flaws and neurotic disturbances, not unlike obsessive rituals (cf. Freud 1907; Ricoeur 1970:285, 534). Unacknowledged resistance is a prime reason for ritual failure.

From therapeutic processes and experimental drama, I learned to appreciate the significance of working with resistance. In both therapy and theater, participants are required to go beyond personal limitations and to continue even when the body is physically exhausted or when emotional resistance impels the individual to stop "playing" (cf. Winnicott 1989). Only then are play processes capable of transforming personal experiences into meaningful wholes. I think that the criterion of going beyond one's limits is the great contribution of the poor theater phase of experimental drama, as it is pointedly stated in Grotowski's famous but inflated image. An actor, he said, does not "exhibit his body, but annihilates it, burns it, frees it from every resistance to any psychic impulse [and] sacrifices it" (1968:34). Grotowski's innuendo of the biblical term *sacrifice* is no coincidence (for he wanted to restore the sacred forces of theater). Only when we sacrifice old scripts will we mature; only when we are ready to overcome resistance will new scripts emerge—both in the sense of discovering new meaning in the biblical text as well as in our "scripted" life.

Players often report that they lose track of time and space, and experience reality more intensely during play processes. "Condensation" describes this intensification and amplification of experience.[2] A single word, gesture, or image can be invested with the emotional content of a cluster of experiences, memories, and associations. Body-centered play processes mobilize creative energies and condense the perception of reality, and biblical narratives can function as a prism through which we perceive our cultural and personal histories and transformations.

When the ritual qualities of ambiguity, transgression, resistance, and condensation are interactive and balanced in play processes, transformations can happen. Furthermore, it is important that instructors and facilitators of serious play observe certain hermeneutic and therapeutic principles (which loosely correspond to ritual qualities).

There is, first, the hermeneutic claim that all texts, speech, or acts possess a "surplus of meaning"; that is, they are multidetermined, multidirectional, and polymorphic (the corresponding ritual quality is ambiguity). Without actively affirming the validity and presence of the principle of surplus of meaning, play will degenerate into mere repetitive play and might as well be abandoned.

There is, second, the therapeutic rule of "protection" (resistance is its corresponding ritual quality). Without creating a safe environment, there is no incentive to enter dangerous territory; the risk to get hurt is simply too high. If protection is not guaranteed, resistance is actually a healthy response, necessary for one's self-preservation. How to make a play safe is in the responsibility of a particular leader or based on a group's mutual consensus, but it certainly requires skill and experience.

There is, third, the need to create a balance between overdistance and underdistance, a condition that cathartic theory calls "aesthetic distance" (Scheff 1979). Underdistanced play overwhelms performer-participants with raw emotions whereas overdistanced play leaves them unmoved. In either case, condensation (the corresponding ritual quality) and transformation cannot take place. Extreme emotions, Scheff writes, are bearable only if an "individual's attention is exactly divided between past distress and present safety . . . [Then] catharsis can occur" (60). Such an understanding of catharsis frees cathartic models from a simplistic and magical notion of transformation and healing. Transformative (or healing) play processes require the active mediation between underdistance and overdistance and the work of ritual participants, be they teacher and student, therapist and patient, or actor and audience.

Finally, efficacious play processes depend on the successful "mediation of narrative structures and freeplay". Play is a free and liberating activity—Derrida called it "freeplay" (1978)—for, as philosopher Hans argues, it is "capable of effecting changes [within] ontological and epistemological fields." Yet it cannot "continually transcend prior ontologies and epistemologies, for the network is not that flexible" (1981:22f). Freeplay becomes, in the process of playing, a structuring activity; play is "the location where we question our structures of understanding and the location where we develop them" (Hans 1981:x). In other words, transformative play processes simultaneously deconstruct and structure. They mediate between the binary positions of openness and structure (the philosophical model), between underdistance and overdistance (the cathartic model), and—when linked to biblical narratives—between text and experience, or narrative structure and improvisatory play.

Tensions, which will emerge as a result of the to and fro movement between these binary positions, are not adverse to play; on the contrary, they are the driving force behind play. Play processes sustain those tensions and are sustained by them. The hermeneutic and ethical task of the interpretive work of play processes is that these tensions, these dangerous "zones of betweenness" (Abrahams 1986:30), are permitted and encouraged. Body-centered play processes set these tensions free, work and play with them, and make them meaningful.

How I Prepare Myself Before Entering a Play

I have conducted enactments of biblical narratives in classrooms (for undergraduate students) and for religious and artistic communities. Here, I want to report and reflect on a workshop that I conducted for two dancers which lasted for four hours. One of the dancers, Billy Yalowitz, asked me to help him enter the story of Jacob and Esau (Genesis 25–29), because he was captivated by the character of Jacob about whom he wanted to choreograph a modern dance piece. The other man, Jonathan Kligler, had extensive experience in improvisational dance (he is, in fact, a teacher of "contact improvisation") and is an ordained rabbi. I mention this because their background and familiarity with movement and textual interpretation enabled us to enter the play process on an advanced level, even though both men were unfamiliar with my specific approach.

I think it is important to realize that playing does not always have to be for "beginners" but that it can be enriched and deepened when players are frequently exposed to its practice (or related processes). Playing can be learned; it can improve and grow. To work with dancers, as in this case, had the advantage that we were able to build on an expanded movement vocabulary which, in turn, assisted in entering emotionally precarious situations and probing veraciously our relationship to the text. In addition, we were able to avoid certain pitfalls, such as (unacknowledged) regression and resistance (cf. Krondorfer 1992).

I prepared myself for this workshop as I usually do: I read the text, underlined descriptive or otherwise vital terms, visualized the relationships between people, and let myself be drawn into the plot. My first reading never follows an analytic mode, though I also hesitate to call it a meditative or intuitive reading for I neither rely on a specific meditation technique nor on purely emotional responses; rather, to use a commonplace, I let the text "speak" to me, or I digest the text as the text ingests me. I am fully attentive to the reading and cannot be distracted by other stimuli. It is as if boundaries between me and the story are dissolved—it is a temporary confluence of reader and text.

These are the scribbled notes from my first reading:

- God's prediction: "the elder shall serve the younger;"

- twins: (Jacob's hand on Esau's heel)
  —Esau: red, hairy;   a skillful hunter; Isaac's favorite;
  —Jacob: quiet, smooth; dwells in tents;   Rebekah's favorite;

- Esau is *hungry* and sells *birthright* for bowl of lentils;
- Isaac (old/dim eyes) will *bless* Esau if he gets to *eat*;

- Jacob *solicits birthright*;
- Rebekah plots against Isaac/Esau; asks Jacob to *solicit blessings*;

- Isaac: your *voice* is of Jacob; your *hand/smell* of Esau;
- Jacob *kisses* Isaac (kiss of betrayal? Judas kisses Jesus);

- Esau *cries, weeps*: "Bless me, even me also, my father;"
- Isaac *trembled violently*: "Your brother has taken away your blessing;"

- Esau hated Jacob (Cain and Abel?).

When I later looked over my notes, I noticed that a structure had already emerged. Interactions between shifting pairs seemed to be the driving force behind the story. Within a larger narrative frame ("the elder shall serve the younger," "Esau hated Jacob"), there were plots and counterplots presented as encounters between pairs and arranged in triangular shapes (see Figure 10.1).

During the reading of a text, I already conceive of movements although I do not organize these ideas until afterwards. I always plan different kinds of movements: preparatory sound-and-movement exercises that are inspired by but independent of the text; movements and sounds that amplify the text; movements substituting for parts of the text (gestures, mime, and so on); movements dramatizing small segments of the story; or movements and sound that exceed the written word, filling in where a text leaves gaps or is silent and opaque. Most of these exercises are informed by experimental drama techniques; some are based on psychodrama and Samuel Laeuchli's *mimesis*.

How I Structured the Play of Jacob and Esau

I met the two dancers in a Philadelphia dance studio with wooden floors, large mirrors on one side of the walls, and a few chairs scattered in the space. I told them briefly that we would begin with a warm-up, then interview the biblical characters and go through a series of reenactments, and end by talking about our experience. I did

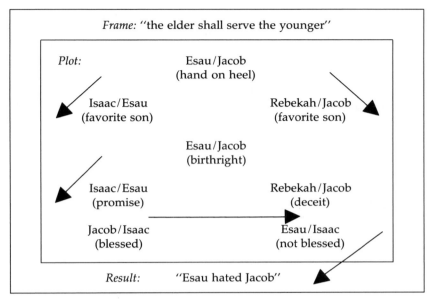

Figure 10.1   *The story's triangular structure*

not tell them the exact nature of the reenactments, since some scenes would be effective only if we sustained an element of surprise and spontaneity.

Warm-Up

After a fifteen-minute movement warm-up (stretching, relaxing, and breathing), we worked on our voice and resonance: breathing, jamming, singing, screaming, groaning, and so on. I consider these sound exercises very important, since they revive the gestural and sensual quality of words (which we later need when recovering some of the emotions coded and contained in language).

Building on these sound exercises, I asked the dancers to combine a particular movement with a particular (verbal) statement, repeat the whole phrase until they would find an emotional connection, and then amplify both phrase and emotion. To give a few examples:

- The statement "Hold me!" is repeatedly articulated as one stands upright with both arms stretched to the ceiling and the head bent backwards, looking up. The emotional equivalents, which most people rediscover, are feelings of dependency and helplessness; or people feel again like a child asking for help.
- "Get off my back!" is repeatedly shouted as one quickly raises both arms and shoulders backward as if to shake off something

or somebody sitting on one's neck. For most people, this phrase has an infuriating and liberating effect.

- "Give me!" is repeatedly said as an arm stretches forward and the hand opens. Many people get in touch with softer feelings whereas others with anger, inadequacy, and blemish.
- "Bug off!" has as its movement equivalent a sudden and violent forward thrust of the pelvis. This exercise is by far the most difficult, because of the aggressiveness and sexual connotation of both movement and language. Some people substitute the phrase with other words (such as "leave me alone" or other stronger expressions), and women sometimes exchange the pelvis movement with a forward thrust of the entire torso. However, it inevitably brings people in touch with their rage and frustration, and they often collapse afterwards with relief and laughter.

Interviews

I asked the dancers to identify with one of the parents who we then interviewed. Billy chose Rebekah. "We will ask you everything we always wanted to know from Rebekah," I said. Jonathan and I began the interview. We asked: Are you happy in your marriage? Can you describe your relationship to Isaac? Why do you like Jacob better? Billy spoke in Rebekah's (and his own) voice, answering to the best of his or her knowledge. "I am fairly happy; . . . it's not that I don't like Esau, it's just that I like Jacob better; . . . Isaac and I get along, but he's getting old and is lately very reserved;" and so on. We then switched roles. Jonathan played Isaac with a feeble voice and sometimes closed eyes ("Isaac was old and his eyes were dim;" Genesis 27:1). Again, we asked him questions: Why only bless Esau? I heard you did not have an easy childhood; could you tell me about it? Do you bear any scars from your childhood that might affect your relationship to your sons? Do you love Rebekah? Then he would answer: "I love Rebekah, but she is a tough woman; . . . Yes, my childhood was painful, but I survived it; . . . Jacob? I don't know. I just never felt very close to him;" and so on.

The two dancers then identified with one of the brothers. I asked Billy first, and he immediately decided to portray Jacob (which did not come as a surprise, since he had been bewildered by Jacob prior to the play and had already identified with Rebekah). We interviewed him: What relationship do you have to your mother? How would you describe your brother? Were you afraid of Isaac? How did you feel after stealing first the birthright, then the blessing? Again, we switched roles and interviewed Jonathan or Esau: Why did you sell your birthright for a bowl of lentils? Did you trust your brother? How did you feel about him after he cheated you twice?

The Play

The play moved through six scenes, most of them lasting approximately fifteen minutes. Between each scene, we took short breaks, in which we remained silent, shared some thoughts, and took notes.

In the first scene, I asked Billy and Jonathan to improvise a dance about the birth of the twins. The duet soon turned into an energetic and passionate wrestling. The two dancers were in close physical contact, lifting each other, sliding down each other's backs, climbing onto each other, crawling through open legs, grabbing their heels, and holding onto hands, necks, and knees. Because of the physical and emotional exhaustion (the term *heavy labor* came to my mind), they began breathing, groaning, and moaning. Interestingly, the dance remained stationary. The twins never moved through the large studio space, as if confined by invisible boundaries. It looked like they were already struggling in the womb over their birthright.

After a short break, we played the first of three encounters between father and son. Jonathan volunteered to play Isaac. I asked him to sit on a rolled-up marley floor (a special mat for dancing), which lay in one corner of the studio, close his eyes, and repeatedly ask Jacob: "Are you really my son Esau?" (Genesis 27:24). Jacob (played by Billy) would only be able to respond to his question nonverbally.

In the ensuing play, it was difficult to watch the growing distrust, fury, and desperation between father and son. We might assume that Isaac, as patriarch and keeper of the blessing, has all the power in his hands. Indeed, he (literally) sat in a higher position on the rolled-up marley, but he was immobile, blind, and absorbed in futile efforts, trying to get hold of his son. Wanting to convince himself that it is really Esau, not Jacob, upon whom he would bestow the blessing, he tried to grab his son, feeling his skin and his smell. Jacob, in turn, first knelt in front and below him, a few feet away, watching his father and listening to his question: "Are you really my son Esau? Are you really my son Esau?" Eventually, Jacob got up, approached his father and touched him lightly on the arms, hand, and torso. He especially groped for his father's hands, but backed away before Isaac had a chance to seize his son. It looked like an aborted handshake. The dance or query thus turned into a to and fro movement. The more desperate the father's plea, the faster and more aggressive the son's touch and withdrawal. "Are you really my son Esau?" Isaac beseeched his son with a voice that betrayed fear, despair, and impotence. (As I was witnessing the two dancers, I thought of the helplessness Isaac must have felt when Abraham tried to sacrifice him; I also imagined Isaac to be afraid of old age, and I was reminded of my own father who had instilled in me the fear and guilt that if I left him, he would die). Jacob continued to hastily stroke and brush Isaac's body, avoiding any close contact. No rapport seemed possible.

In a brief interlude, I asked Isaac (Jonathan) to request a kiss. "Come near and kiss me, my son" (Genesis 27:26). Jacob (Billy) approached him and kissed him on the forehead. Isaac took the opportunity to embrace his son, putting his arms around his neck, touching and smelling him. However, neither kiss nor embrace could revert the mistrust: Isaac feared betrayal; Jacob feared disclosure.

The third father-son encounter took place between Isaac (this time played by Billy) and Esau (Jonathan). Isaac sat again on the rolled-up marley and Esau squatted cross-legged in front of him. Esau would implore his father, "Bless me, even me also, my father" (Genesis 27:34,38), while Isaac would remain mostly silent. Only sporadically, he would interject, "Your brother has taken away your blessing" (Genesis 27:35).

Esau's continuous plea, "Bless me, even me also, my father!" slowly grew into a lament, or a tormented cry, which began to fill the whole space, echoing from the walls and reverberating in our heads. Esau (Jonathan) performed the phrase with such empathetic rigor that it transformed into a rhythmic and haunting tune: "BLESS me, even me ALSO, my FATHER! Bless ME, EVEN ME ALSO, my father!" However, Esau failed to get through to his father. Isaac (Billy) passively watched his son, his shoulders sunken in, shaking his head and his hands. He had nothing to offer. Silently, he endured Esau's anguish. Once or twice, he said, "Your brother has taken away your blessing," but his feeble response was drowned out by Esau's wailing.

Whereas in the first father-son encounter, it was Jacob who seemed pitiless, now it was Isaac who had a cruel part to play. In both instances, Isaac seemed disempowered. (Again, I was reminded of the Abraham episode. Perhaps, it was the fury Isaac had felt as an abused child that was now played out against his own son—a cycle of violence and abuse passed on from generation to generation and from father to son.) Esau, too, was disempowered, for his desperate pleas were only met by rejection. We were deeply saddened after we ended this scene.

We know from the biblical text that, years later, in the well-known nocturnal encounter, Jacob wrestles with a nameless man (or angel or God?) "until the breaking of the day" (Genesis 32:24). I asked Billy to improvise a solo dance in which he would explore this nightly encounter. Before he started, I read him one sentence, "I [Jacob] will not let you go, unless you bless me" (Genesis 32:26).

Jonathan and I watched Jacob as he began to dance, sometimes soft with undulating arms and legs and sometimes harsh with impulsive movements in the upper body. Often, he reached behind as if to relate to or fight something invisible. Unable to get hold of this effigy, or this shadow, the dance did not find a conclusion. When it became apparent that Billy would continue dancing without coming to an end, I spontaneously decided to send Jonathan to the rescue. I instructed him to join Jacob and, at an appropriate moment, ask him, "What is your name?" (Genesis 32:27).

Jonathan got up and cautiously circled Billy. "What is your name?" Jacob refused to answer. Eventually, Jonathan embraced him tightly from behind, and they began to wrestle again, as Jacob tried to free himself. Finally, Billy gave the answer: "Jacob, my name is Jacob," he whispered with a coarse voice. (As I looked on, I was struck by the similarity between Jacob's wrestle with the angel and the very first scene, the birth of the twins. Were we witnessing another kind of birth? The nocturnal struggle both wounds and heals Jacob. Hurt at his thigh, he finally receives a blessing without having to pretend to be someone else.) Billy later said of his dance that he "was able to feel the contact of the blessing only in the inner thigh region. I felt the wounding here as authentic contact, establishing a relationship with God, and blessing."

I originally planned to conclude the play with the twins' reconciliation: "And Jacob lifted up his eyes and looked, and behold, Esau was coming . . . But Esau ran to meet him, and embraced him . . . and they wept" (Genesis 33:1,4). However, Jacob's solo dance was a powerful ending in itself. I decided to get back into a circle and simply talk about the brothers' final meeting. It was Esau who was first able to reach out to his brother, and we suggested that he most likely had reconciled himself with the betrayals he had suffered in his youth. Jacob, on the other hand, was burdened by unresolved feelings for many years, perhaps ashamed of his deeds or pained by the fact that he, as Jacob, had never received a paternal blessing either. Jacob, it seemed, finally matured during the night when he revealed his real name and got an authentic blessing. Interestingly, Billy perceived Jonathan's tight embrace from behind, which brought Jacob's solo dance to a halt, as an embrace not only of a stranger, angel, or God but also of Esau. "As Jacob," Billy later wrote, "I experienced readiness for the real human contact with Esau. . . .Esau was embracing and supporting me from behind."

Concluding Talk

As we looked back at what we had played, we were amazed by the intensity of the workshop—by how much the story had spoken to us, how we had explored the emotional background of the biblical characters, and how much the narrative had provided an opportunity to get in touch with our own relationships to our fathers. A tragedy had been played out in front of our eyes, embodied in our own bodies.

Familiar pains were resuscitated: fathers incapable of blessing their offspring; fathers possessing only a limited quantity of available blessings; sons yearning and struggling for those blessings; unhealed wounds passed on as hurt (from Abraham to Isaac and from Isaac to Jacob and Esau); the sons' revenge by cutting off all bonds to their fathers; attempted and desired infanticides and parricides. As we were concluding the afternoon, we were immersed in sadness and grief, remembering our own fathers and reflecting on a culture with broken and injurious father-son relationships. We could have wept (like Jacob and Esau) but we did not.

What We Learned From the Play

A few months later, Billy Yalowitz's modern dance piece premiered at Temple University. It was entitled "Jacob and Esau" and divided into three parts. It began with the twins' wrestling, reminiscent of our play, though now choreographically refined and expanded. In the second part, Esau crawled around stage while Jacob walked upright, smiled, mimed a handshaking, and announced repeatedly, "Looking good! Fantastic! Fantastic!" His whole behavior mimicked a corporate salesperson. At the end of this scene, Esau left the stage in a threatening posture (his "death threat," as Billy explained). In the third part, Jacob, alone on stage, was confronted with images of body parts and X rays projected onto the backdrop. The monotonous voice of a doctor commented on those pictures. However, amidst this medical prating, the audience could clearly distinguish the phrase, "Nothing is wrong with you, but, okay, we will take a look." As I was watching the performance, this scene immediately reminded me of Jacob's thigh injury from his nocturnal wrestling. For Billy, however, the doctor represented Laban, Jacob's uncle, who, according to Genesis, was even more clever than Jacob: Laban deceived the deceiver.

"My personal revelation about the story's meaning," Billy later wrote, "came through our playing of it—namely that Jacob, having received a false blessing from Isaac, one that was not meant for him, must go through an initiation of a kind (at the hand of his even more deceptive trickster uncle, Laban), before being able to fight for and receive a real blessing. When we played the scene in which Jacob deceives Isaac, my movement vocabulary as Jacob was centered around the handshake—as false offer, as manipulation. In working with this movement motif later, Jacob became a salesman, selling false goods to both Esau and Isaac."

With respect to the effects of play processes, Billy's choreography is illuminating. It shows that play processes can serve as preparation for further artistic explorations (although play is integral and complete in itself). It also demonstrates that play stimulates creativity but does not prescribe one viewpoint or interpretation (Billy's performance was different from our improvisatory play). Finally, it shows that a new performance is also a new ambiguous script which, in turn, requires interpretive work (for my interpretation of the "doctor's voice" differed from the choreographer's intent).

Personally, I was less intrigued by Jacob's "corporate behavior," as Billy called it; I felt more saddened by the antagonistic relationships between father and sons, which had effectively transpired in our playing. I sensed that Jacob, Esau, and Isaac must have felt disempowered, betrayed, and rejected. Instead of establishing intimate bonds, they tried to solve their problems by regaining power. After our playing, I found myself grieving over the loss of an intimate relationship with my father and being angry about his refusal to give a wholehearted blessing to my life's choices. I felt, and still feel, that the story of Jacob and Esau is applicable to today's crisis of male identity, as it is described, for example, in Osherson's psychotherapeutic study, *Finding our Fathers*.

I would like to conclude this investigation into the seriousness of play by returning to the aforementioned hermeneutic and therapeutic principles. By and large, our playing of the Genesis story was efficacious because we followed those principles. The structure of both narrative and play provided sufficient *protection* for emotionally difficult situations to emerge. As a result, we were able to express and experience anguish, anger, rejection, and powerlessness without being overwhelmed by emotional distress (*aesthetic distance*). We oscillated between textual references and our own movements (*mediation of narrative structures and freeplay*), and remained open to the possibility of multiple interpretations (*surplus of meaning*). Furthermore, the ritual qualities of ambiguity, transgression, condensation, and resistance were present at various stages, sometimes more forcefully and other times less forcefully, and the careful reader certainly noticed their workings.

Two additional principles need our attention, because they, more than any other, attest to the hermeneutic relevance of play. First, there is a *hermeneutics of disclosure* at work when we play. We discover passages previously ignored, gaps to be filled, ambiguities to be interpreted, gestures waiting to be visualized, and sounds to be expressed. We discover the emotional relevance of words, images, and symbols. We disclose the hidden in the manifest, go beyond surface meaning, invert priorities, and invent our own dramatized play. During these acts of disclosure, we become creative explorers in our own right. Disclosing is the "fun" part of playing, "the liberation of human capacities of cognition, affect, volition, creativity" (Turner

1982a:44). We discover the arduous, at times comical, struggle of Jacob and Esau in the womb; we invent a movement as response to Isaac's query; and we give voice to Esau's desperate plea.

Analogous to a psychotherapeutic journey into the interior space and memories of individuals, we enter the interior space of a text. We revive cultural memories hidden in biblical narratives and weave them into our own memories and experiences. In the Jacob-Esau episode, we also relied on an experimental drama technique known as *via negativa*. *Via negativa*, a term used by Grotowski, achieves genuine creativity by reducing, eliminating, and amplifying; it searches to express "extreme emotions," and discovers "hidden faces" and "intimate truths" (Grotowski 1968:15–53). But beware—this process also resuscitates forgotten pains, fears, and desires stored in cultural memory systems, such as biblical narratives. Body-centered play processes are passionate and joyful but they are also agonizing and antagonizing. The fun of discovery is inevitably paired with seriousness. Sharon Welch, though in a different context, spoke of the insurrection of "dangerous memories" and "subjugated knowledge" (1985); her insights are applicable to the enactment and embodiment of biblical narratives.

Keeping the seriousness of play in mind, we arrive at the second hermeneutic principle, a *hermeneutics of suspicion*. Whenever we enter a play, and whatever we think the outcome of such playing is, we need to remain suspicious of particular results and of our endeavors in general. We know that play releases powerful and dynamic forces that make transformation possible. However, we are in need of frameworks that help us evaluate those transformations. How do we know that transformation takes place? What kinds of transformation do we achieve? A good deal of playful "disclosure" is currently going on but precious little is done when it comes to a hermeneutics of suspicion. Applied to the Jacob-Esau play, we can ask, for example, whether Billy's choreographic choice of focusing on Jacob's negative traits (the deceiving salesman) avoids Jacob's hidden pain and anger, which we had discovered in our play that afternoon. Is this a sign of resistance, denial, or regression? Similarly, we can ask whether my own emphasis on the denied blessing clouds my judgment of Jacob's character (after all, he betrayed his brother) and steers me in a direction where I want to overprotect him.

A hermeneutics of suspicion reminds us that playing has no *a priori* hermeneutic privilege, although it has all the potentials of opening up new avenues of learning and a new mode of knowing. Having participated in numerous workshops and read literature on various experimentations, I am convinced that many of those processes, despite their claims to the contrary, have backfired and misfired, and are flawed, ineffective, or hollow (cf. Grimes 1990:191ff). Unless we are able to develop categories and frameworks that assist us in applying a hermeneutics of suspicion, play processes are at risk of deteriorating to purely self-referential, regressive, or naïve levels. We need to take this critical step; otherwise, our playing might soon be discarded as another whim of the postmodern era.

Notes

1. Anthropologically informed theory, particularly about festivals, acknowledges the ubiquity and importance of transgression (cf. Caillois 1959; Bakhtin 1969; Turner 1982b; 1986). Festivals, it is argued, are public and communal acts of transgression, often religious at their roots and sensual in expression. They are periodic carnivalizations of society and culture, potentially dangerous, or, as Freud put it, "an obligatory excess" (1913:140).

2. Ethnological studies on festivals and rituals confirm the existence of the ritual quality of condensation. Kerenyi, for example, argues that a festive mood heightens the perception of reality and pushes life to the point of boisterousness (1938). Play theologian and bibliodramatist Gerhard Marcel Martin similarly observes that festive play engenders "enlargement and intensification of consciousness and life" (1976:11).

References

Abrahams, Roger D. 1986. "Play in the Face of Death: Transgression and Inversion in a West Indian Wake." In *The Many Faces of Play*, ed. Kendall Blanchard. Champaign, Ill.: Human Kinetics Publishers.

Alter, Robert. 1981. *The Art of Biblical Narrative*. New York: Basic Books.

Auerbach, Erich. 1953. *Mimesis: The Representation of Reality in Western Literature*. Trans. Willard R. Trask. Princeton: Princeton University Press.

Bakhtin, Michael. 1969. *Literatur und Karneval: Zur Romantheorie und Lachkultur*. Trans. Alexander Kämpfe. München: Carl Hanser Verlag.

Caillois, Roger. 1959. *Man and the Sacred*. Trans. Meyer Barash. Glencoe, Ill.: Free Press.

Derrida, Jacques. 1978. *Writing and Difference*. Trans. Alan Bass. Chicago: University of Chicago Press.

Douglas, Mary. 1984. *Purity and Danger: An Analysis of the Concepts of Pollution and Taboo*. London: ARK Paperbacks.

Freud, Sigmund. 1904. "Freud's Psycho-Analytic Procedure." Standard Edition. Vol. 7. Ed. James Strachey. London: Hogarth Press.

――――. 1907. "Obsessive Actions and Religious Practices." Standard Edition. Vol. 9.

――――. 1913. "Totem and Taboo." Standard Edition. Vol. 13.

――――. 1917. "A Difficulty in the Path of Psycho-Analysis." Standard Edition. Vol. 17.

_____. 1926. "Inhibitions, Symptoms and Anxiety." Standard Edition. Vol. 20.

Grimes, Ronald L. 1990. *Ritual Criticism: Case Studies in Its Practice, Essays on Its Theory.* Columbia: University of South Carolina Press.

Grotowski, Jerzy. 1968. *Towards a Poor Theatre.* New York: Simon and Schuster.

Hans, James S. 1981. *The Play of the World.* Amherst: University of Massachusetts Press.

Kerenyi, Karl. 1938. "Vom Wesen des Festes." *Paideuma: Mitteilungen zur Kulturkunde* 1 (December):59–74.

Krondorfer, Björn. 1992. "Bodily Knowing, Ritual Embodiment and Experimental Drama: From Regression to Transgression." *Journal of Ritual Studies,* 6 (Summer).

Laeuchli, Samuel. 1987. *Das Spiel vor dem dunklen Gott: Mimesis—ein Beitrag zur Entwicklung des Bibliodramas.* Neukirchen: Neukirchener Verlag.

Martin, Gerhard Marcel. 1976. *Fest: The Transformation of Everyday.* Trans. M. Douglas Meeks. Philadelphia: Fortress Press.

Osherson, Samuel. 1986. *Finding Our Fathers: The Unfinished Business of Manhood.* New York: Free Press.

Rardin, Jared J. 1979. "The Rites of Resistance: Image and Drama in Pastoral Psychotherapy." *The Journal of Pastoral Care* 33 (September): 175–84.

Ricoeur, Paul. 1970. *Freud and Philosophy: An Essay on Interpretation.* Trans. Denis Savage. New Haven, Conn.: Yale University Press.

Schechner, Richard. 1977. *Essays on Performance Theory, 1970–1976.* New York: Drama Book Publishers.

Scheff, T. J. 1979. *Catharsis in Healing, Ritual and Drama.* Berkeley: University of California Press.

Sternberg, Meir. 1985. *The Poetics of Biblical Narrative: Ideological Literature and the Drama of Reading.* Bloomington: Indiana University Press.

Tillich, Paul. 1952. *The Courage to Be.* New Haven: Yale University Press.

Turner, Victor. 1982a. *From Ritual to Theatre: The Human Seriousness of Play.* New York: PAJ Publications.

_____, ed. 1982b. *Celebration: Studies in Festivity and Ritual.* Washington, D.C.: Smithsonian Institution Press.

_____. 1986. *The Anthropology of Performance.* New York: PAJ Publications.

Welch, Sharon D. 1985. *Communities of Resistance and Solidarity: A Feminist Theology of Liberation.* Maryknoll, N.Y.: Orbis Books.

Winnicott, D. W. [1971.] 1989. *Playing and Reality.* Reprint. London/New York: Routledge, Chapman & Hall.

Lot's Wife Looks Back:
Biblical Stories as Therapy and Play

Evelyn Rothchild-Laeuchli

Remember Lot's wife. Whoever seeks to save his life will lose it; and whoever loses it will save it and live.

Luke 17:32–33

Amy's Story

Amy sat in her chair, her body frozen, her hand clenched
around a crumpled ball of Kleenex, and her face an unmoving
mask. The only sign of the storm raging inside her was the tears that
slid down her cheeks. She saw so many images: the flowers at her
grandmother's funeral, her father throwing a chair in rage, and her
mother's face turned away, unfocused, seeing nothing.

There were dark shadows that haunted her. Could she dare to
look? What she saw might kill her. The word *incest* spun in her head
but would not attach itself to the bits of memory or the feelings in her
body. If she could move, she knew that she would scream or throw
up. Finally she said, "I've got to know, even if I die!"

Amy was a member of a small group in a psychiatric hospital who
had just played the story of Lot. Amy played Lot's wife, a woman
without a name. Her husband Lot, faced with the angry and lustful
men of Sodom, offered his two young daughters to be raped in place
of the two angels who were his guests. He then fled God's wrath
against his neighbors and ran to save his life. "Flee for your lives; do
not look back. . . . But Lot's wife behind him, looked back, and she
turned into a pillar of salt" (Genesis 19:17–26). Later, in a cave above
the town of Zoar, Lot had intercourse with his two daughters.

As a group leader and therapist, I had been playing Bible stories
and myths with groups for ten years; yet each time, the power of the

191

story hits me viscerally, like a punch in the stomach. I understood why Amy held her arms tightly against her middle and why she sat rigid and unmoving, a monolith of pain.

Amy had chosen the role of Lot's wife. (These choices always have a reason.) She played it brilliantly, using her own mother as her model. Just as in the Bible, she was faceless, voiceless, "a good wife." She did not protest when her husband said, "Look I have two daughters, both virgins; let me bring them out to you, and you can do what you like with them . . ." (Genesis 19:8). In Amy's family, it was not angels but her two brothers that were protected and preferred; and the angry voices crying "Bring them out so that we can have intercourse with them!" (Genesis 19:5) were not the voices of the men of Sodom but the unspoken voice of her father.

For Amy, a door had opened to memories and awareness. She had been running for a lifetime through alcoholism, bulimia, and brutal relationships. She was desperately trying to save her life by shutting out the pain and quieting the voices that reminded her of what she could not know. Now at last, she was looking back into a childhood of violence and abuse—the burning city of Sodom.

Amy, like so many victims, blamed herself. "I was his favorite. I was too pretty. My mother was ill. The family would have fallen apart. If I hadn't slept with him, he would have left my mother." There is a psychological truth in Genesis 19:30–38 when we are told that it is the daughters who feel responsible for the incest.

During the discussion of our play, someone said, "This is a horrible story. Why would God put such a terrible story in the Bible?" Amy answered simply, "It's the story of my life. Somehow I feel better that it's in the Bible." A pillar of salt is something precious—salt of the earth and salt of our tears—it is an example that nourishes the spirit of the community. Amy's courage to look back healed us and gave us hope.

This is not theology. Working closely with human suffering and tragedy, there is little room to worry about theologically correct interpretations; rather, the focus is on how the story resonates or screams into and through the minds and bodies of my patients and myself. Yet there is a consensus, an understanding, and a common reality in the group at the end of our play. It may be difficult for our language to convey, but we "know" where we have been and what we have witnessed. It is very personal and at the same time something shared.

Using Stories to Heal

The process of using stories as a context and method of healing is both antique and modern. An audience watching a tragedy at a temple of Asklepius and a patient participating in a psychodrama that objectifies her personal circumstance are both entering a mythic reality to transform consciousness. Myths contain a deep awareness of life on a personal, family, cultural, and universal level. They deal with issues of lifetime development: loss and separation, the development of self, initiation, conflict within the family, and the achievement of intimacy.

Myths are multilayered, condensed, and coded. They contain paradoxes. In playing myth, we decode, extend, and reexperience the primal dramas of humankind. Myth speaks to the third ear. It slips under our defenses and communicates unconscious to unconscious.

Therapists and patients are mythmakers. The mind apprehends and creates its "reality" through mythic lenses. Bible stories, myths, and fairy tales are vehicles for insight, expression, and exploration of one's personal predicament, as well as containers of the condensed wisdom of our predecessors. In myth, our private tragedy is universalized.

As a therapist, one struggles to find meaning in suffering and to find order in what appears arbitrary and random. One listens for themes, patterns, and currents in the patient's description of her situation, the details of her childhood, or the events of her week. Work with patients is in part an attempt to help them know and understand their story, to see their role in the larger drama, and to find purpose and value in playing their part. When a person sees their role clearly, they can begin to have choice; they can alter their role or learn a new one.

The Group Plays the Story

It all seems so simple and naïve. The group sits in a circle. There are empty chairs in the middle, one for each character in the tale. Even at the beginning, they have a strange presence. One tells the story, which is sometimes read. At times, there are changes in perspective. For women's groups, I have played the Prodigal Daughter, the Sacrifice of Sarah's Son, and Lot's Wife. During the telling of the story, I ask the group to allow the characters to speak to them. "Who fascinates or repulses you? Are there people from your own life in this tale? With whom do you identify? Perhaps you would like to learn more about a character you find troubling." The group chooses roles freely. There is never any pressure.

Depending on the time available to the group, a few parts or all of the story is played. With Lot's Wife, I like to start with the scene in which God, hearing that the town of Sodom is in a state of grave sin, decides to send two angels to investigate. At different times, I use meditation, imaging, or movement to help the group enter the process. "What is grave sin today?" I ask the group, and there is a period of silent meditation followed by sharing. "We are destroying the earth." "We ignore the suffering of the homeless." "I am an alcoholic and I am destroying my own life and that of my family." "We are all addicted to status, money, and success, and we refuse to see reality; how empty we really are and how desperate." "We are filled with self-hatred and show it in the way we judge others." "I don't know what it is that I have done, but I have always had an oppressive sense of guilt and shame." In all the groups with which I have worked, the sense of sin becomes visceral, heavy, and suffocating.

The group members sitting in the circle have become the people of Sodom. We listen and watch as God tells Abraham, Lot's uncle, of his plans to destroy our town. Abraham argues with God: "Wilt thou really sweep away good and bad together? Suppose there are fifty good men in the city; wilt thou really sweep it all away, and not pardon the place because of the fifty good men? Far be it from thee to do this—to kill good and bad together; for then the good would suffer with the bad" (Genesis 18:23–25).

It is a very different experience to listen to God and Abraham when it is the fate of your own family, your parents and children, and your neighbors and friends that is being decided. "Am I one of the just? How can it be that the innocent will suffer?" As Abraham begins to barter with God, there is fear and tension in the room. "May I presume to speak to the Lord, dust and ashes that I am: suppose there are five short of the fifty good men? Wilt thou destroy the whole city for a mere five men?" (Genesis 18:27–29).

"Abraham is clever but he is afraid," someone reflects. It is very quiet after that comment, and the group is riveted as Abraham works to save us. In the end, he is able to get God to commit to sparing the town if there are only ten just men. We eye each other nervously. Someone mentions the concentration camps—how arbitrary it was to be chosen to live or die. A woman says softly, "Sometimes I feel like I am evil and I deserve God's punishment; that I am responsible for the terrible things that have happened in my life. The next moment I feel that I am innocent, a victim, and then I am filled with sadness and anger about the unfairness of God, of life."

This issue of the good and bad suffering equally and the lack of justice in life is a theme that the group grapples with as they struggle to make sense of their own histories and current situations. Childhoods of abuse and neglect, disabilities and illnesses, deaths and losses of loved ones and friends, chronic depression, and emptiness lead the patient to say, "Why me Lord?" Some have elaborate rationalizations to explain their anguish as a just punishment for some imagined wrong. It is easier to accept such punishment than to face a world without justice. Some refuse to acknowledge their pain because their rage and sorrow might drown them, and no God has heard their cries. Others fight desperately for some sense of control, even if it means starving to death, as it does for the anorexic.

To be healed would mean to be able to know "reality" without the need for defenses that are too limiting or too destructive to oneself and others. In *The Future of an Illusion*, Freud argues that it is only when we have the strength to see reality, with all its unfairness, that we are able to be truly compassionate and to act humanely (1961).

Then there are the two angels. We are the people of Sodom, and the angels walk around the circle looking at us sadly or coldly, with great distance or great compassion. No matter how the angels are played, we learn quickly that they are powerless, without a voice or choice. They are only here to report what they see and hear. Sometimes they are silent observers listening to the townspeople discuss their fears and concerns. They do not interact but are invisible. At other times, they are investigative reporters who ask probing questions to individual members of the group. Often the people in the circle get angry with them. "Don't tell me that you're only following orders! Get out of here! I can't stand your holier-than-thou attitude."

A woman patient, when asked why she thought she deserved to be spared, said to the angel: "You remind me of a goddamn therapist; so distant and untouchable. You don't have any idea what it's like to be me; the hell I live in minute to minute. It's you that's evil, not me! How dare you judge me!"

We have entered the story. Play has added a depth to our experience. Our defenses are down. We are raw. The Greeks called this process catharsis; as a therapist, I also see it as a process of mastery. All play is an attempt at mastery, or an attempt to achieve new levels of integration. It is a form of communication with ourselves and others. Through our play, we learn about our roles, the roles of others, and the dynamics that drive us. Even a year later, group members have told me, "I am still struggling with the Abraham in me," or "I feel so much closer to my mother since I played her part. I had no way of understanding her before."

The story brings up conflict, and the role allows defense. One is both actor and observer, and there are subject-object shifts. A patient once stopped me in the cafeteria to tell me that she had finally figured out why playing stories was so helpful and powerful for her: "I got it! This play allows me to see as much of myself and my problems as I can tolerate. Then when it's too much, I can say that it isn't me—that it's only the character that I am playing."

As group leader, I also play the role of director, although it is often my experience that the play is directing me. The group has the freedom to rework scenes, to change the format of our play, and to switch actors. It is often stunning to see that when the group has demanded a more compassionate God or a more vocal Abraham the story does not change. It is just held differently. Loss is loss; tragedy is tragedy.

The role of Lot's wife can be played in many ways. She can be compliant or defiant, or a victim or a rebel, but the story grinds forward. Her husband offers their children to be raped by the angry mob. Do his reasons matter to the mother or the children? No matter what explanations are given, the children are frightened and horrified. One child lays her head on her mother's lap; the other turns away from her family and lets out a piercing scream. Despite the fear and pain of the children, it often seems to the group that it is easier to play the childrens' parts than to play the role of Lot.

The play is nearing its end. Lot's two daughters are holding each other frightened, tearful, and unable to speak or understand the events that have befallen them. Lot and his wife sit on two chairs, back-to-back; he can only look forward, she can only look back. Lot's wife is being played by a young woman physician who is just completing her training; Lot is a local parish priest.

The group that sits in a circle around the players begins to question Lot's wife about what she sees: "Why did you look back? Are you glad that the men who threatened your daughters are being destroyed? How do you feel about your husband after he sent your daughters out to be raped by a mob? Can you bear to look him in the face? What has God done to your town? What has happened to the woman who lived next door with the three small children? Are you relieved that you don't have to go on after experiencing all this?"

At first, it is hard for her to speak. It is too much to know or to communicate. Then she begins slowly, "I see people crying in pain, suffering without relief or reason. I want to believe that they deserve this so that it will make sense." I interrupt at this point to push it further. "Have you ever seen a child die?" She begins to weep. It was only the day before this group that she experienced the first death of a child in her care. "I did everything I knew how. Her injuries were too severe. . . . She was so little. . . . Her parents were so desperate." The group begins to mourn with this young physician. There is a bond that grows as the group supports her and struggles to carry her vision and sorrow. Tears are being shed for so many losses and for once we can mourn and be comforted, not alone but as a community.

It suddenly becomes clear to me that Lot is totally alone and that he is the most lost and vulnerable person in the room. There is community among those who mourn the death of a child, a city, or their own naïve belief in justice. Lot, who cannot see this reality, cannot be comforted. I go and rest my hands on his shoulders. It is too hard for him to carry this role alone. It is only when he is touched that he too can weep.

Coming Back to Reality

After the play, there is a time for sharing and a time to come back to our everyday reality. People tell stories of memories that have come up during the play. Some cry in relief and sorrow for their new understanding of themselves. Others give support to the players and express appreciation for what they have been given. A few distance themselves by quoting theories or arguing about how a role was interpreted. Everyone is supported. Each person's experience is validated. We are—each of us—both Lot and Lot's wife; at any given moment, we can only see as much as we can bear.

How has this play been healing? What in all of this is therapeutic? The use of dramatic play creates an integration of intellect and affect that is often missed in regular therapy. From the stories, one gains insight into family and personal dynamics, and there is the ability to accept and experience feelings that have previously been threatening or overwhelming. There is also a healing of loneliness; an individual's concerns are shared, and, from this sharing, a deep sense of connection with others, or a sense of community, is created. We are known and accepted at our most naked and vulnerable.

A new respect for the self grows as we see ourselves reflected in others. "She was also sexually abused, and she is such a courageous and sensitive person. Perhaps I am also worthy of respect." This reflection of oneself, in and from the group, is in my experience the best way to heal shame. In my years of work as a therapist, I have come to believe that it is the healing of shame and low self-esteem that allows the individual to become fully alive and creative.

The Transforming Power of Stories

With my husband Samuel Laeuchli, as part of my work for the Mimesis Institute, I have lead literally hundreds of workshops and growth groups using biblical themes. Watching how different groups respond to and enact the same story has given me a sense of the underlying structures in these stories; what is mutable and what is constant. There is a difference between playing Bible stories with therapy groups and playing them with educational groups in churches and academic settings. With patient groups, there is much more openness and trust, and much more acknowledgment of human vulnerability and pain. I have often wondered if any therapist could risk having as clear a perception of life as some of the individuals whom we label as sick or "crazy." It is from my work with patients that I have gained a trust in my current conception of these tales.

The stories are often horrible and tragic. Even stories of celebration have dark undercurrents. As we rejoice in Christ's birth, we anticipate his death. Mary's face is so often touched with sadness, her tender glance sweetened by her pain at knowing she can only hold her child a little while. Part of the healing of these stories may be that they provide an avenue into the core of our experience and allow us enough distance to see it without being overwhelmed. There is an opportunity to experience horror and to mourn. The Murder of the Innocents is juxtaposed with the peace and serenity of the manger.

There is no single approach to understanding biblical texts that is adequate. One cannot fit the power and depth of these stories into a psychological, theological, or historical framework. Within my own field and training, the narrowness of a Freudian or Jungian perspective limits rather than enables. At best, one brings to the text all that one has learned and has experienced, the reactions and sensations of the body, a thousand associations, and thoughts and feelings. These can all be guides to understanding and entering the tale.

All symbols and metaphors are multidetermined; they have many levels of meaning, some of which are contradictory. In my work with groups, the individuals are supported in meeting the story without expectation or prejudice, to tolerate the tension of paradox, to accept confusion and contradiction, and to respect and allow their inner process. One does not work to understand the story; rather, the story works on the mind, emotions, and body until it is known. This ability to suspend one's usual judgments, to be aware of one's spontaneous responses, to permit inner and outer conflict, and to contain one's reactivity and need to act is essential to any process of knowing or transforming. Ultimately, the task of therapy is more than understanding; it is transformation. There is something within a myth or story, when it is deeply experienced, that transforms.

Themes Make a Difference

I have played Bible stories as a form of therapy with groups in numerous settings—psychiatric hospitals, a residential treatment center for emotionally disturbed teens, and a special classroom for deprived and abused 5-year-old children. I have also used these stories as a group training method for individual and family therapists. Although it is exciting to use Bible stories, biblical figures, and biblical quotes in working with individuals, it is, in my experience, the group work that is most dynamic.

In clinical settings, I try to select stories that bring specific issues into focus. The staff often asks me to play a story dealing with intergenerational or sibling conflict, abandonment, loss, or shame—whatever concerns are reverberating in the community at that time. After playing stories with these themes, the patients can address these problems more directly in their individual treatment and in other groups. At times, patients have requested to play a particular role, and the group cooperates to provide them with this opportunity. "I would like to play Sarah as the barren wife, because I am struggling with my own infertility," or "I want to play Elohim creating the world, because as a woman I have felt so powerless."

I find certain stories particularly helpful in preparing new patients for therapy. I play the parable of the Good Samaritan as "helpers who cannot help." The patient who plays the person in need sits in the center of the group and expresses a real or ficticious problem. Another patient plays the role of the priest or Levite—someone from whom we expect help and support but who emotionally walks by. There is always a mixture of tears and laughter as the "helper" mouths the platitudes that have been given so often by counselors, clergy, teachers, and family members. "You have to pull yourself together; think of the children." "Count your blessings, don't think about your troubles." "Your parents love you; they only did it for your own good." "It could be worse, at least you have your physical health."

The patients are asked to identify why this "help" fails to touch their pain. "They don't really hear me, their words push me away." "They make me feel so lonely and ashamed." "I feel so put down; they don't want to know how hard it is." "They make me feel guilty that I am suffering. They think that if I wanted to, I would simply change." The question is then asked "Why can't the priest and Levite help?" There is a surprising compassion in the group: "They are afraid; underneath they feel despair; they have too much pain in themselves; they're afraid if they see my pain, they will be overwhelmed by their own."

The entire group then plays the Samaritan—the half-breed, the one who is not acceptable, the one whose own pain has taught him empathy. The patients are deeply moved as they learn that their suffering has given them a gift of understanding and that they can sensitively touch one another's lives.

The Prodigal Son is a good model for patients about to begin family therapy. The split between the "good" child and the "prodigal," the tensions between father and older brother, and the absence of the mother's voice can create recognition about one's own family dynamics. The prodigal son's inability to separate from his family and to establish himself in his own life successfully is an important key to underlying issues. It also gives insight into other family member's behavior and vulnerability.

Patients recognize their own role as good child or rebel. They struggle with the difficulty of separating from a family in which one child sacrifices himself to support and remain loyal to the parents and the other sacrifices himself to fulfill the father's or mother's unconscious wishes. I have played this story many times with many different groups, and no matter how the roles of mother and father are enacted, there is always difficulty in the parents' marital relationship. The marital problems result in the parents using the children for emotional gratification.

The Role of The Group Leader

There are rules for the group work and play. The group leader sets the tone. Creating a safe space is the ultimate concern. There is an acceptance of each individual's contribution and perspective. Each person is joined with and valued. Their pain, confusion, anger, and fear are acknowledged and held by the group. There is no attempt to find solutions; rather, there is a "being with" the problem. If there is safety and openness, I find that people can let go of defenses, become vulnerable, and share painful secrets. There is a willingness to see things in a new way. All of this can be done without confrontation. Aggression between group members is deflected onto the group leader. Attacking statements are decoded or reframed and integrated into the flow of the group process. The fear that is hidden under the anger is gently brought to light.

Gradually and organically, there is an interweaving of voices and perceptions. Some people in the group give expression to the son's experience, some to the father's or mother's. Each character is heard with compassion. Words are used to acknowledge and to comfort. There is a need to name our experience and to use words as markers for what cannot be said. There is permission to mourn, to share our deep sadness, and to cry out. Perhaps it is only the angels or God who can contain the whole, see the tragedy, and have the strength to carry it alone, in silence.

Rilke, *Lament*

Whom will you cry to, heart? More and more lonely,
your path struggles on through incomprehensible
mankind. All the more futile perhaps
for keeping to its direction,
keeping on toward the future,
toward what has been lost.

Once. You lamented? What was it? A fallen berry
of jubilation, unripe.
But now the whole tree of my jubilation

is breaking, in the storm it is breaking, my slow
tree of joy.
Loveliest in my invisible
landscape, you that made me more known
to the invisible angels.

Rilke, *Klage*

Wem willst du klagen, Herz? Immer gemiedener
ringt sich dein Weg durch die unbegreiflichen
Menschen. Mehr noch vergebens vielleicht,
da er die Richtung behält,
Richtung zur Zukunft behält,
zu der verlorenen.

Früher. Klagtest? Was wars? Eine gefallene
Beere des Jubels, unreife.
Jetzt aber bricht mir mein Jubel-Baum,
bricht mir im Sturme mein langsamer
Jubel-Baum.
Schönster in meiner unsichtbaren
Landschaft, der du mich kenntlicher
machtest Engeln, unsichtbaren.

(Buch der Bilder, I–2)

References

Campbell, Joseph. 1970. *Myth, Dreams and Religion*. New York: E. P. Dutton.
Eliade, Mircea. 1959. *The Sacred and the Profane: The Significance of Religious Myth, Symbolism and Ritual within Life and Culture*. New York: Harcourt, Brace and World.
Freud, Sigmund. 1961. *The Future of an Illusion*. New York: W. W. Norton and Company.
Rilke, Rainer M. 1982. *The Selected Poetry of Rainer Maria Rilke*. Ed. Stephen Mitchell. New York: Random House.
Yalom, Irvin D. 1985. *The Theory and Practice of Group Psychotherapy*. New York: Basic Books.

Contributors

Tom F. Driver will retire in 1993 as the Paul Tillich Professor of Theology and Culture at Union Theological Seminary in New York, where he has been a faculty member since 1956. He has held visiting professorships at Fordham University, Vassar College, Barnard College, the University of Otaga in New Zealand, Doshisha University in Japan, and Columbia University. He has written extensively on theater as well as theology. His most recent book is *The Magic of Ritual*.

Gerhard Marcel Martin is Professor of Practical Theology at Marburg University, Germany. He has studied in Tübingen, Heidelberg, Bonn, New York, and St. Louis. In coordination with artists, psychologists, teachers, and theologians, he has developed *bibliodrama* as a holistic and multidimensional approach to biblical texts. He has written extensively on theology and art, and religious experience and bibliodrama.

Björn Krondorfer has taught at Temple and Lehigh Universities. His PhD thesis is an interdisciplinary study of avant-garde theater and religion. He conducts workshops on enacting biblical stories and is cofounder of the binational performance company, *The Jewish-German Dance Theatre*. He also works as a translator, and has been a consultant for the U. S. Holocaust Museum in Washington, D. C.

Samuel Laeuchli is Professor of Religion at Philadelphia's Temple University, where he teaches mythology, symbolism, ritual, and play. He is also the executive director of the Mimesis Institute, a center for art, play, and psychology, which he and his wife, Dr. Evelyn

Rothchild-Laeuchli, founded and developed. Three books and several articles on his work have been published in German.

ALIX PIRANI is a psychotherapist and writer based in Great Britain. Working within the traditions of humanistic and transpersonal psychology, she runs workshops in dynamic mythology and spirituality. She is the author of *The Absent Father: Crisis and Creativity* and the editor of *The Absent Mother: Restoring the Goddess to Judaism and Christianity.*

DAVID RHOADS graduated from Duke University in New Testament Studies in 1973. For fifteen years, he taught at Carthage College in Kenosha, Wisconsin. He now teaches at the Lutheran School of Theology at Chicago. He is the author of *Israel in Revolution 6–73 C. E.* and *Mark as Story* with Donald Michie. He has given performances of the Gospels and conducts workshops for pastors on the Gospel narratives.

EVELYN ROTHCHILD-LAEUCHLI is a clinical psychologist in private practice in Yardley, Pennsylvania. She treats children, families, and individuals. She has done group work and individual therapy in numerous settings, including a residential treatment center for emotionally disturbed teenagers, a therapeutic nursery for abused and neglected preschoolers, and a private hospital for eating disorders. She is a founder of the Mimesis Institute.

TIM F. SCHRAMM is Professor of New Testament Studies at Hamburg University. He has published extensively on the New Testament and bibliodrama, and he conducts workshops. He was visiting professor at Temple University. His books include *Fest und Freude* (translated into English, *Festival and Joy,* Abingdon Press), *Unmoralische Helden* and *Selbsterfahrung mit der Bibel.*

ARTHUR WASKOW lives in Philadelphia. He is a Fellow of the Institute for Jewish Renewal, director of the Shalom Center, coeditor of *New Menorah,* and the author of *Godwrestling, Seasons of Our Joy, These Holy Sparks,* and many other works on Jewish renewal.

WALTER WINK is Professor of Biblical Interpretation at Auburn Theological Seminary in New York City. He is the author of two works on biblical hermeneutics, *The Bible in Human Transformation* and *Transforming Bible Study.* His other works include a trilogy, *The Powers; Violence and Nonviolence in South Africa;* and *John the Baptist in the Gospel Tradition.* In 1989–1990, he was a Peace Fellow at the U. S. Institute of Peace in Washington, D.C.

Index